ALASKA

Utqiagvik

Beaufort Sea

Prudhoe Bay

Sea

Inu

Kotzebue

YUKON

Wales

Fairban

Yukon River

Nome

Galena

Yukon River

Talkeetna

McCarthy

Anchorage

Whitehorse

Bethel

Seward

Juneau

Kodiak

Islands

Akutan

Unalaska

Nikolski

Pacific Ocean

CROSS WINDS

CROSS WINDS

ADVENTURE AND
ENTREPRENEURSHIP
IN THE RUSSIAN FAR EAST

STEVEN MYERS

Bletchley
Press

DEDICATION

To the peoples of the Russian Far East, who toil
in obscurity in a part of the world few have heard of,
and only a lucky few have ever seen.

CONTENTS

Acknowledgments ix

Introduction xiii

Prologue. xix

1 Two Men with Guns 1

2 Non-Negotiable Demands 7

3 They Called My Bluff 29

4 Planning for the Improbable. 37

5 North to Alaska 55

6 Adventure of a Lifetime 77

7 It Felt Like Lindbergh Landing in Paris. 93

8 Kamchatka: A Place of Wonder 107

Photographs 127

9 Entrepreneurial Inspiration 165

10 Be Careful What You Ask For. 175

11 The Concept Takes Form 193

12 Negotiating with Russians 211

13 Spooling Up the Enterprise 225

14 First Revenue Flight 243

15 Aggravation 253

16 Money, Fuel, and Nefarious Intentions. 271

17 Exfiltration 277

Epilogue. 295

Glossary of Important Names. 299

ACKNOWLEDGMENTS

This extraordinary adventure has been very challenging to write about because there was so much to share. It was only with the help and encouragement of my family, close friends, and colleagues that I was able to sift through the massive accumulation of materials to arrive at a manuscript capturing the essence of what happened.

Jennifer Harrison, my eldest of three daughters and son, is a brilliant clinical psychologist. She was fourteen when this adventure began and had no real appreciation for most of what occurred in those early years of her life, or why. In her late thirties, she read an early draft of the manuscript, and her astonishment at my story inspired me to press on.

For all of my children, now adults in their thirties and forties, this book has been a unique opportunity to share with them an extraordinary period in my life of which they previously had only been casually aware. But it was a period that impacted their lives and mine in so many unforeseen ways.

My wife, and best friend Vivian, a blossoming novelist and former management consultant, appreciated more than most what it takes to construct a story that others would want to read.

Paula Mathis, my wife during the period, managed our burgeoning family. Her devotion to our children allowed me to pursue ambitious projects.

Dr. Tom Heinsheimer, SM&A's brilliant Chief Scientist for a dozen years, had the remarkable skill to sell what seemed like an absurd idea to the Russians, and then sell it to me. He worked relentlessly to make our adventure a reality.

Dr. Viktor Kerzhanovich, also known as Viktor #1 in the book, is a brilliant Russian scientist who was, from the very beginning, our "indispensable man" on the ground in Russia. Viktor and Tom Heinsheimer met each other, thanks to Dr. Louis Friedman, Co-founder & CEO of the Pasadena-based Planetary Society. Lou worked for years to bring together the American and Soviet Mars programs. He sponsored and participated in the trip to the Kamchatka Mars site with Tom, described in Chapter 2, which led to our adventure.

Ken Colbaugh, my Chief Operating Officer at SM&A for a decade, was the great enabler. Without his superb leadership and support at SM&A, I would not have had the discretionary time needed to pursue this extraordinary adventure.

Dennis Crosby, my Chief Operating Officer at CKC, the entrepreneurial venture that came out of our first flight, had the day-to-day responsibility for managing what he characterizes as the most difficult, most challenging, and most rewarding assignment of his career. He devoured the original manuscript and provided me with many useful ideas and details to help flesh out the key events.

Chuck DeVore was my "utility infielder" at SM&A for thirteen years, an Army intelligence officer, and later a three-term California state legislator. There was never a responsibility I gave him that he didn't enthusiastically embrace. His tireless energy and creativity were critical to ramping up the CKC enterprise.

Boris Gurevich, a Russian business consultant, translator, and negotiator, went with me to Moscow for the joint venture negotiations in March 1993. He was crucial in helping me make sense of the many communication issues involved in dealing with the Russian authorities.

Dr. Jerry Green, my good friend and President of the Pacific Council on International Policy, first encouraged me to write this book in the spring of 2009 over lunch, after I told him about what had occurred. He was relentlessly persuasive, and a valued contributor, reading several drafts and providing candid feedback on many contentious issues.

Rob Begland, one of my closest friends, ski buddy, attorney, and former Army officer, offered very helpful insights into the parallels between Lindbergh's adventure in 1931, mine in 1992, and our shared tolerance for uncertainty.

Jerry Dauderman, another of my closest friends, favorite golf buddy, Harvard graduate, and fellow international relations enthusiast, read several drafts and provided me with the kind of feedback only he could give.

There are others, too numerous to mention, and a few who must remain anonymous, to whom I am forever grateful for their contributions to our efforts, and for their help in making this story a reality.

Why has it taken me more than 25 years to write this book? It's been much more challenging to tell my story in a digestible way than I ever imagined. I cared more about sharing with you a deeply personal experience of the heart, rather than merely providing a travel log. I've tried to capture the essence of how I felt about what we experienced as it was happening, from the extraordinary people we met, to the incredible places we went, to the food we ate. I couldn't stop writing about it. I'd put the manuscript down for a while. A few years would pass. Then I'd pick it up and rewrite it . . . yet again! Reading the biographies of my aviation heroes last year—the Wright brothers, Eddie Rickenbacker, Jimmy Doolittle, and Charles Lindbergh—inspired me to finish. Enjoy!

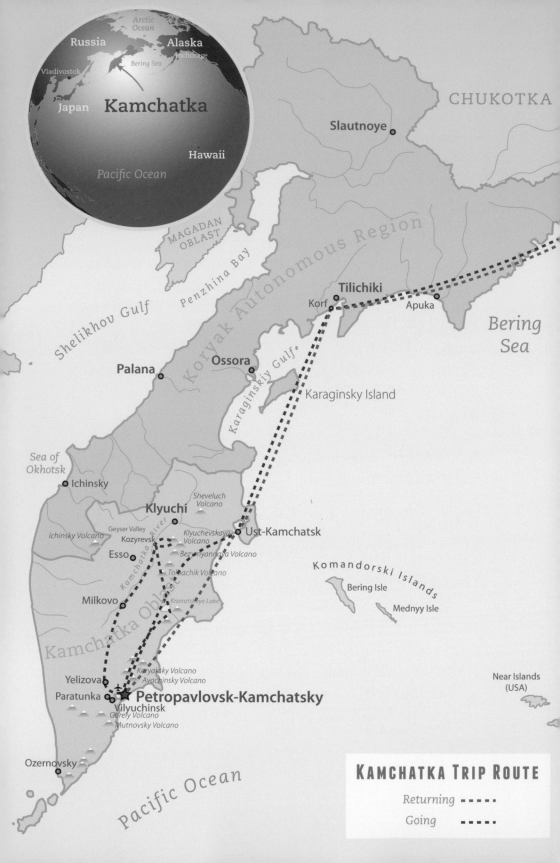

Arctic Ocean

Russia   **Alaska**
                    Anchorage
Vladivostok   Bering Sea

Kamchatka

Japan

                Hawaii

Pacific Ocean

CHUKOTKA

Slautnoye

MAGADAN OBLAST

Penzhina Bay

Koryak Autonomous Region

Tilichiki

Korf   Apuka

Shelikhov Gulf

Bering Sea

Palana

Ossora

Karaginskiy Gulf

Karaginsky Island

Sea of Okhotsk

Ichinsky

Sheveluch Volcano

Klyuchi

Geyser Valley   Klyuchevskaya Volcano   **Ust-Kamchatsk**
Ichinsky Volcano   Kozyrevsk

Esso   Bezymyannaya Volcano

Kamchatka River   Tolbachik Volcano

Komandorski Islands

Bering Isle

Milkovo   Kronotskoye Lake

Mednyy Isle

Kamchatka Oblast

Near Islands (USA)

Koryaksky Volcano
Avachinsky Volcano

Yelizova

Paratunka   ✈ ★ **Petropavlovsk-Kamchatsky**

Vilyuchinsk
Gorely Volcano
Mutnovsky Volcano

Ozernovsky

Pacific Ocean

KAMCHATKA TRIP ROUTE

Returning -----

Going -----

INTRODUCTION

This is the true story of my extraordinary experiences in the Russian Far East and Moscow shortly after the end of the Cold War. In July of 1992, just seven months after the fall of the Soviet Union, I flew an airplane and six-person crew into the Russian Far East and down the length of the Kamchatka peninsula to Petropavlovsk. Our feat was made possible only because of the remarkable cooperation of the new, post-Soviet Russian Government. At the time, I believed we were the first Americans to ever fly into this little-known and virtually inaccessible region of the globe.

Some twenty-seven years later, in the summer of 2019, I was astonished to learn that Charles Lindbergh and his wife, Ann Morrow, had flown to Kamchatka in 1931, an incredible achievement history had largely forgotten. In a terrific biography of Lindbergh by Winston Groom, their flying to Kamchatka merited only a passing observation. He noted that Anne Morrow had written a book in 1935 about their 1931 adventure called *North to the Orient*.

As I researched the topic, I became increasingly amazed at Lindbergh's aeronautical daring. A fledgling Pan Am Airlines wanted to start an air travel service to the "Orient," as Asia was called at the time. Pan Am asked Lindbergh to explore possible routes from the United States and report on their feasibility. Using a piece of string, he drew a line on the Pan Am office globe from New York City to Tokyo and committed to flying the "great circle path," some 7,000 nautical miles to Japan, nearly twice the distance from Long Island to Le Bourget.

Flying over the Arctic, Alaska, and Kamchatka was the most direct, fuel-efficient route, even though it was, and still is, the most isolated, barren, and by far the most inhospitable route. Lindbergh intended to accomplish this feat using a custom-built Lockheed Sirius airplane, a single-engine, open-cockpit monoplane on floats.

The Lindberghs spent a year positioning provisions and fuel along the planned route and preparing their airplane and themselves for the mission. Anne earned her private pilot license and learned Morse code so she could accompany Charles as the radio operator, collecting weather information and reporting on their position as she could.

They departed on July 27th, 1931, from Long Island, New York. They flew no more than several hundred feet above the ground. They navigated point to point by dead reckoning, using the primitive navigational charts and terrain information then available. They frequently found themselves in fog, clouds, and storms, navigating with little more than a basic altimeter and a magnetic compass. To his great credit as one of the most exceptional airmen ever to have lived, Lindbergh and his wife eventually reached Tokyo on August 26th, 1931.

Sixty years later, in March 1992, I was invited by the Russian authorities to observe and opine on the potential of their post-Soviet space program activities taking place on the Kamchatka peninsula. I agreed to go if I could fly there using my company airplane. To my astonishment, they agreed.

I was anything but disappointed to learn I was not the first; being second to Lindbergh is an honor for which anyone should be grateful. And by being second, I learned something important I might have otherwise missed: that the great attraction in common to adventure, aviation, and entrepreneurship is not in trying to be the first to do something, or even arriving at a particular destination. Instead, it's that exceptional achievement comes from having the courage to knowingly embrace uncertainty and push through to success. But from where does such courage come? As you'll read, I learned early in life that the cornerstone of courage is optimism.

The second half of the book shares with you the extraordinary story of entrepreneurship and intrigue that then ensued once we reached Petropavlovsk. Partnering with the governor of Kamchatka and several key leaders of the region, I led the formation of one of the first Russian-American joint ventures in Moscow the following winter. My entrepreneurial concept was audacious in the extreme: to create something akin to the Hudson Bay Company in the Russian Far East. The Hudson Bay Company, chartered in London in 1670, controlled the fur trade throughout much of North American for several centuries, and had a prominent economic and political role in Canadian history.

Over the last fifty years, I've had the good fortune to fly much of the world in many types of aircraft. I've accumulated more than 6,000 hours of flight time and 11 jet-type ratings. But what I achieved in the experiences you'll read about in the first half of the book was the culmination of my lifelong calling for aviation adventure. No experience I've had compares with the sense of adventure, the challenges of uncertainty, and the tremendous sense of achievement that flying in that part of the world was for me in 1992.

It is also humbling to realize how much higher was the uncertainty Lindbergh faced. Becoming aware of and acknowledging his achievement allowed me to create the context through which you can better appreciate the uncertainty I faced and overcame. These reflections have also left me feeling a unique connection to him.

In the sixty years between our adventures, aviation had been transformed. World War II ushered in an era of vastly more capable aircraft, reliable instruments, and support infrastructure . . . even in Russia. Although frankly, flying in Russia in 1992 felt like time travel back to the 1950s.

In the nearly thirty years since my adventure, aviation has yet again been transformed, primarily driven by satellite navigation (GPS), computer technology, and resulting advances impacting every aspect of aviation, from avionics, to materials, to manufacturing capabilities. Tools like the iPad, with no end of flight support applications, have revolutionized flight operations. Continuous improvement in training, safety, reliability, tools, and technology is what aviation has always been about, starting with the Wright brothers.

I hope to share with you a story that encapsulates the spirit of a flying adventure in a time when the technologies that are so common in cockpits today were the stuff of science fiction. I had to do everything "the hard way" by today's standards. But in all fairness, not remotely as hard as Lindbergh and so many other adventurers that came before me.

I've also learned from my various entrepreneurial experiences that success is not a journey for the faint of heart. A "better idea" is only the first ingredient in an opaque process that must survive many, many challenges, obstacles, and detours on an uncertain path to success. It was very early days for the fledgling Russian Federation in 1992. In the Wild West that Russia was, and in many ways still is, no one could be sure what the rules were.

KAMCHATKA TRIP ROUTES

`- - - - -` *Lindbergh's 5,200 nm Route from NY to Petropavlovsk in 1931*

`- - - - -` *Our 5,200 nm Route from SNA to Petropavlovsk in 1992*

PROLOGUE

In 1983, Cold War tensions between the United States and the Soviet Union escalated to a level not seen since the Cuban Missile Crisis. The U.S. deployed the Pershing II missile system in Europe and held the most extensive U.S. Navy exercise ever in the North Pacific. Soviet General Secretary Yuri Andropov and President Ronald Reagan were deeply suspicious of each other's intentions, and each feared a preemptive nuclear strike.

Many factors drove the escalation, but most notably Reagan's Strategic Defense Initiative, a program to shield against a preemptive nuclear attack, and Andropov's Operation RYaN (Raketno-Yadernoe Napadenie), a program to detect a potential U.S. nuclear sneak attack.

The Kamchatka peninsula, closer to San Francisco than to Moscow, was one of the most mysterious and inaccessible military security areas of the Soviet Union for more than sixty years. Access to the region was forbidden to all but those with the highest security clearance. What went on there that was so important?

Against this backdrop of escalating tensions, on the night of September 1, 1983, Korean Air Lines Flight 007 (KAL007), a Boeing 747 carrying 269 passengers and crew, on a scheduled flight from Anchorage to Seoul, was shot down by the Soviets after deviating from its assigned route by several hundred miles into the prohibited airspace over the Kamchatka peninsula. The Soviets claimed KAL Flight 007 was on a spy mission, whose purpose was to probe the air defenses of highly sensitive Soviet military sites there, some of which were most certainly part of Operation RYaN.

1

TWO MEN WITH GUNS

"We are here to speak to you about a matter of grave national security. As you know, you're on the protective watch list because of certain projects you're read-on."

They were very large men. One look at them made me feel that I was about to line up on the scrimmage line with the Pittsburgh Steelers. Black suits, black ties, black gun holsters. When I shook their hands, I wondered if they had the wrong guy. I hoped they did.

A few moments earlier, my assistant had walked into my office and said, "Steve, there are a couple of gentlemen in the lobby who want to speak with you." She looked quite concerned—her eyes formed large white saucers.

I replied casually, "Really? Who are they?"

She repeated nervously, "There are a couple of guys out there, and I think you should speak with them."

I got up and followed her out to the lobby to see what had so taken her aback. The sheer size of these guys wasn't something people usually encountered. They were each at least six-five and 275 pounds. Guns were visible through their open coats.

"I'm Steve Myers. How can I help you, gentlemen?"

They were very polite as they showed me their credentials. Their credentials were instantly recognizable and made clear where they came from.

"We've been asked to meet with you on a matter of significant urgency."

Without saying another word, I turned around, led them into my office, and asked them to take seats at my conference table. I closed the office door, sat down, and squeezed out a smile. A feeling of anxiety and foreboding came over me as I asked to see their credentials again. I wanted a closer look.

"Gentlemen, how can I help you?"

The lead agent began, "You are Steven Myers, chairman of the California Kamchatka Companies?"

"Yes sir, I am."

On that morning in mid-June 1995, when these two US government agents showed up at my office, I was finalizing my plans to attend the Farnborough Air Show, south of London, the following month. Farnborough was, and is, one of the world's largest international aerospace and defense exhibitions. The California Kamchatka Companies (CKC) was one of the first post-USSR Russian-American joint ventures and one of the largest, if not *the* largest, entrepreneurial endeavors in the Russian Far East. I was the chairman of the joint venture.

In addition to CKC, I led another enterprise called SM&A (Steven Myers & Associates, Inc.). SM&A was a very successful boutique management consulting business serving the aerospace and defense industry. While the business purposes of CKC and SM&A were very different, many of the same business development strategies applied. Many of the crucial customers for both enterprises attended Farnborough, providing us with an efficient, target-rich environment for cultivating existing relationships and developing new ones. Between the two businesses, we planned so many meetings and events during the week that I needed a team of six people with me to deal with them.

I had planned a two-week family driving tour around Germany and Austria after Farnborough, and then to be in Moscow for the scheduled CKC quarterly board meeting in August.

The two government agents knew my plans in detail and more. No surprise there. But why did they care? As I sat listening to them, my mind flashed back to several years earlier. SM&A's clients primarily supported US government agencies. Over the years I had spent a great deal of time in government facilities in Washington, DC, and around the country, an alphabet soup list of three- and four-letter agencies: DOD, NSA, NRO, NRL, NSSC, CIA, and NASA among many others.

I recalled being alone in an elevator at the CIA headquarters at Langley, Virginia, when a large man got into the elevator with me. I made a concerted effort not to stare at him. He was undoubtedly a field agent from his manner and attire, a character straight out of a Tom Clancy novel, back from a far-off corner of the world only an hour earlier. He appeared to be on his way to some incredibly time-sensitive meeting to brief somebody in charge about something fascinating, I'm sure. I would have loved to go to that meeting. I wondered what he had been doing and what the future held for him. One thing I presumed—I wasn't going be crossing paths with him, or anyone like him, any time soon.

But here I was, and the agents sitting across from me had me wondering the same thing. Where had they come from, what had they been doing, and why were they in my office?

"Mr. Myers, we've been directed to convey that you are very well known to the national security establishment. You have an excellent reputation for the important services you've provided to the nation and you're recognized as a prominent citizen, a patriot, and a friend to the US government."

"Thank you for those kind and gracious remarks. Please, continue."

"We are here to speak to you about a matter of grave national security. As you know, you're on the protective watch list because of certain projects you're read-on. We don't normally do this. But considering what you've been doing in Kamchatka, and considering SM&A's activities, you urgently need to have the information we are about to share with you."

My heart began racing. I was thinking, "Wow! What is this all about?"

"A high-risk situation will likely develop while you are in Moscow in August. If we are correct, it will become a tragedy for you and an international incident for us. We have hard intelligence that you are going to be kidnapped."

In one sudden, dramatic moment, time nearly stopped, and everything began to move in slow motion. It felt like being in a movie scene. Of the many topics running through my mind that I thought they might have wanted to talk to me about, being kidnapped wasn't on the list! My coping mechanisms struggled to kick in. A million thoughts ran through my mind as I worked to focus on what they were saying.

"We are not here to tell you what to do, Mr. Myers. We wouldn't presume to know. However, the 'powers that be' wanted you to have this information as soon as possible. Whatever you decide to do, speaking for myself, I'm sincerely hoping you won't be going to Moscow in August. If we have to try to rescue you, the chances are high that you won't survive."

I sat there for what seemed like an eternity, attempting to process what they had told me. Finally I said, "Thank you so much for sharing this intel with me. Can you give me any specifics?"

Their responses were vague. I knew the rules. They weren't going to give me any information that might reveal sources and methods. That was for some good reasons, the most important one being that what I didn't know, I couldn't divulge. They were only going to share with me what I needed to know. But they were also in no hurry to leave. They wanted to be sure I got the message.

My first instinct was to ask about Russian Mafia involvement. I knew they would not reveal sources and methods. But I asked anyway about how this intelligence had come to their attention. I thought it was probably communications intelligence (COMINT), perhaps through phone taps or microwave intercepts. It could have been human intelligence (HUMINT), maybe a mole somewhere. What I desperately wanted to know was if my Russian JV partners were part of the plot.

Finally, I asked the agents to convey to the "powers that be" that I appreciated their informing me this way. I asked the agents to assure them that, while I didn't know what my plans were for dealing with the situation, I would not be going to Moscow for the board meeting in August. I would not be going to Russia anytime for the foreseeable future.

The agents were visibly relieved at my response. Did they actually care? There was a lot more going on here than they were telling me. They were here to sell me a story to take me out of play. But why?

2

NON-NEGOTIABLE DEMANDS

Osipov was not about to talk to anyone within the new Russian government, and then initiate all of the bureaucratic coordination needed unless he was certain I would do it.

In February 1992, I was running my aerospace and defense consulting business, SM&A, out of Lockheed Missiles & Space Company's facilities in Sunnyvale, California. It had been going on like this for four years. Sunnyvale sits in the heart of Silicon Valley, in the Santa Clara Valley between San Francisco and San Jose. In 1992, Lockheed was one of the largest employers in the county.

A decade earlier, I had invented a new kind of consulting service that provided exceptional value to my clients. The services we offered were so extraordinary that no one believed we could actually do what we promised. We wildly exceeded Lockheed's expectations most of the time. They came to adore our people. We loved working with them, and they loved us back. They couldn't get enough of our services. The result was that Lockheed management wanted us there all the time. In particular, they wanted *me* there all the time. Supporting Lockheed meant *being* at Lockheed. Cell phone service was still in its infancy. Laptops were a dream.

No email, no internet, no Google. I carried a pager on my belt. They gave us offices in their facilities. I was permitted to use those offices as SM&A's base of operations for all of our business. This unusual Lockheed relationship made for some challenging personal logistics.

My home was three hundred nautical miles to the southeast in Irvine, some forty miles south of Los Angeles. Fortunately, I had been flying for more than twenty years by then, and I owned an airplane. High-frequency travel at odd times between my home and my office was the perfect opportunity to build flight time. I owned a twin-engine Aero Commander 690B propjet. It was a workhorse, ideal for this mission: fast, reliable, and definitely a pilot's airplane.

Every Monday morning, I flew the Aero Commander from Orange County's John Wayne Airport to San Jose. I took off at 6:45 a.m., ahead of the 7:00 a.m. commercial flight departure crush. I arrived at Lockheed in time to lead a 9:00 a.m. mandatory management meeting, attended by dozens of Lockheed executives, managers, and engineers. Every Wednesday afternoon, I flew home around 4:30 p.m. for dinner and time with my family, flew back north on Thursday mornings, and finally flew home again on Friday late afternoon. I flew this trip hundreds of times. I worked about sixty hours a week on Lockheed programs, and logged five hours a week of flight time.

Winning US Government contracts is the foundation of the aerospace and defense business. In the early 1980s, I developed industry-changing processes and tools for enabling companies to compete more effectively for large, complex programs. After more than a decade in business, SM&A had managed nearly a hundred government proposal efforts for our clients and won most. Our win rate was over 90 percent on dollars awarded.

If the numbers were indisputable, there was no end to the skepticism, particularly from prospective clients who had not worked with us, as to why we won so often. They found it hard to believe that we could change the behavior of our clients' people in ways that positively impacted their probability of winning. They preferred to believe that they would win because they were the "xyz" company, and their brand somehow translated into an insurmountable competitive advantage. It wasn't true then, and it's not true today.

You win when you provide better value to your customers. We became the leading experts in the world at working with our clients to discover, for any given competition, what "better value" meant, how to provide it, and how to sell it. Of all the things that matter most in business, there's no higher value you can deliver than to win business for your customers. But here's a tip: make sure they know who did it! SM&A was becoming a well-oiled winning machine, and Lockheed knew it.

We also worked extensively with Rockwell and McDonnell Douglas (both now part of Boeing), and General Electric (now part of Lockheed Martin). Key industry people began to notice that whoever hired SM&A won the contract and knew it was no coincidence.

My chief operating officer, Ken Colbaugh, and I shared an office in one of Lockheed's dozens of buildings on their sprawling Sunnyvale campus. Before joining me at SM&A, Ken and I had worked together for four years. He was a Lockheed executive working with me on an extraordinarily large and complex NASA proposal to replace the Space Shuttle's solid-rocket motors following the Challenger disaster. We clicked instantly and became good friends. After the Lockheed/Aerojet team won the program, he became my COO. I owe much of SM&A's many years of success to our remarkable working relationship.

In 1992, in the wake of Desert Storm, the US urgently needed a more capable missile system to shoot down Saddam Hussain's Scud missiles, among other threats. Twenty people from SM&A, two hundred from Lockheed, and one hundred from other contractors were working on what rapidly became one of the most critical proposals I ever led: the US Army Theater High Altitude Area Defense System (THAAD). Today it's called the Terminal High Altitude Area Defense System.

For political and technical reasons, this particular program had become a critical national security priority. Despite all the hoopla in the press about how well the Raytheon Patriot system had worked during Desert Storm the prior year, those of us working in missile defense knew differently.

There were significant vulnerabilities in Patriot's ability to shoot down Saddam's Scud missiles, particularly before they reached Israel's metropolitan areas. Desert Storm uncovered three significant missile-defense weaknesses central to US strategy for responding to future conflicts. First, the Patriot missiles weren't able to intercept all of the Scuds. Some got through. This put tremendous pressure on coalition combined forces to find and destroy Saddam's well-camouflaged mobile missile launchers before their missiles could be launched.

Second, the intercepted Scuds were scattering debris, causing as much, or more, damage than if the Scuds had been allowed to continue. The Scuds were so inaccurate that their warheads didn't pose a credible threat against any specific target. But for obvious political reasons, the Scuds could not be allowed to appear effective, nor the US appear defenseless because of a lucky shot.

Third, there was great concern about what could happen if Saddam launched Scud missiles with chemical or biological agents. A Patriot missile worked by exploding in front of an incoming missile, creating a debris field the Scud warhead would crash into and break up. Shooting the Scuds down actually increased the area of the debris field, making the potential for chemical or biological exposure significantly worse.

The THAAD strategy was to intercept the Scud warheads much earlier in flight and much higher in the atmosphere. The THAAD warhead would fly to and crash into the Scud warhead and break it up. This was a tremendous technological undertaking, akin to hitting a bullet with another bullet.

At the time of Desert Storm in 1991, THAAD had already been in conceptual development as a mid-course, anti-ballistic missile interceptor. It was quickly repurposed into a theater-level area defense system with the highest government development priority.

Winning a high national priority program wasn't easy. Nothing attracts fierce competition like a high-priority development program with legs. Hughes and McDonnel Douglas were competing against Lockheed for THAAD. I knew the leaders we were competing against in those companies. They were first-rate.

Because of the national urgency, the Army's missile systems people in Huntsville, Alabama, worked with each of the three contractor teams early in the competitive process to establish a stable set of common requirements that each contractor would be required to meet as part of their proposal. This approach led to significant strategy-shaping efforts by each of the three teams to influence the requirements in their favor. Every week it seemed like the Army proposed another change in requirements. We had to develop a very proactive advocacy approach to neutralize the efforts of the other teams while advancing our approach.

Ken and I shared an office in the THAAD facility so we could more easily and quickly communicate and coordinate on all matters. The arrangement suited us well. Things went on like this for all of 1992 and well into the fall of 1993, when the

US Army finally awarded the Lockheed team the development contract.

In addition to our THAAD responsibilities, Ken and I also had a business to run, with people at other facilities, working on different proposals and projects for Lockheed, Rockwell, McDonnell Douglas, and others. Ken and I took turns traveling to other facilities as needed to check on our people's progress and meet with our clients.

Tom Heinsheimer, one of my first hires at SM&A, was our chief scientist. Tom is a brilliant guy on so many levels. He earned his Ph.D. in astrophysics in Paris. He speaks French and German with high fluency, along with several other languages. Tom has the rare ability to see situations from a very imaginative perspective. I greatly valued his counsel. He provided an endless stream of interesting ideas. With brilliant people, it is always about knowing which ideas are feasible.

In my Lockheed office on a fateful morning in February 1992, I was doing what program and proposal managers do: preparing for upcoming meetings, writing memos, reviewing documents, interviewing or interrogating people, and making phone calls.

Tom walked in. I hadn't seen him for a while.

"Hey Steve, I just got back from Kamchatka and have something I need to talk to you about."

"Great to see you, Tom. How was the trip? Is it urgent? I have a meeting in a few minutes."

"Extremely."

"How long do you need?"

"Thirty minutes."

I picked up the phone and called the people next up on my schedule to see if they could move to a later time slot. They were more than happy to oblige. A progress review meeting with me was something people looked forward to with a certain trepidation. A good proposal manager is like a good sports coach, always demanding high standards, inspiring his players to do better than they ever have. I was a taskmaster, always challenging everyone for more. A little more time to prepare was like found money for them.

Two hours later, Tom and I were still talking. It was going to be a very long day. Two hours of meetings had been rescheduled into the evening, and we were still talking. Fortunately for Tom, or perhaps it was fate, Ken was at another client facility that day. Ken was practical and very focused. Had Ken been there, I am quite sure none of what was about to unfold would have happened. Any serious talk about a "boondoggle into a swamp" was not going to happen if Ken had a say in the matter. He would have very quickly intervened in the conversation, brought the meeting to a swift close, and helped Tom to the door.

On the whiteboard opposite my desk, Tom had diagrammed an idea and wanted my involvement. When he finished, I just stared at him. At the time, I didn't connect with my emotional reaction. But I should have. I felt a combination of frustration over having my time wasted, and great trepidation of becoming involved in something for which I neither had the time or resources.

I simply said, "Tom, you're out of your mind. There is no way in a million years this could happen. This is the silliest idea I have ever heard. There isn't any way I'm going to do this. Please go away."

But Tom didn't leave. Instead, he smiled, stayed calm, and just waited for me to cool off.

"Tom, we are working day and night, running this superhigh national priority proposal and running our business at the same time. We have more opportunities than resources. And you're asking me to investigate a *swamp*? Forget about it!"

He looked at me sideways, grinned knowingly, and said, "Steve, this is an opportunity of a lifetime. You could do something profound. Nobody's ever done anything like this. You'll even be in the record books as the first Westerner to fly an aircraft into the Kamchatka peninsula."

Tom, himself a world-famous high-altitude balloonist, knew how deeply passionate I was about flying. He had begun reeling me in like a dangling fish.

During the prior four years, Tom, along with his other responsibilities, had been a consultant to NASA at JPL, the Jet Propulsion Laboratories in Pasadena, and IKI, the Soviet Institute for Space Research in Moscow, on a bold new program for the exploration of Mars. In the 1980s, NASA and JPL had one disappointment after another with Mars exploration. It seemed as if every time that NASA launched a probe for Mars, it failed, blew up, crashed, or just disappeared.

To reduce the risk, NASA began partnering with the Soviets to take advantage of their considerable expertise in this area. The Soviets loved their space program. The US and the Soviet scientists agreed to pool resources. The next series of planned missions to Mars became a joint venture for the US and the Soviet Union. JPL, for NASA, built the spacecraft, while the IKI built six-wheeled rovers to explore the Martian surface.

Under an SM&A contract with JPL, through the Planetary Society, Tom was sent to the Soviet Union many times, beginning in 1988, to work with IKI scientists on the program. He cultivated many business relationships and personal friendships with Soviet leaders, scientists, and engineers. These relationships would later prove crucial in ways even he had not foreseen.

Extensive testing of the rover was critical to success. The way to test a rover for conditions on Mars was to find a place on earth that had similar features and then take the prototype there and test it under every conceivable scenario. In the Russian Far East, on the Kamchatka peninsula, there is a volcano called Tolbachik with terrain that looks like images sent back from Mars. The Russians set up a testing facility on the slopes of Tolbachik and took the rover prototype there to test it, modify it, and test it again. Tom was able to go with them on several occasions.

On August 18, 1991, Tom was on his way to Kamchatka to meet up with his IKI colleagues for scheduled rover tests. This happened to be the first day of the attempted coup against Mikhail Gorbachev by hardliners in the Communist Party Politburo. For the next several days, it was uncertain when, or even if, Tom would be able to get back to the US. It was a surreal experience for the peoples of the Soviet Union, and Tom had a front-row seat. Gorbachev was captured and held under guard at his dacha in the Crimea near Yalta. The public didn't know. The coup leaders nervously held a press conference to announce that Gorbachev was ill and that emergency measures were being put in place. The public reacted with a mix of incredulity, fear, and anger.

The events that followed have no parallel in history. The attempted coup ultimately failed because a white-haired Boris Yeltsin courageously stood on a tank in front of the Soviet White House in Moscow and faced down the Soviet military. On December 31, 1991, the Soviet Union ceased to exist.

In January 1992, Russia and its new independent neighbors, to the west in central Europe, and the south along the Black and Caspian Seas, formed the Commonwealth of Independent States (CIS). But Russia and her neighbors were left without functional governments. Their economies collapsed. Many former satellite countries to the west, ecstatic to be free, quickly ran into the open arms of the European Union and NATO, who offered financial aid and security.

The western nations celebrated the great victory over the collapse of the "Evil Empire," while life for the Russian people entered a period of chaos, desperation, and even greater deprivation. The value of the ruble collapsed, leaving pensioners penniless. Older people were left to beg in the streets. Many people were left starving. Tens of thousands, particularly the old and frail, in the face of no hope, committed suicide. More than 90 percent of the population found themselves living below the poverty line. Alcohol consumption skyrocketed.

Chaos breeds opportunity, and not all of it good. Plant managers began showing up with new business cards proclaiming themselves the CEOs of their companies. Oligarchs were created overnight as a mad scramble to control Russia's assets began. Yeltsin seemed not to notice or care. The Russian people were left to fend for themselves with a crash course in market economics. Survival became all about how to make a dollar, and depended on how to keep whatever they were doing going. Entrepreneurs from Europe began pouring into Moscow. The US dollar was the safe-haven currency.

Things were no different for the leaders at the former Soviet Space Program. The IKI leadership and their superiors at the former Soviet Academy of Sciences worked to keep their programs alive. Partnering with the US on everything they could was their highest priority. The Mars rover program, already a proven model for Soviet/US relations, became an extremely high priority.

In the months following the attempted coup, Tom and his colleagues from IKI had many conversations about the future of Russia. In meetings with people such as Yuri Osipov, the president of the Soviet Academy of Sciences, and Albert Gallev, the director of IKI, Tom suggested that Russia focus on creating a safe environment for entrepreneurship. Tom argued that Russia could never solve the many challenges it was facing alone. Russia had neither the knowledge nor the experience needed to build a new, more prosperous nation. Tom was convinced this was the only way forward. "What Russia needs is rapid economic development entrepreneurs who could make things happen more quickly. Entrepreneurs will know what to do. Just get out of their way and let them do whatever they want to."

In late January 1992, Tom and Yuri Osipov were having one of their endless series of vodka dinner conferences. It was a very cold, blustery evening in Moscow. No one knew how the new Russia would survive the winter. Yuri said to Tom, "I have been thinking a great deal about your thoughts on the future of Russia. Tell me why entrepreneurs would want to come to Russia in particular. Why now?"

Tom replied, "Cheap labor. It's simple Darwinian economics. The current Russian economic environment offers the potential for substantial economic advantage because of cheap labor. Business-minded people will rush in to take advantage of the cheap labor disparity until costs level out. You have economic leverage as long as you are cheap. The problem is you have no way to monetize your leverage with the west. You have no way to exploit it on your own because you don't know how to."

Tom continued, "Take a guy like my boss, Steve Myers. He is a very typical entrepreneur who created a very successful business from nothing. He saw opportunities that few others saw, and those that did couldn't figure out how to exploit. He was able to create jobs and then profits because he was willing to act on his vision and was willing to take risks to turn his visions into reality. That's what entrepreneurs do!"

"Great! Let's get him over here!"

Tom smiled and said, "Yuri, Steve isn't coming over here! I was just using him as an example."

"What?"

"There is no way!"

"Why not?"

Tom replied, "If I go to Steve and suggest he make a trip over here, he's going to laugh at me."

"Why would he laugh at you?"

"Because he has a world of opportunity in front of him where he is. Successful entrepreneurs know how to take advantage of the right opportunities and know which opportunities to ignore. There is no reason for him to come over here. You need entrepreneurs to come over here who have little to lose and much to gain. Or entrepreneurs who already have businesses in basic industries that are a natural fit with opportunities here. Neither of those situations applies to Steve. So why would he come?"

After several more glasses of vodka were poured and enjoyed, Yuri exclaimed, "There must be something Steve wants! Sure, the kind of people you're talking about are going to come. There is no stopping them. But they're just going to want to exploit us, take advantage of us, make their money, and leave. We need guys like Steve to come over here, who are experienced, have means, and can figure out what is possible to do here in an entirely different context. It is precisely because he is not already invested that his perspective could be very helpful. There must be something he wants!"

Tom thought for a while and finally replied, "Well, there *is* something. There is some leverage I could apply. But you guys would never agree."

"What leverage?"

"Steve is a serious and accomplished pilot. He's been flying for a long time. He was in the US Air Force, twice. He owns a twin-engine propjet. It is a very capable airplane. He flies it back and forth between southern California and the San Francisco Bay Area all the time, almost every week. He also uses it to get to his other clients in the western US. I have flown with him many times. You could invite him to fly his airplane to Kamchatka, and we'll mix it in with a Mars rover test. Then all you need to do is just stand back and watch what Steve does. He's an entrepreneur. He won't be able to stop himself. It is what he *does*. It'll blow your mind."

Yuri went pale.

"Tom, be reasonable. Do you know what you're saying? There is no way that could happen! That has never happened! It is a closed area. Special permission is required for even Soviet citizens to go there. You're one of the few non-Russians who have ever been there. No one from another country has ever flown into the Kamchatka peninsula and lived to talk about it. My God, those maniacs shot down that Korean airliner a few years ago for going near the place, and that plane flew there *accidently*."

Tom replied, "Well, there you go! You want Steve . . ."

Tom wasn't pushing. He was just brainstorming over vodka with Yuri and some other Russian scientific leaders. But he knew the result was inevitable.

Tom is a consummate master of out-of-the-box thinking. He doesn't see his role as making it happen, but rather to conceptualize what and why. A brilliant, strategic thinker, much of SM&A's success was due to his bold insights. He also knew one of the reasons SM&A had succeeded was because I knew a good idea when I heard it, even if it sometimes took a while for me to get it.

Yuri sat back, smoking a cigarette, sipping his vodka, thinking about what Tom had suggested. Finally, he said, "Well, look Tom, before I'm going to push a crazy idea like that through the Soviet, I mean through the *Russian* bureaucracy, I need more than you telling me Steve might come. You need to talk to him and then come back and tell me you are very certain he will come.

Otherwise, I will look foolish. I know nothing about Western aviation. Does he really own an airplane that can do something like this? Can he really fly a mission like this?"

"Yes, he does, and yes, he can."

"Really? That is amazing. Are you sure?"

Yuri Osipov was not about to talk to anyone within the new Russian government, especially Foreign Minister Andrey Kozyrev, and then initiate all of the bureaucratic coordination needed with the various aviation and military authorities unless he was certain I would do it. It seemed like an impossible task in any event. But he was willing to try. First, he needed proof that I was for real.

I sat in my office staring at the whiteboard, and at Tom. "Fly? What do you mean *fly*?"

"I told them you would fly your propjet into Kamchatka if they give you permission."

"Yeah, Tom, I'm going to navigate an aircraft out of US airspace, across the Bering Strait, into former Soviet Union airspace, fly through Siberia, and into the Kamchatka peninsula. You can't be serious. What are you thinking?"

Tom said, "Steve, look, I can see you hate the idea. But I have to tell them something. So why don't we plan out what it would take to do it and put together a list of your impossible demands. I'll present it to them, and then they'll go away. And then I'll save face with Yuri Osipov. If I tell Yuri you threw me out of your office, I'm going to look like a fool and lose all my credibility with him."

I glanced at him suspiciously. I knew this game. He stared calmly back at me, the picture of innocence.

"Okay. So, we'll just go through the exercise of figuring out what it would take to do it."

"I just need to cover with these guys. The faster we get through this, the faster I'm out of here."

In my mind, any possible threads of interest in actually doing this stunt were quickly discarded. After all, why did I need all the drama? I had a lot to lose. It's not like I was a bachelor looking for adventure. I had a thriving business. I had a young family, with a wife and four children. Why would I want this aggravation? "Right, Steve," I said to myself. "I don't want it. Yeah, I'm just going through the motions for Tom. I have no intentions of doing this."

I started asking Tom a lot of questions. Something in my brain whispered, "Well, okay, let's make it impossible so he will go away. I have to give him something he can go back with. He can't just go back and say, 'Steve said nyet.' We need Yuri to save face too. Tom needs to go back and tell him, 'Yes, Steve will do it, but these are his requirements.' Impossible requirements to be sure. Then they can say 'nyet,' and this aggravation will go away. I won't give it another thought. There is no way they are going to end up saying 'da.' It's not possible."

I erased the whiteboard and started to fill it up again. I drew a map. I created a timeline, lists of information needed. We began to fill in the blanks. Calculations were made. Questions were asked. Phone calls were made. More data was filled in. We outlined the basic plan for how to organize and execute this mission. Tom loved it. That's one of the things we liked about each other. We knew how to work together to get the answer we needed. That's what leaders, engineers, scientists, and planners do.

I was an electronic technician and computer repairman during my first tour in the Air Force, before college. At one point, I had the good fortune to work on what was then the largest computer system in the world. I studied science, engineering, and mathematics at Stanford University, and then went back into the Air Force for a second tour as a pilot. The end of the Vietnam War put an end to my Air Force flying career. There were too many pilots and massive cutbacks. It was time to move on.

I then had a nine-year run as an engineer, project manager, systems engineer, program manager, director of this, and VP of that, as I worked my way through four companies. That was until the right opportunity came along, which introduced me to my life calling, consulting. I love solving complicated problems. The more complicated the problem, the more I like it. And I like working with people to solve problems.

On the whiteboard was a list of essential questions needing to be answered:

1. Where would we need to land on each leg to reach Petropavlovsk?

2. Can we get jet fuel at the end of each leg?

3. What is the most stressing leg of the trip, and why?

4. Are the leg distances, times, and fuel requirements reasonable, given our maximum gross weight limit?

5. How much weight could we carry (our useful load) if refueling to full capacity is required?

6. How many people could we take with what weight assumptions at full fuel capacity?

7. With full fuel and people allocation, how much weight budget could we allocate for stuff?

8. What supplies and equipment (stuff) are essential, requiring how much weight?

9. How are we going to navigate in areas where there are no charts?

After a couple of telephone calls, I found that there were no charts available for the Russian Far East. I thought there had to be Russian charts available *somewhere*. But I had no idea how to get my hands on them. There were US Geodetic Survey maps available for the region. These were not useful for navigation as aviation instrument charts, but I could use them for visual flight rules (VFR) flying. Also, because they were large area charts without fine details, they had serious limitations even for visual flying.

I made a note to try an experiment to see if I could navigate from Orange County to San Jose using only the survey map for the California area. I'd pick a day with good VFR weather and use a route that avoided running afoul of the many airspace restrictions in effect. I would still need departure and arrival charts with radio frequencies and other information to leave Orange County and arrive at San Jose. But if I couldn't find San Jose airport by this method alone, then what chance would I have over there? I wasn't convinced it would be a very useful test. I knew the route so well I could probably fly it with no charts at all.

"Okay, Tom, I'm going to navigate an aircraft out of US airspace into former Soviet Union airspace with no aviation charts and no instrument approach charts? Get real."

"You're not going to Steve. We're just going through the motions. We're having fun!"

"Oh, right. How am I going to navigate?"

Tom was grinning at me. "They've got beacons."

"What are the frequencies? How am I going to communicate?"

"Take a fast course in Russian, Steve."

"Yeah, right! What if the weather is bad? How will we get down?"

As a practical matter, no competent pilots are going to fly an aircraft into the wilderness without a very well-thought-out plan for getting themselves, and their passengers, home in one piece. There would be a tremendous amount of planning involved in undertaking something like this. There was no end of things that could go wrong, and each thing that could go wrong had to have a work-around solution. If not properly planned, the mission could quickly turn into a deadly nightmare.

On the other hand, the opportunity to do this kind of flying was extremely rare. There is a wonderful book called *Fate Is the Hunter* by Ernest K. Gann, in which he describes stick and rudder flying with a compass and flying by road in the United States before World War II. No radar. Few radio communication facilities. Occasional high-power AM radio stations that served as beacons and provided music for long, slow flights over the endless countryside. You were completely on your own.

Speaking with Tom, this felt like an opportunity to do the kind of flying Gann describes. I had to admit to myself that pioneering sounded pretty exciting. Again, I thought, "We are just concentrating on getting the job done for Tom and having a good time doing it." Yeah, sure. That's what we were doing.

"You know, this could be quite the pioneering expedition," Tom said with a half-amused gleam in his eyes. Was he reading my mind, or was it already written all over my face?

In flying, there are three basic rules: Don't crash. Don't run out of gas. Don't get lost.

My biggest challenge was to figure out how to make this mission work with a minimal amount of external navigational support. It was quite an issue. In 1992 the GPS (Global Positioning System) was still being created. The US Air Force had a few satellites in orbit and was planning launches of several more each year. GPS-based commercial-user equipment was just beginning to appear on the market for land and boat use only. There was nothing on the market for aviation use.

By the time our meeting ended, Tom and I had a plan. We had a route and a timeline. We had figured it out to the first order. We had a lot of work to do to sort out the details. But conceptually, this is how flight planning gets done. It's a top-down process with successive iterations of more and more details. Top-down planning also surfaces most of the biggest issues early.

We knew the capabilities of the aircraft. The significant advantage of a propjet for this kind of mission was that it could also fly as low as a few hundred feet off the ground. Because of its slow approach speed and quick stopping ability, we could land on gravel or grass strips, or even on dirt roads if need be. We needed flexibility. The primary tradeoff for high or low altitude was fuel consumption. How far we could fly was a function of how high we flew. There was also a limit to how much the aircraft could carry, which led to tradeoffs among fuel, passengers, and cargo.

We quickly concluded that we needed to launch into Russia from Nome, Alaska, and so the first part of the exercise was figuring out how to get to Nome. Once we flew across the Bering Strait into Russia, we figured out where the cities were and assumed that there were airfields there. We also assumed that we'd be able to get jet fuel at those airfields. Propjets use the same type of kerosene that jet aircraft use all over the world, including Russia. They were certain to have fuel we could use if they had fuel at all.

Flying generally adds an entirely new dimension to the concept of doing your homework. Planning for this mission, with its extraordinary complexities, involved putting my life and the lives of others who would be with me in my hands. We had to know what we were talking about. We had to know what the numbers we were calculating meant. We took it very seriously.

As we worked through the details, I began visualizing the entire flight. Visualization made it easier for me to think about how things were going to work. Just as importantly, what to do if things didn't work. All pilots have to learn to never allow ourselves to get into situations we can't fly out of. Going for a swim in the Bering Strait was just one of a long list of unacceptable outcomes that I needed to consider.

Frankly, the entrepreneurial spirit was not in any way present in this moment. But the adventure, that was something else. The opportunity to fly where no Westerner had ever flown was a rare opportunity. It was great fun imagining the experience, even knowing that it was never going to happen. I had to keep telling myself this was just an exercise to help Tom save face.

"Okay, Tom, let's go over the basic plan. We'll fly out of Orange County and make our first stop at Truckee, north of Lake Tahoe. Then we'll make our second stop and overnight in Seattle at Boeing Field. We'll fly from there up to Juneau, and then through the Wrangell Mountains, and the glacier fields, into Anchorage. We'll give ourselves a rest day and some buffer time before flying from there west and north, along the Yukon River and the Iditarod Trail. Then we'll fly west along the southern coast of the Seward peninsula and into Nome. What fun!"

Tom loved it. We finished up with lists of unresolved issues, action items, supplies and equipment, and possible candidates for the mission, along with a timeline and a navigational plot. We knew where, how, and who. Now we needed to talk about when. Schedule management is how I've always run my life. It's not real until I put it on the schedule. Scheduling for me is where life starts. I subscribe to Woody Allen's philosophy that "Eighty percent of success in life is showing up." I've always believed that where I choose to show up determines what my priorities are and what I've chosen to invest my energies in. So, when I decide where I'm going to show up and when, I'm ultimately deciding the course of my life. Scheduling is affirmation. It's why I've been an obsessive schedule organizer my entire adult life. Said another way, my operational definition of freedom is, "Control your time and the resources to take advantage of it!"

So here we were, integrating a schedule for something that was never going to happen with my clients' schedules, my SM&A

schedule, my family's schedule, and my personal schedule. What had been, up to this point, an exercise seemed suddenly very real. The biggest driver in this entire exercise had come down to *when*, not *if* it could happen.

It had to be July; it was the best weather in that part of the world and the most daylight. Daylight was critical. We couldn't control the weather, but the last thing we needed was to run out of daylight over there. I had spent some time in Alaska in prior years and was generally familiar with the flying environment. Daylight was your friend. The trip had to start on the Fourth of July, Independence Day, the beginning of a three-day holiday weekend. We needed to be able to return by July 25th, at the latest. Three weeks was plenty. It was the time period when I would be missed the least. Things were always slow in July. It was far enough out that I could plan around it. No other start date was acceptable. We, therefore, had to be able to cross into Russian airspace on July 8, 1992.

Many details still needed to be sorted out, like where we were going to stay. But we didn't need to know those details to finish this exercise. We had a credible list of non-negotiable demands, starting with a non-negotiable date that they'd have to agree to for us to come. Finally, the meeting was finished.

Tom said, "Great! I'll write Yuri a long communiqué explaining these demands. He'll love it. It's very credible. He'll be able to save face when the authorities blow him off."

"Great! Thanks, Tom. It was a fun exercise."

People were lining up outside my door. It was going to be a very long day. I had reviews scheduled with people until late in the evening. I went on with the business of the day: Lockheed, THAAD, SM&A, the family. I knew there was no way it was going to happen. I didn't even bother to mention the meeting to Ken, or my wife. I didn't give it another thought.

3

THEY CALLED MY BLUFF

*"I am in it for the flying. It is an adventure. We'll
fly over there, have a great time, take some pictures,
and have a cool story to tell the kids."*

A month after Tom's visit, in March 1992, I was in my office at Lockheed, Sunnyvale, happily grinding away on the THAAD proposal, when the phone rang. It was Tom. "They've accepted everything!"

"What?"

"Yeah. I went back to Yuri. I called him in Moscow, and I said, 'Look, this is what Steve wants.' There was a lot of screaming and yelling on the other end of the phone. I was on a speakerphone with Yuri and his staff. They didn't want to do any of it at first. They seemed shocked you actually thought you could do it. I don't think they thought I was ever serious about it. After I went through each of the issues, they asked a lot of questions."

I sighed. "Yes, I know exactly how they felt. Go on."

"They had a lot of questions I wouldn't have been able to answer if we had not gone through that two-hour preliminary planning effort on your whiteboard. As I went through it with them, they began to realize how serious and capable we were. By the time we finished, I had sensed a certain resignation in their tone. They were going to have to try."

As Tom talked me through the details of the call, I began to realize that Yuri and his people were cornered. Yuri had committed to Tom that he would take this idea to his superiors if Tom confirmed I would do it.

"I think they're going to agree. Yuri asked me to call back after they had a chance to make some calls and have some meetings about it. I called Yuri back, and they agreed. They're preparing a memorandum now. I should have the fax in the next couple of days. That's the first step. Once we have an agreement in principle in writing, they'll have something they can take to their superiors."

"Great. Get back to me when it's in writing."

After some pleasantries, I hung up the phone. I still didn't believe it. No way was this going to happen. I went back to work and just forgot about it—a second time.

Several days later, Tom called, again.

"I've got the letter. They've agreed to everything you demanded."

"Crap!"

"I'm faxing it to you right now so we can read it together."

"Crap!"

We went over Osipov's letter line-by-line. They would agree to everything, and more. I thought to myself, "Oh, my. Am I really going to be a pioneer?" Then I thought, "Oh, my. What am I going to tell my wife?"

The 1980s were, in many ways, the happiest and most transformational years of my life. It was the decade in which most of my children were born. I met and married my second wife, Paula. My life path became clear, and my business prospered. It was also, by the way, the best decade for music ever. We had four children: two daughters from my first marriage, a son from Paula's first marriage, and a daughter with Paula. We were a prospering, prototypical, blended family.

I started a consulting business in the aerospace and defense arena the year that Ronald Reagan became president. Listening to his inauguration speech on January 20, 1981, I knew that opportunity was at hand. The core of Reagan's agenda was a massive buildup in US military capability to confront what he called the Evil Empire. I spent the entire decade working in significant roles on many programs of national importance, including the Strategic Defense Initiative, aka "Star Wars."

Then, on January 28, 1986, I witnessed the Space Shuttle Challenger explode. It was a heartbreaking, horrific, and needless thing to have happened. Needless because one of the first things all pilots learn, and something constantly reinforced in recurrent flight training, is never to operate an aircraft outside its operating limitations.

It was an exceptionally cold morning at Cape Kennedy for the Challenger launch, close to 31 degrees Fahrenheit. The O-rings, rubber gaskets that provided a critical double seal between the solid rocket motor segments, had become stiff and brittle. Flaming hot propellant was able to escape through the dysfunctional seals and ignite the main fuel tank.

Challenger was a disaster in every way imaginable. It was a tragedy for those seven brave lost souls, for their families, for NASA, for the US, and the world. A tragedy still playing out today in a Space Program that is no longer viable.

One of the first consequences of the Challenger disaster was the decision by the Air Force to move its satellite launch manifest from the Space Shuttle onto a new generation of expendable launch vehicles. They didn't have a choice. One of the Air Force's highest priorities was launching the first generation of

Global Positioning System satellites into orbit. They needed a new launch vehicle to make it happen, and they needed it now.

McDonnell Douglas pulled me away from my work on Strategic Defense Initiative projects at Rockwell to manage their proposal for a new vehicle specifically designed to launch GPS satellites. The Air Force called it a medium launch vehicle (MLV). This may have been the single most important project of my career. We eventually won a very hard-fought competition against Martin Marietta and General Dynamics that we were handicapped to lose. This win set up a long string of nationally significant competitions I led in the years following. These included the proposal to NASA for the Space Station for McDonnell Douglas, the replacement program for the solid rocket motors that had failed on the Challenger for the Lockheed/Aerojet Team, the space-based infrared satellite system, and the Theater High Altitude Area Defense (THAAD) system for Lockheed, all of which we won.

The MLV is still carrying GPS satellites into orbit to this day, without a single launch failure. McDonnell Douglas, now Boeing, has done a magnificent job over the last three plus decades of this program. People today, all over the world, take this extraordinary technological capability for granted. They have no appreciation of the enormous gift that the United States has given to the world with GPS. I am very proud to have been one of the many people who made it possible.

When Tom first began working with the Soviet system in 1987, he quickly discovered how complicated and difficult it was to get anything done at all. Everything was a negotiation. The Communist Party, the Soviet military, and the KGB were in the middle of every activity. Everyone had to be lined up to proceed with whatever you wanted to do. It was usually an impossible task. They would just wear you out.

This is the kind of frustration that drives entrepreneurs crazy. Entrepreneurs are not known for being rule followers. The entrepreneur's guild motto is, "Better to ask forgiveness than permission." By contrast, in the Soviet culture, the motto seemed to be, "Anything not expressly permitted is forbidden." Any request made which could be denied *would* be. Imagine the impact such a concept would have on the psyche of any culture.

Perhaps this difference in mindset, more than any other, is the reason for the enormous economic prosperity of the US. Make the sandbox safe for entrepreneurs, create some hardline boundary conditions, and then just get out of the way. Smart entrepreneurs make sure that they have plenty of rule followers around them to keep them from going too far afield. The bottom-line impact is that the US today is 25 percent of the global GDP. Russia is 2 percent.

The Soviet Union may have fallen, but the "Union" was still very much in place as a way of life. Nothing had changed in the day-to-day lives of most of the people except their level of uncertainty and anxiety. The people in charge scurried around more than ever, struggling to find their relevance in the new order. Tom developed an excellent strategy for dealing with the Soviet mindset: tell each of the three groups (the government bureaucrats, the KGB, and the group you were working with) that the other two were on board, and they (the third group) were the only ones causing trouble.

The letters we began receiving from the Russians were not the typical draft letters of intent, in a business sense, I was used to seeing. They were in English but had more of the characteristics of diplomatic engagement. There were a lot of code phrases requiring us to read between the lines. The first letter said that they thought they could work out the details. The next letter, which was still general in content, linked the trip to the Mars rover project. This was all about "cover" for them.

I began to understand how this clash of cultures could become an insurmountable obstacle. After a great deal of back-and-forth, we finally received a letter permitting us to proceed. It came in a strange, negative way, so customary of the Soviet culture. The letter began, "Nyet, no, you can't come. Absolutely you cannot come." And then the very next sentence read, "You cannot come farther than Anadyr." Anadyr was our proposed second stop after crossing the Bering Strait.

"Oh, so then we can't go," I said to Tom, with some enthusiasm.

"No, no, this is okay," Tom replied. "They say we can't go, but we *can* go. They're just negotiating." Tom had become an expert in Soviet banter.

Eventually a letter came which said, "Well okay, as long as you're in Anadyr, do you want to come all the way to Petropavlovsk?"

Tom's reply was simple enough, but did the trick: "Yes, we want to come all the way."

For a project not supposed to happen, this situation was beginning to feel positively surreal. The chances of this adventure's actually happening seemed to have gone from zero to maybe 30/70. I felt the need to tell both Ken and Paula what was up. I started with Ken, probably because I didn't have a clue how to explain it to Paula. Ken reacted surprisingly well to the news. It sounded to him like a great adventure, and he thought my July timing was good. He particularly liked that I'd be the first American to do it.

Paula's reaction was more incredulous. She knew how much I loved flying and thought I'd have a great time. But she was also worried about the risks involved, as any wife would be. She was particularly concerned about the travel team getting stuck in Russia, for any number of reasons, and not being able to get out for quite a while. I tried to assuage her concerns. I promised her and the kids a grand flying vacation around the US shortly after my return in late July to celebrate our achievement.

Entrepreneurs are a rare and peculiar breed of people: driven, never satisfied, never content, hungry. What are we hungry *for*? Every entrepreneur has something to prove. Some, like myself, are born into impoverished circumstances. We rise out of poverty and fight our way to the top. Perhaps it's about legitimacy. We tend to overcompensate. For some, the motives may be different, but the result is the same. Eventually, some of us discover our destinies, and if we are lucky, embrace them wholeheartedly. The entrepreneur in me was starting to take control.

The telltale rationalizations were becoming evident in my thoughts: "I am in it for the flying. It's an adventure. We'll fly over there, have a great time, take some pictures, and have a cool story to tell the kids." The Russians needed their cover story; I needed mine.

4

PLANNING FOR THE IMPROBABLE

Despite the Russian consulate being officially closed, Katya
was able to walk into the consulate and get our visas. Without
Katya, the entire mission would have most certainly blown up.

On June 4, 1992, we were deep into planning for our July
4th mission departure. True to form, I received a package
from the Consulate General of the Russian Federation in San
Francisco. The letter in the package read, "Unfortunately, as
the proposed places of visit are located in closed areas, the host
organizations are in no position to issue invitation letters directly.
Instead, they should clear their invitations through the Russian
Foreign Ministry, and only upon receiving such clearance can
visas be processed by our office. We are returning the documents
and advise you should contact your hosts in Russia and ask them
to initiate all necessary procedures in Moscow. Hopefully, there
is enough time to undertake all required actions before your
proposed visit."

"Yes, I hope so, too!" was my reaction.

I faxed the letter and a cover note to Tom: "This letter came
with the applications and our returned checks this morning.
What now?"

Tom's response was positive, as always: "Don't worry. It's going to get fixed. Viktor is all over it."

Viktor Kerzanovich, an engineer at IKI, had become a very close friend of Tom's and had become our invaluable paperwork expeditor on the Russian side. He was planning to rendezvous with us in Provideniya, the first landing point across the Bering Strait. But the big news buried in Tom's reply was about a Russian navigator. This was stunning news. The navigator would sit in the co-pilot seat, the right seat in the cockpit, and handle all my communication and navigation needs while in Russia. He'd provide everything I had been fretting about: charts, frequencies, beacon codes, contacts, relationships, interpreting, etc.

It was time to begin preparing for the mission in earnest. We didn't have a lot of time, especially when talking about flying the first mission into the post-Cold War Russian Far East. This wasn't going to be a pleasure flight through Canada and Alaska. Flying to Nome, in the far western reaches of Alaska, was certain to be an adventure all by itself.

My two most significant concerns about the mission were navigation and weather. We were going to be operating in a part of the world that very few people on our side of the Pacific Rim knew anything about, and almost no one knew in sufficient detail to be useful. I needed precise latitude and longitude coordinates to use as waypoints and to find the places we were going to. The weather, at best, was expected to be broken cloudiness with occasional overcast, just like Alaska. We certainly needed to know the terrain. How high were the mountains? At what altitudes could we safely operate? Going as high as possible was not generally a good strategy for this kind of scenario. High meant that we'd inevitably find ourselves over cloud cover. How would I know where we were? How would we get down?

The Russian navigator meant that we'd have everything we needed, but he introduced other issues. Would I be able to read the charts he carried? How good was the navigator's English? How would I verify the information he was giving me? The key to resolving these navigational issues was GPS.

In an ironic twist of fate, I had persuaded McDonnell Douglas six years earlier to offer a faster launch schedule in the medium launch vehicle (MLV) proposal I was managing for them than the Air Force required. It was a key element of our win strategy (see chapter 3). The faster launch schedule resulted in more GPS satellites in orbit in July 1992 when I needed them! The coverage was still patchy, with accuracy degraded, but still way better than my alternatives.

Unfortunately, the satellites would be no help without a GPS receiver, and there were no GPS receivers on the market for civil aircraft in 1992. But I had an idea.

Long range area navigation (LORAN) is a ground-based system commonly used by ships and aircraft during the 1980s. I had a LORAN receiver in the cockpit dashboard of my Aero Commander, manufactured by a company called NorthStar. It worked exceptionally well. But LORAN would not work in the far northern latitudes we'd be flying in. I had heard a rumor that NorthStar was developing a combined GPS/LORAN receiver that could easily retrofit into the dashboard slot of an existing LORAN receiver. All that would be needed was a GPS antenna and cabling. It was tailor-made for my mission.

I reached out to the NorthStar VP of marketing and persuaded him to use my mission as a beta test of their new receiver. I offered to come back with a detailed technical report on their receiver's performance, including pictures and a great endorsement that they'd be able to use for advertising. To my great relief, he loved the idea and was able to sell it to NorthStar management.

They all loved the idea, but there were concerns. Their engineers didn't know how well the unit would work at the latitudes we'd be flying in. Mine was precisely the kind of beta test they needed to get answers about coverage limits.

The prototype receiver arrived via FedEx within a few days, along with the cables and a 110 VAC power converter. I needed the converter to program the unit at my desk with lat/long waypoints. I also needed to play with the unit's new features. I wanted to be comfortable with using it before installing it in the airplane. I programmed every waypoint of significance I thought we'd need for the trip using the geodetic survey charts of north-eastern Russia that I had received from NOAA.

On June 5, 1992, with a month to go before departure, our five-member travel team held an extensive planning meeting at Zamperini Field in Torrance, California. I was very fortunate to meet Capt. Louis Zamperini and hear his remarkable story before he died in 2014. He was a juvenile delinquent, a 1936 Berlin Olympic track star, a WWII B-24 bombardier, a Japanese POW survivor, and a Christian evangelist. His is an inspiring story of courage and determination. His autobiography, *Devil at My Heels*, is a great book and the subject of the 2014 movie, *Unbroken*.

I needed to familiarize the travel team with the Aero Commander's operating and emergency procedures and give those who had not flown with me before some time to become comfortable with the airplane. The meeting turned into a lengthy detailed, planning, and status discussion. There was a great deal to go over. For example, how the flight segments were organized and why. How weight was allocated and why. Who would be responsible for which tasks. What we would do under all kinds of contingencies, and so forth. There were many questions to be answered, and lists were compiled of action items. It was a mission that we all wanted to conduct safely, but that we also recognized had some potentially significant risks. The more we talked, the more the team got pumped up for it.

The team consisted of me, Tom Heinsheimer, Julie Heinsheimer, Ed Beall, and Mike Stoner. Julie, Tom's wife, had several responsibilities, one of which was the team's healthcare. What if someone became ill? What contingencies should we plan for? The group agreed that if someone died, the others might have to leave that person. Later, the survivors would try to recover anyone lost, but the priority had to be the survival of the living. We agreed not to risk the lives of the living over the dead. This wasn't the Army. It wasn't a "no soldier left behind" kind of mission.

Ed Beall was an architect, artist, and journalist. He would document the trip from beginning to end. Mike Stoner would be our videographer and photographer. Tom would sit right seat and help me with navigation as far as Provideniya. Julie and Ed would sit in the back, where there were large panorama windows and tables that they could use for drawing and writing during each leg. Mike would sit in a middle seat facing aft, where he'd be able to move around quickly to take pictures and video. I broke the outbound trip to Petropavlovsk into six flight segments:

4 July	Orange County to Truckee to Seattle Boeing Field
5 July	Seattle to Juneau to Anchorage
6 July	Anchorage to Nome
6/7 July	Nome to a still TBD waypoint (in the Bering Strait at the International Date Line) to Provideniya.
8 July	Provideniya to Korf
9 July	Korf to Petropavlovsk

The plan was to take off fairly early in the morning on July 4th, make a fuel and rest stop at Truckee airport, just north of Lake Tahoe, and arrive in Seattle by midafternoon. The next day we'd leave Seattle and fly along the coast of British Columbia to Juneau for a fuel and rest stop, then through the Wrangell Mountains, over the glacier fields, and on to Anchorage, arriving midafternoon. With some twenty-three hours of daylight in the far north, the concept of midafternoon took on an entirely different context. We were not going to run out of daylight.

We hoped for good weather and agreed to continue past Anchorage and fly north up the valley to Denali National Park. After circling Mount McKinley, renamed Denali in 2015 (the highest mountain in North America, at 20,310 feet), we'd return to Anchorage for some dinner and a good night's sleep. If we were not able to see Mt. McKinley on the fifth, we would try again on the way to Nome on the sixth and, failing that, try again on the return trip. Every leg was about weather, navigation, and fuel management.

We needed to fly from Anchorage to Nome on the morning of July 6th to be fed, rested, refueled, and prepared to cross the Bering Strait to arrive at a specific waypoint on the International

Date Line at a precise time on July 7th. We had not yet been given either the waypoint or the time.

There were several unknowns we had to accept to make the mission work. The single most stressing of these was what to do if an engine failed taking off from Provideniya or jet fuel wasn't available at Provideniya. I planned to carry enough fuel to fly back to Nome or Anadyr, or possibly Korf, if we had enough fuel. The Russian navigator would be a great help sorting this out if it came to that. We had options. We'd deal with whatever happened.

What this meant operationally was that we needed to take off from Nome with full fuel (2,573 pounds) and five people at maximum gross takeoff weight (10,350 pounds), fly to Provideniya, land, add two people (about the same weight as we'd use flying there of 400 to 500 pounds), take off, lose an engine on takeoff, and then fly back to Nome. If all went well on takeoff, we'd fly on to our next destination, which could be no further than three hours flying time away.

Given these requirements, there were 1,550 pounds available for the five of us and all the stuff we'd need to take with us. The five of us weighed about 975 pounds, fully clothed. We were each allocated a 50-pound personal allowance, for a total of 250 pounds. We allowed 527 pounds for airplane spare parts, food, water, other supplies, a raft, gifts, charts, emergency equipment, and medical supplies.

The Aero Commander 690B propjet is a remarkable airplane. The numbers show why it was ideal for this mission. It could take off in 1,500 feet from a gravel runway, which is what we'd have at Provideniya. It could climb 3,000 feet a minute, nominally cruise at 265 knots, and fly 900 to 1,300 miles with 2,573 pounds of fuel (about 384 gallons), depending on altitude. It could fly as high as 31,000 feet or as low as we needed to, which at times would at 500 feet for considerable distances.

The 10,350-pound maximum gross weight was based on how well the airplane would perform on a single engine. If an engine failed during takeoff, this was critical. At sea level, the plane would climb 900 feet-a-minute on a single engine. And every flight for the trip, except the fuel stop at Truckee, would be at sea level.

Center of gravity (CG) at maximum gross weight is usually a limiting factor in how much can be carried and where people and stuff are stowed in an aircraft. A CG too far forward or too far aft makes an aircraft increasingly difficult to handle during an engine failure. Demonstrating how remarkable the design of the Aero Commander is, the airplane can fly at maximum gross weight, with 600 pounds in the cargo hold and someone in every seat, and stay well within the CG limit.

The gravel runway at Provideniya was a major concern. I had never landed an aircraft on gravel. I called some people who had. We discussed soft landing and soft takeoff procedures for the 690B. I had done these kinds of landings with single-engine aircraft, but I had never needed to with an aircraft of this size. I was much more concerned about the takeoff than the landing. The issue was that gravel could get into the engine during takeoff. Propjets were designed to make that unlikely to happen. The spinning propeller acted as a barrier to potential foreign object debris (FOD) or gravel getting into the jet engine intake, but this was by no means a sure thing. "Get the airplane into the air as fast as possible," was the best advice pilots who had done it could offer.

Right on cue, my aircraft insurance broker called with bad news. Russia was not on the list of countries that my airplane was approved to fly in. I needed the underwriters to approve an amendment to my policy to include Russia. I should not have been surprised when my agent said that the underwriters had freaked out at the suggestion and did not want to do it.

"What? No way can this trip happen without insurance. You've got to fix this."

After much imploring, my agent was able to persuade the underwriters to take a serious look at covering the trip. They sent two representatives to meet with me. They inspected the airplane and went over a long list of questions about my flying experience and what I would do under various scenarios to protect their interests. The gravel runway at Provideniya was at the top of their list of issues. They specifically wanted to know what I would do if an engine failed on takeoff.

Fortunately, I had done my homework and was able to explain to them, in detail, my plans for this contingency. They were both surprised and relieved to learn that I intended to fly the plane back to Nome on one engine. They required me to do some practice takeoffs from unimproved airstrips using soft- and short-field takeoff techniques in the Acro Commander. I was already planning to do this anyway. The underwriters went away happy with my answers, approved the trip, and sent me a bill for a very substantial one-time increase in premium. I was more than happy to pay it.

My navigational strategy for flying in Russia was to use easily identified landmarks as waypoints and program each into the beta-test NorthStar GPS unit with their latitudes and longitudes. If the GPS unit failed, I had chosen waypoints that I thought I could recognize from the air and use for dead reckoning using the US Geodetic Survey charts. I thought I could navigate safely using geodetic charts without any additional navigational aids if I had reasonable visibility. This was a big "if."

My biggest concern was the weather. The weather could be very unpredictable in the far north. We'd have reliable weather data as far as Nome. From there westward, it would be a complete unknown. The prior July had seen very good weather in

Alaska. But the summer prior to that had been poor. There was no way to know what the weather would be like. We'd just have to deal with it in real-time and make prudent choices. Again, it was all about whether the Russian navigator had his act together. If we couldn't see well enough to identify landmarks, we might find ourselves grounded for days while we waited for acceptable weather conditions. What if we were forced down by mechanical failure? I could land the airplane on a road or flat terrain in an emergency, but we might be stuck there for quite a while. Emergency supplies were critical. How would the Russians treat us under such circumstances? Even having Viktor Kerzhanovich with us was no guarantee that the locals would be cooperative.

We assumed that the Russian navigator assigned to us would also be an ex-KGB/FSB representative. He'd be there to watch us and report—not just navigate for us. I was counting on his ability to help out if unforeseen circumstances arose.

There was still a great deal to do, and fewer than thirty days to go. A letter had to be written to the district director for US Customs in Anchorage to arrange for out-of-port service in Nome if we had to make an emergency return from Provideniya, and later, when we returned from Petropavlovsk. We were uncertain of our return date and our point of departure. We assumed that it would be Provideniya since we were entering Russia there. There were forms to complete, and people to call.

I got a tip from a friend about a pilot working out of LAX who had Russian instrument approach plates for some of the airports in the Russian Far East. How he came by these charts is a bit of a story. He had been flying cargo flights into Vladivostok and Khabarovsk on the Mongolian border and bribed an Aeroflot pilot for his charts. Those charts would be extremely helpful, but he wouldn't give them up. I finally persuaded him to let me make copies of some of them for a small fee.

I couldn't read Russian, but I was able to sort out most of the Russian instrument approaches because they were based on the use of non-directional beacons (NDBs). NDB instrument approaches were invented by General Jimmy Doolittle, of World War II fame. He was the first aviator to fly on instruments in the late 1920s. He invented many of the primary instruments required to do so. NDB approaches are rarely used in the US today but are still in everyday use in much of the third world, and Russia in particular.

In 1992, NDBs were still in everyday use in many parts of the US. These approaches could be challenging because they weren't very accurate, and wind conditions could make them even harder to use, especially if the pilot wasn't proficient. I rarely used NDBs. This meant I needed to take a very conservative approach to using them. For example, I'd have to raise my weather minimums to twice the published "minimums" on the chart, the lowest altitude I could descend to without seeing the runway.

My cockpit happened to have an instrument in the dashboard, called a radio magnetic indicator (RMI), specifically for use in executing double NDB approaches. An RMI is a gyro-driven compass with two needles that could point to two different NDB transmitters, precisely what I needed for Provideniya. I was concerned about what to do if the gyro failed, or one of the NDB receivers failed during the trip. I figured out how to fly the approach with the gyro inoperative or with only one NDB. It wasn't going to be easy, but I had a plan.

Yet another issue was altitude conversion. The Russian charts presented all altitudes in meters. My airplane's two altimeters displayed altitude in feet. I had never worked with meters and had no confidence in my ability to convert one way or the other in my head, under any kind of stress. While stationed in Germany in the late 1960s, I learned to drive on roads using kilometers for speed and distance instead of miles. This was an entirely different exercise. Getting the speed wrong might get you a ticket. Getting the altitude wrong in Russian airspace could get you killed. I developed a practical conversion table mounted on the dashboard was easy to use.

The planning process went on like this every day. Another issue or contingency emerged, and every day we came up with solutions. We just kept grinding away at the list.

"Tom, do you have our Russian visas yet?!"

"No," was the short answer.

One day Viktor sent us a message that we had to have a CDS number from the Russian government entered into the international flight plan that we'd be filing in Nome. He emphasized that we couldn't go without the CDS number.

"Great. What is a CDS number, and how do we get one?"

Ed Beall's wife, Suzie, helped Julie put together medical and emergency aid supplies. Ed and Julie started packaging all of our trip food supplies and equipment. We needed 220 VAC electrical power adapters for recharging our batteries for the video equipment. We needed all kinds of spare batteries for our cameras and flashlights.

Since everyone was bringing a camera, we all agreed to use the same kind of slide film for easier integration and processing later. Mike Stoner, our videographer, and I had been experimenting with a new Kodak slide film recently introduced, Ektachrome EPZ-100. The quality was excellent. We purchased an ample supply of 64-, 100-, and 400-speeds. Kodachrome 25 was just too slow for aircraft use.

We hired a publicist, and she started putting together hundreds of press kits for all of the press conferences she was scheduling before our departure. Tom designed a large logo for our flight with the title across the top, California Kamchatka. We put decals of the logo on both sides of the Aero Commander fuselage. Tom also made some stick-on decals and baseball caps with the same logo, so we could give them away to people we encountered on our trip.

We planned two more travel team meetings before departure. The next meeting was on June 16th. We needed to verify that all arrangements had been made and review equipment and supply details. Our publicist wanted to brief us on PR and press plans.

"Viktor and Tom, do we have visas yet?"

"No," was the short answer.

The team planned to rendezvous at my house on July 3rd at about 4 p.m. for a final trip briefing, a discussion session, a farewell dinner party, and a sleepover. We planned to stage everything in the garage, weigh everybody and everything to be sure we were within our 1,552-pound limit, and load the airplane to make sure everything fit.

"Tom and Viktor, we'd better have visas by then! How's it going?"

On June 14th, Tom called to say, "We've run into more visa problems, which Viktor is all over." Tom didn't sound particularly concerned.

"What does that mean?" We had twenty days to go.

The next day Tom and I received a letter from Viktor. First, he reported that there was a problem with the runway in Provideniya. "It is covered with 'broken stones,'" which I interpreted to mean gravel. However, he reported that Russian passenger planes were landing there, including AN-26s, with forty passengers. He wanted to know whether I could land in such conditions.

Second, we had to choose between two different waypoints from which to cross into Russian airspace—Larsa or Valda. They needed to know which for our final flight planning. After studying the charts, I picked Valda.

Third, we had to plan to pay with cash for everything. The Russians did not have any means to take credit cards. Navigator, fuel, services, etc.—all cash. We needed to bring plenty, along with a very large stack of one-dollar bills.

Fourth, he was having trouble getting the authorities to agree to let us land in Korf, located at the north end of the Kamchatka peninsula, and was suggesting alternatives that were out of range, given our fuel capacity.

Viktor finally assured us, yet again, that he was "working for permission."

"Visas, Viktor!"

We informed Viktor we could indeed land on their "broken stones" and we would cross into Russian airspace at Valda on July 7th at 23:00 Zulu, now called Universal Coordinated Time (UTC). I did not tell Viktor or my team about my plan to make a low pass over the runway at Provideniya before landing and, if I didn't like what I saw, return to Nome. I didn't see any reason to tell anyone. I didn't want them to worry about it. I explained in detail how Korf was vital to our mission. We simply didn't have either the range to reach their alternative fields or the range from their alternatives to reach Petropavlovsk. For example, they suggested Anadyr, but the range from Anadyr to Petropavlovsk was over 1,000 miles. I couldn't fly that far with our passenger load.

We also needed the mythical CDS number for the international flight plan we had to file in Nome.

"Where is the CDS coming from? How are you going to get it? Where are the visas?"

At this point, I had my fingers and toes crossed. June 25th. Nine days to go.

We received a fax from Viktor saying that he had heard from the Kamchatka authorities. They had promised to give permission by June 30th or July 1st at the latest. He said he would send a fax to their consulate in San Francisco immediately after he received this permission. He was in daily contact with Kamchatka. They were proposing a backup plan whereby they would provide Viktor with visa papers so he could do everything needed in Provideniya.

I am not the nervous type. It is not my style. But I was beginning to feel nervous. We were nine days from launch and still didn't have visas and didn't have the mythical CDS number. These, plus so many other details, were still coming together and running through my mind. I knew in my gut that it was going to happen. But how?

On June 29th, with five days to go, Tom received a letter from Moscow, which said, "Space Research Institute and Institute of Volcanology of the Russian Academy of Sciences invites you to visit Russia for discussion of the results and preparation for the future tests of the Mars rover in the Mars 96 Project. The meeting will be held at town Kozyrevsk, Kamchatka. Your visit there is approved by the authorities. You may apply for your Visa to the Soviet Embassy/Consulate using this Telex as your Visa support."

Phew! Interesting that it said "Soviet" and not "Russian."

I sighed the biggest sigh. Little did I know . . .

I relayed the fax to Tom, Julie, Ed, and Mike, saying that the flight planning was complete and included the final itinerary with the latest dates and phone numbers.

Ed was making the hotel arrangements on the North American side. Our publicist was scheduling a press conference at Orange County Airport for July 3rd. This trip was happening!

Or was it? Where were the visas? What's the CDS number?

Tom called the Russian consulate on July 2nd and found that there were no visas because the consulate in San Francisco was going to be closed on Friday, July 3rd, for the 4th of July weekend!

"Are you kidding me?" We needed a miracle.

The miracle's name was Katya Linkin. Katya had been on loan from IKI, working temporarily at the Planetary Society in Pasadena for about a year. She was a very capable scientist with a physics degree from the Moscow Pedagogical Institute. She is also the daughter of a famous Russian space scientist by the name of Slava Linkin. She was in California to help prepare the Russian rover Marsokhod for tests, organized by The Planetary Society, to be conducted in the Mojave Desert. It was her first trip to the US, and she was in culture shock. Life in the States was so very different from the life she had known in the USSR.

Katya happened to be visiting with Tom and Julie when the visa crisis came to a head. Tom told her about it, not because he thought she could help, but just because she was a sympathetic ear to his massive sense of frustration. To Tom's astonishment, Katya picked up the phone and called the Russian consulate in San Francisco. After several minutes of conversation, which Tom did not understand, Katya said that she'd be back the next day. She drove to the airport, caught the next flight to San Francisco, and took a taxi to the consulate. There she presented the consul general with our letter of invitation and, with his permission, telephoned Moscow and had the consul general speak with Prof. Roald Sagdeev, the director of IKI, the Space Research Institute. The consul general then gave his permission, but only if Katya presented the documents the next day.

So, Katya stayed in San Francisco overnight. Or more accurately, she stayed awake in San Francisco. Tom had given her a credit card to use for expenses, but she couldn't bring herself to use the card. In Russia, it was considered morally unforgivable to use a stranger's credit card. Instead, she spent the night aimlessly walking the streets in San Francisco with a bar of Ghirardelli chocolate for her dinner.

Despite the Russian consulate's being officially closed on July 3rd, Katya was able to walk into the consulate and get our visas. Without Katya, the entire trip would have most certainly blown up. It would have been the beginning of the following week before we would have had the visas; the flight planning would have been void, our launch window missed, and our passing across the Russian border at the approved time missed. Planning with the Russians was that specific. Everything had to be cleared all the way through—no improvisation with these people.

On July 2nd, the *Los Angeles Times* blasted the Metro page headline, "Making History with Flight to Once-Secret Area." I was proud, excited, and relieved. I eagerly read the article:

"Our flight there is not just for adventure," said Heinsheimer, who has been a Rolling Hills councilman since 1972. "The flight is a symbol of serious commitment to open Kamchatka for major business development. The location of this area on the Pacific Rim provides enormous potential for business opportunities with Japan, Canada, and the USA. There is also a potential for Tourism."

"We're going to be the first non-Russians allowed to fly an aircraft into Kamchatka," said Myers. "It's a real thrill, and I'm honored to do so."

The *Orange County Alert* front-page headline announced, "Flight to Siberian Peninsula a 1st for Americans," and quoted me as saying, *"This flight is a historic aviation achievement and will document air routes and territory never before flown by civilian aviators."*

Another Orange County newspaper described our mission as "a flight into the unknown." Indeed. I felt the adrenaline pumping through my body like a drug. I loved everything about the adventure before us, the planning, the fits and starts, and the notoriety. It was quite a rush. I was all in!

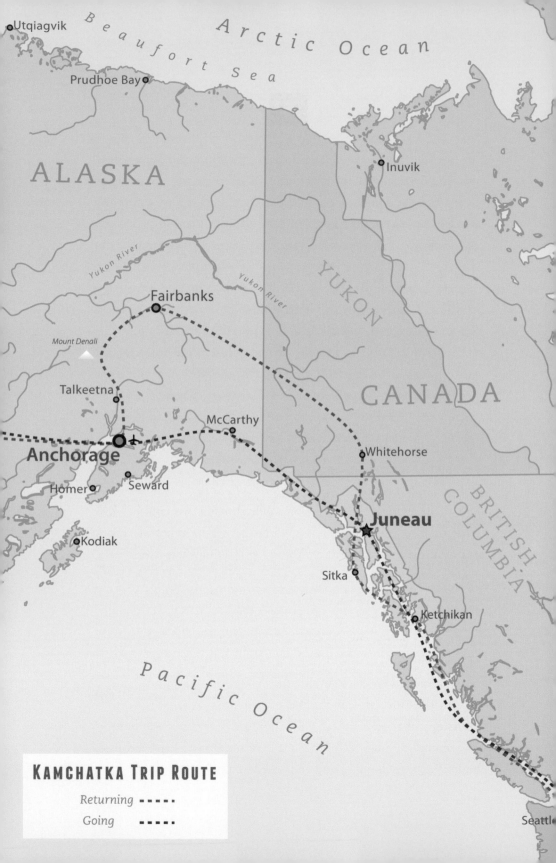

Utqiagvik

Beaufort Sea

Arctic Ocean

Prudhoe Bay

ALASKA

Inuvik

Yukon River

Yukon River

YUKON

CANADA

Fairbanks

Mount Denali

Talkeetna

McCarthy

Whitehorse

Anchorage

Homer

Seward

Juneau

BRITISH COLUMBIA

Kodiak

Sitka

Ketchikan

Pacific Ocean

Seattle

Kamchatka Trip Route

Returning -----

Going ▪▪▪▪▪

5

NORTH TO ALASKA

This was a very rare opportunity for some incredible sightseeing. It was also an opportunity to practice flying in unfamiliar terrain at low altitude while using charts as our only means of navigation.

The weigh-in ceremony held in my garage midafternoon of July 3rd turned into quite a show. We each had a fifty-pound personal allocation. Everyone managed to come in overweight. Tom came in twenty pounds over the limit. Some tough decisions had to be made about what we each thought we couldn't live without. Cameras and film were a must. A warm jacket was more important than extra clothes. The right walking shoes were more important than excess underwear. The garage turned into what looked like a flea market with stuff dumped out all over tarps, reorganized, and reweighed. No one was happy about it. Paula organized a buffet dinner for the team and our kids with some of our favorite foods, wine, and conversation, which put everyone into a better frame of mind.

As the sun rose on the 4th of July, the house came alive. Footsteps, chatter, laughter, and a mixture of frenzied excitement and serene calmness filled the air. Five months of trip planning, bureaucratic diplomacy, organizing lists, completing innumerable tasks, flight planning, weighing, and calculating, and now it was time to go. Every nerve in my body tingled.

The local morning newspaper headline read, "California to the Russian Peninsula of Kamchatka an Aviation First."

We would be flying over areas that were, until now, forbidden to any non-Russian aircraft, in an area of the world closed to foreigners since the late 1930s. The interviews with the media went well. They were clearly intrigued by what we were doing.

At 9:07 a.m., our families, along with several media outlets, joined us on Martin Aviation's ramp at Orange County's John Wayne Airport for our departure. As I started each of the Aero Commander's two Garrett 715 shaft horsepower turbine engines, each made a deep, powerful purr. After completing my pre-taxi checks, I unlocked the propellers and began taxiing north to the end of runway 19R. I completed my cockpit checks and was immediately cleared for takeoff.

For our families and the media watching from the ramp, we were all too present, and then suddenly, in an instant, we vanished into the overcast. Paula later recalled standing on the ramp, holding our youngest daughter in her arms as we departed, hoping I would return safely to her and our children.

The Aero Commander climbed quickly through the overcast and into the clear blue sky. A short ten minutes later, as we passed Los Angeles International Airport (LAX) heading northwest, we were already cruising at 16,000 feet, with a ground speed of 265 knots. I expected headwinds, but for the moment, they were non-existent. A digital readout on the NorthStar GPS predicted our time en route to Truckee (TRK) at less than an hour.

As Bakersfield appeared ahead, I began briefing the travel team on a long list of matters. Everyone wore a noise cancellation headset, which made it easy to hear what we were saying in the cockpit. They could hear me transmit and receive over the radio, or

I could speak to them without transmitting. Mike Stoner plugged a cable from his video camera into the intercom system so he'd be able to record what was being said while he was filming.

I began by reviewing safety procedures: "No one is to open the main door under any circumstances while the propellers are turning. The window behind the jump seat on the starboard (right side) of the cabin can be removed in an emergency. We may have to use it if we have to land wheels up, or if we have to ditch. Make sure that you each examine the door and the handle, and are comfortable with how to use it. If you're not sure how to use it, ask me about it in Truckee.

"There are airline-type oxygen masks above each of the seats behind the small rectangular panels. We probably won't need them as we plan to fly the entire trip below 18,000 feet and below 10,000 feet most of the time. However, if the masks drop, it's for a reason. So, put them on immediately. They work just like an airline passenger mask. Air conditioning and heat are available that I can adjust from the cockpit as requested. You will be able to hear my communications in the cockpit with whoever is sitting in the co-pilot seat, and all communications with ATC."

We flew over Yosemite Valley—gorgeous—dotted with lakes and snowdrifts. It became increasingly bumpy as northwesterly winds banged into the western slopes of the rugged Sierra Nevada mountain range below us, then forced up and churned the air in front of us. At 10:35 a.m. I could see the Truckee airport over the foothills to the north of a magnificently clear, deep-cobalt-blue Lake Tahoe.

I love Lake Tahoe. I never get tired of visiting it. My children have so many happy memories of childhood summers on the west shore of one of the most beautiful lakes in the world and winter sports at the ski resorts circling the lake.

My reason for landing at Truckee was more than senti-
mentality. It's on the great circle path from Orange County to
Seattle, and the 5,904-foot field elevation saved considerable
descent and climb time, and fuel. While the airplane was being
fueled, we had an early lunch in the cafe. For some reason, we
were all still hungry after having had a full breakfast just a few
hours earlier. Perhaps it was adrenaline.

By 11:30 a.m., after being wished well by Sunny, the control
tower operator, we were off for Seattle Boeing Field. Everyone
was in good spirits. Julie wanted to sit up front. Everyone would
get a turn. Being in the cockpit, even though it was no more than
ten or so feet forward of the passenger seats, created an entirely
different experience. By sitting with me, asking questions, and
seeing what was involved in flying an aircraft, they began to
appreciate the complexities of what was required.

We continued our flight northwest along the Cascade Range.
At 12:10 p.m., we passed the 14,162-foot Mount Shasta. Then
came Crater Lake, Mount Hood at 11,245 feet, and Mount
St. Helens. The vast devastation of the May 1980 eruption was
still all too apparent from the air, with its mile-wide horseshoe
crater, remnants of the vast avalanche, and splattered debris field
extending for miles to the east.

The Pacific Northwest offered a stunning patchwork of green
meadows, and darker green forests that seemed to extend forever,
occasionally punctuated by a prominent volcanic mountain or
lake. The view from the air was stunning. I wondered what Russia
would look like from the air. Would it look like this? Would it
be green, brown, or red? I had no visual image of what to expect.

As we crossed the Columbia River, marking the boundary
between Oregon and Washington, I saw the 14,411-foot peak
of Mount Rainier off in the distance to the northeast. It looked
much closer than it was. It was still more than fifty miles away.

Seeing Mount Rainier again caused the same emotional reaction in me that I always felt whenever I saw it.

Twenty-six years earlier, I should have been killed at the bottom of a crevasse in Cadaver Gap, after a terrible fall during a mountain climbing trip. It had been a long fall, at least thirty feet before hitting anything. Miraculously, my final landing pad had been the only flat rock area around. I hit so hard that I bounced back into the air, did a somersault, and hit the rocks a second time. I was a mess, with a fractured pelvis and a compound fracture to the right arm. My backpack's gear spread out for a yard sale among the rocks, gravel, ice, and snow. Worse, I nearly suffocated. The wind had been knocked out of me so badly, I couldn't breathe and couldn't move.

I lay there for what seemed like an eternity, staring back up at the crevasse, wondering why I wasn't already dead. After a while, I realized that I wasn't breathing and couldn't. The thoughts running through my mind at that moment were astonishing to me: "If I could figure out how to get one breath, just one, then maybe I could figure out how to survive." I began focusing on trying to get my body to relax and take a breath. On the verge of passing out, I was finally rewarded with one breath—just one. And the process started all over again.

Eventually, I began breathing. I realized then that the three climbers I was with would assume I was dead. I was the anchor, the fourth climber on the line, and my safety line snapped when the ledge I was on had collapsed. There was no way for them to reach me, and no way they could tell if I was alive or not. My only hope was that they'd go for help.

Later I began moving. I slowly slithered among the rocks retrieving some of my gear. It was painful. Everything hurt. I couldn't hope to stand. I began giving myself first aid. I stopped the bleeding and made a sling for my arm. Certain of internal injuries, I didn't dare drink or eat anything. It was already midafternoon. It would be dark soon. There was no chance of rescue by my buddies before the following day.

The deafening sound of the waterfall upslope was the source of glacier water streaming through the bottom of the crevasse and meandering downslope. It was freezing. I was already going into shock. With one hand, I dug a pit in the gravel and buried myself in my sleeping bag to conserve heat. I lay awake all night counting the stars I could see through the narrow gap between the top of the crevasse walls on either side, some sixty feet above. I thought about many things I had never thought about before. Powerful ideas came to mind that would later transform my life in ways I could not have imagined.

By morning I concluded that it was, indeed, far too dangerous for my buddies to try and climb down into the crevasse to look for me, if they were even there. They undoubtedly thought I had been killed. They probably went for help. It would be at least another day, probably two, before the rangers arrived to recover my body. That was unless the weather turned bad, in which case it would take longer.

Desperate for the warmth of sunlight, I started crawling downslope, hoping to find some. Eventually, I came across a fossilized tree branch. What was it doing in there? I used it to help me stand. I felt better standing, more emboldened. While shaky on my feet, I could very slowly hobble. A couple of hundred yards and a couple of hours later, I was no closer to sunlight. The sun angles just didn't work.

Eventually, I found myself looking up at a wall that was distinctly better than the hopeless vertical faces dominating my view in every direction that morning. With two good hands, arms, and legs, I could easily climb that. But all I had to work with were one good hand, one arm, and legs that could do little more than support my weight. Climb? This was my best shot, maybe my only shot. I didn't hesitate.

As I slithered up the slope a few inches at a time, I knew I wouldn't survive a fall. My left hand reached up to grip whatever it could and then pull my body up, with my legs doing whatever they could to provide stability and the slightest push.

Several hours later, sitting on a rock in the open air at the top of the crevasse, I felt the sun's warmth reinvigorate my body. I knew I would survive. The truth is, I had never thought otherwise. Eventually, I connected with the rangers on their way up the mountain to recover my body. For the first week in the hospital at Ft. Lewis, I couldn't lift my head off my pillow. But I was young, and I recovered quickly. I had also changed; first, in subtle ways but soon in ways that began to overtake me.

In the years that followed, I began asking myself why it had never occurred to me that I wouldn't survive. The entire experience had been about how to survive. I did whatever I had to do to survive. Where had this come from? A strong survival instinct wasn't a quality I'd realized was within me.

I became fascinated by the experiences of others I read about or met who had also survived the seemingly unsurvivable. The optimists seem to survive most often. The pessimists and realists rarely did. Why is that? As I thought about it, the reason became clear. People can do extraordinary things when they find the courage to do what is required. Courage comes from the optimism they feel about their purpose, whatever they believe their purpose is. My mantra ever since has been, "The cornerstone of courage is optimism!"

We flew through fluffy clouds and over blue rivers on our way into Seattle's Boeing Field International airport (BFI). I never grow tired of how beautiful it is to fly and how much joy it gives me. At 2:38 p.m., we touched down at BFI and taxied to the transit ramp. Not surprisingly, it was raining. Two guys from the fixed-based operator (FBO) came running out with umbrellas.

Everyone in the terminal was so friendly, especially when they learned what we were doing. There was much excitement, and the other pilots and the staff had many questions. We sounded confident. I was also thinking about how difficult the coming days would be. I felt a great sense of responsibility not to screw it all up. We borrowed a crew car from the FBO and drove over to the Federal Aviation Administration (FAA) flight service station for a long talk with the people there. I wanted as much tactical information as they could give me about the weather ahead. We made an early evening of it. Everyone was tired. I was out like a light when my head hit the pillow.

I jumped out of bed at 6:45 a.m. It was July 5th. I enjoyed the view of the Port of Seattle as I opened the window and felt the cool breeze. It had stopped raining, leaving broken cloudiness. As we walked out of the hotel after a hearty breakfast, we saw and heard trains roaring by. The sounds of gulls screeching and of boats on the waters of Puget Sound were captivating. I was in the mood for flying.

By 9:45 a.m., we were taxiing for takeoff. Loading was much easier this time. The team was getting the hang of aircraft operations and how to organize their stuff for easy in and out. We all felt great. Now that we were well on our way, we each felt the full effect of the great adventure on which we had embarked.

Julie sat in the co-pilot seat again. We climbed quickly into the heavy overcast sky. By 10:00 a.m., we were on top of the clouds and continuing northwest at 11,000 feet. I was planning to go lower to sightsee and reviewed the calculations with Julie, who expressed a great deal of interest in understanding how the numbers worked. We started with a full load of fuel, 2,550 pounds, which also put us at maximum gross weight for the takeoff. I wanted to get the feel of the airplane at its heaviest as expected for the entire trip.

I wasn't sure of the leg distances in Russia, because I couldn't be sure what routes we'd be assigned. I assumed that every flight would require a maximum gross weight takeoff, carrying all the fuel we could to the weight limit, no matter where we were going. The number of people who would be on board would determine how much range we had. I anticipated seven when we took off from Provideniya, which would reduce our range by 400 pounds of fuel (the added weight of two people), or about 50 minutes and about 200 nautical miles.

The flight from Seattle to Juneau was about 800 nautical miles, the longest leg between Orange County and Provideniya. At a ground speed of 250 knots, with the headwind, burning 600 pounds per hour, the math said 3 hours, 15 minutes, plus the time for an instrument approach if we needed one. Forecasted weather was pretty good—no need to worry about an alternate. We had at least 4 hours and 20 minutes of fuel, which was more than enough to do all the sightseeing we wanted. We were on an instrument flight plan. We could fly lower altitude on the routing we had been assigned by air traffic control (ATC). I began requesting lower altitudes in 1,000 feet increments, hoping to break out. But it didn't work. By 10:32 a.m., it felt like we were flying in a light bulb. The world outside was opaque. As we approached Ketchikan, tantalizing views of Misty Fjords became visible as we began going in and out of clouds.

Misty Fjords National Monument features some of Alaska's most spectacular scenery. Many thousands of years ago, the area was covered in ice. Glacier movement carved long saltwater fjords into cliffs soaring some 3,000 feet into the air. The scene below us formed a spectacular, colorful plethora of tidewater estuaries, mountains shrouded in mist, sky-blue lakes, waterfalls, and seemingly endless evergreen forests. We hoped to see more of it on the return trip.

At 12:50 p.m., we began an instrument approach into Juneau. We broke out of broken clouds to the sight of stunning snow-capped mountains appearing to be very close. Bright green mountains with rivers of snow on their slopes dominated our views. There were mountains everywhere. The team loved it. Juneau was a gorgeous airport to land at, with the bay alongside for floatplanes.

Greeting us in the Juneau FBO was the local newspaper Headline, which grabbed our immediate attention. A search-and-rescue effort was in progress for seventy-nine Russian Eskimos traveling the Bering Strait in small, wooden boats. They had left Provideniya on Monday, attempting to cross 90 miles of seas that, on Tuesday, turned into 30-foot waves and winds to 25 knots. Low clouds and poor visibility were hindering the search, along with faulty telephone connections, making coordination with the Russians even more difficult than usual.

We hoped the weather would blow out by the time we arrived in a couple of days. The briefers in Seattle had forecast good weather. We hoped they were right.

My immediate focus was on getting us to Anchorage safely. I had been looking forward to the flight from Juneau to Anchorage with particularly high expectations. The terrain promised to be spectacular only if we could safely fly low enough to see it.

We headed over to the Juneau flight service station. The briefer was highly experienced and was used to working with pilots who flew low and stayed within the visual flight rules (VFR). As a general rule, pilots in Alaska remain below the clouds at all cost. If it means flying at 500 feet, then so be it. Very few airports in Alaska had instrument approaches. General aviation pilots did not want to find themselves in clouds or above them, with no way to get down safely. Everyone listened intently as the briefer went over suggested routings with me.

"Whitehorse is good—you'll be okay going over there at 6,500 feet, then on to Gustava, Glacier Bay, Haynes, Burwash, Northway—you're good—just follow the mountains. Then Volcanava, Gunright Lodge, Chickaloon, and Anchorage."

I heard Ed say to Julie, "Are you kidding? We're not asking for directions in Orange County! Follow the mountains, he says. Well, there's a truckload of mountains out there. How will Steve know which ones to follow?"

Julie's reply gave me a sense of the confidence she had placed in me. All she said was, "He'll know."

The briefer continued, "Minimum altitude in Glacier Bay is on your chart at 2,000 feet. Call on 122.25 for Juneau Radio to report your position."

I asked the briefer, "If I have to divert, where can we get Jet A fuel?"

We went over the options. I calculated the point at which we'd committed to continuing to Anchorage, irrespective of the weather. We could always go high and make an instrument approach into Anchorage.

Tom was in the right seat for this leg, as we taxied out of the ramp at 4:02 p.m. With his substantial experience as a high-altitude balloon pilot, he knew how to read aeronautical charts. For many years he had run the Gordon Bennett Cup, the oldest and most prestigious international, high-altitude gas balloon race in the world. In 1975 his balloon crashed during takeoff from the dirigible hangar at El Toro Marine Corps Air Base while he and Malcolm Forbes were attempting to be the first transatlantic balloonists.

I placed the charts we'd need on Tom's lap and discussed with him the procedure for marking our position on the chart as we proceeded. He needed to make it easy for me to see where we were on the chart at all times. Ed was right—there was a truck-load of mountains out there!

Ed Beall had already staked out his position on the aft bulkhead, port side forward-facing seat for the entire trip. He liked having the pullout tables to use for his drawing and writing materials. Ed is a brilliant architect and a very creative individual. He brought several artist workbooks with him and spent much of his time drawing pictures of what he saw out of the large picture windows that are one of the Aero Commander's great passenger features.

Everywhere we visited, Ed picked up odds and ends, such as postcards, magazine clippings, something from a hotel, or whatever interested him. He brought drawing tools, scissors, tape, and glue to cut and paste things into what became a marvelous scrapbook. He said doing the scrapbook as the trip proceeded kept him in the moment and increased his sensory perception. I greatly admired Ed's talent and creativity.

Looking at the scrapbooks later, we found many notes of what had been happening in real-time. For example, he wrote down conversations we had in the cockpit during the leg from Juneau to Anchorage that made for some exciting reading:

"I don't see how to get to the other side of the mountain, Tom."

"What we really want is to go up there?"

"What's the highest peak?"

"6,075 feet."

"This is the pass, right?"

"Can you see how to do it?"

"Well, maybe."

"Glad you're up here with me, Tom!"

"Where is the glacier?"

"No, no, no, we want to go west; we don't want to go in here."

"You want to go north."

"There?"

"No—there!"

"Oh, there."

"Yes, here."

Ed mumbled to Mike and Julie over the intercom at one point, "Do you get the feeling we have a Mutt and Jeff routine going on up there?"

Julie didn't respond. I was too busy to turn around to see if this was fun for them, or they were worried. I wasn't worried at all. I knew we'd figure it out.

"Sorry, guys. We'll get it right shortly."

It was 4:30 p.m.

"We don't want to go in there!"

"I'm having trouble with this scale!"

"But hey, the view's terrific!"

There were chunks of ice floating everywhere and the brightest blue-green water we had ever seen.

Tom and I eventually got the navigation sorted, and we continued over the Grand Pacific Glacier, the Albert Glacier, and the Tweetmeme Glacier. Just as I was admiring the sight of the runoff on the glacier, Tom said, "Dead ahead is a 20,000-foot peak!"

"But that's almost as high as Mt. McKinley! What is it?"

"I don't know. But over here, it's only 12,000 feet."

"Now there's a 19,000-footer! Stewart Glacier should be right here!"

Julie was yelling, "Look at that peak!"

Tom said, "It's only a 12,000-footer."

The valleys were now cloud-covered. The outside temperature was 36 degrees below zero Fahrenheit. Tom said, as he pointed out the window with one hand and at the chart with the other, "I think I goofed! This mountain is here, and that mountain is over there."

"So, are you telling me I need to go left? Tom?"

"Okay, I got it. Here's an 18,000-footer. Mount Logan is over to the left, Mount Steel is 16,644, and Mount Lucian is 17,147. We have to avoid them."

"Let's switch to the new chart—but be quick about it."

"What a way to get to Russia! Flying around a 16,390-footer right now."

It was 5:20 p.m. The shadows were becoming wonderful. Tom and I started up the dialogue again as we tried to compare what was on the chart with what we were seeing. The GPS unit wasn't working very well in this terrain. The surrounding mountains were degrading the signals. Dead reckoning was our only option.

This was a very rare opportunity for some incredible terrain sightseeing. It was also an opportunity to practice flying in unfamiliar terrain at low altitude while using charts as our only means of navigation. It was much harder than I had expected to keep our bearings. I was grateful for the opportunity to practice in decent weather. Tom and I both needed the practice; we didn't know what to expect in Russia.

"Don't you think we're here?"

"No."

"We couldn't be down here!"

"Do you think?"

"There are the Wrangell Mountains over there!"

"Okay."

"We're doing well on fuel. Let's go down to 8,000 to get a little closer."

"Let's follow this river. The clouds are lifting now."

"Oh right—I've been tracking here while we've really been over there!"

"Okay, we're following the Copper River. It's pretty muddy but looks great against the forest."

We were at 8,000 feet, and it was turning into a beautiful day for flying. I was feeling on top of the world, and getting more and more adventurous.

"We're going down to 6,000 feet to follow the river more closely and to get around the rain showers. Look at how beautiful that is. What's the name of that lake?"

It was 6:00 p.m., and we were having the time of our lives. We flew over Cazinia Glacier and lake. The lake was emerald green, and the mud was a beautiful pale purple. Highly localized rain showers were in every direction, punctuating the beauty of the landscape below us.

"Shall we go down to 4,000 feet?"

A chorus of voices unanimously sang out, "Yes!"

"You got it."

6:38 p.m., as we descended to 2,000 feet and approached Anchorage International Airport, I told the group, "This has been the most exciting flight of my life!"

As we unloaded the gear we'd need in Anchorage on the FBO tarmac, a car dealer from the Los Angeles area we recognized, named Cal Worthington, walked out of the FBO wearing his famous cowboy hat. This was the guy with the Western twang who did funny automobile commercials with animals during the 1980s and 1990s, and maybe even longer. He always called the tiger, or bear, or whatever, his dog "Spot." I said hello to Cal and asked him what he was doing in Anchorage. With his cowboy twang, he said he was going hunting. I wished him luck and asked where Spot was. He just laughed as he walked to his Learjet, jumped into the left seat, and started the engines. He looked calm and professional behind the wheel as he taxied by us on his way out.

After checking into our hotel, cleaning up, and calling home with the news of the day, we treated ourselves to a lovely meal at

Elevation 92 Seafood Bar and Grill. Everyone was clearly having a great time. We talked all evening about what we had seen. We walked back to our hotel in daylight at 11:15 p.m., still talking about our beautiful flight from Juneau. The sun was just setting. It was a magical evening. I turned to watch the sunset and thought to myself how good it was to be alive, and how wonderful it was to have this opportunity.

Monday, July 6th, was our reserve day. We needed to be in position to make the Valda Intersection at the appointed time on the 7th. Everything had gone beautifully so far. The previous day's adventures had created the opportunity for Tom and me to practice scenarios we might have to deal with in the days to come. Our confidence was increasing in our ability to execute the mission. We had a day in Anchorage to relax and do some shopping. We planned to be off early the following morning.

Anchorage is a charming little city. The people who live there are surrounded by endless beauty.

Ed was up at 6:00 a.m. jogging. It was low tide, and the water was a long way out in the bay. With only one hour of total darkness this time of year, the constant light took a bit of getting used to. Tom and Ed liked to collect stamps from everywhere we went. So, they visited the post office. Tom forgot his razor in Seattle and decided he needed to shave. I needed more versatile clothes than I had brought. So, I went shopping at Nordstrom's. They had exactly what I wanted: clothes more fitting for Alaska than the southwest. They hemmed the pants on the spot. I dropped the clothes I no longer needed at the Salvation Army.

Five-thirty a.m. on Tuesday, July 7th, was chilly and cloudy. I took a brisk walk and saw mountains in every direction, except to the west. It was too hazy to see much in that direction, and that was the direction we were flying. I spent a few minutes quietly enjoying the beautiful mountain views. The mountains are home to me. I have been a skier most of my life. I did back-country wilderness helicopter skiing in British Colombia every winter for fifteen years. I never tire of the beauty of being in the mountains.

After an early breakfast, we drove to the Anchorage airport FBO and began going through what was becoming a very familiar and routine. The others dealt with loading while I checked the weather, reviewed my planned routing to Nome with Tom, filed a flight plan, and paid the bill for the fuel. The Flight Service Station briefer reported Mt. Spur was active with some volcanic action. We'd need to stay clear of it. Visibility was generally poor at Anchorage. It was drizzling with low clouds. We'd need to stay low after departure, find the Stony River, and follow it west.

At 8:56 a.m., we taxied out of the FBO ramp to Runway 33 for takeoff, immediately turned west, and quickly found ourselves over wildly beautiful country with rivers, lakes, and pines. But no roads, animals, or people; at least none we could spot. We flew at 900 feet to stay under the cloud cover and kept the speed down to 200 knots while looking for useful landmarks to follow west. The visibility was good enough to see hundreds of small lakes and huge flat muddy rivers below the overcast. We found the Stony River and began following it to the west.

As we continued west, the Stony River became wider and deeper, and the weather sunnier and clearer. We tried cruising for a while at 1,500 feet. But at that altitude, it was impossible to see animals. I decided to fly lower. Still, we didn't see a single animal.

I wondered if they heard us coming and ran for cover. Mike observed the airplane's tinted windows were affecting the color on the video of the landscape. He planned to make corrections in the lab after the trip if he could. Mike continuously took photos and shot video for the entire leg. He was a very serious professional at his craft.

By 10:52 a.m., the weather was again starting to deteriorate. It was raining. We stayed below 1,000 feet. I was much more concerned about maintaining visual contact with the terrain than about what the altimeter said. Tom marked our position on the chart every few minutes based on the longitude/latitude digital readout on the GPS unit. It was a great technique. I could quickly glance at the chart and know exactly where we were. This procedure only worked if the GPS worked. If not, we'd just go back to our Mutt & Jeff routine.

We were down to 500 feet. Flying so low over the river allowed us to see much more than would otherwise be possible. After merging with the Yukon River, we turned north and passed Anviko. I did some quick fuel calculations and announced I wasn't comfortable with our fuel reserve status. We needed to get some fuel at Galena, before proceeding on to Nome. Low flying had increased our fuel consumption significantly. But it had been worth it.

Galena is a small village in west-central Alaska, some 350 miles northwest of Anchorage along the north bank of the Yukon River. There are only two ways to get there—by boat or by plane. Adjacent to the village is an airfield, and associated buildings used to support military operations out of Elmendorf and Eielson Air Force bases. During the Cold War, this was one of the most forward fighter-interceptor bases US and Canadian air forces operated from. We taxied in and parked next to two Canadian Air Force F-16s sitting on the ramp. In Alaska, you never knew what was going to show up on the ramp. There didn't seem to be anyone around.

We walked across the airfield to the only bar and restaurant in town. The weather was beautiful. The rays of the sun felt wonderful on my face. It was 90° Fahrenheit. Unfortunately, we also experienced our first encounter with Galena mosquitoes, and oh my, we had forgotten to bring mosquito repellent! Cheeseburgers and fries all around for lunch. Then Julie went hunting around town for mosquito repellent while we self-fueled the Aero Commander. She came back empty-handed. We were sure to need bug repellent where we were going. We hoped to find some in Nome.

By 1:50 p.m., we were off to Nome, less than an hour away. More heavy rain en route, and bumpy. Pilots get used to the bumps. After a few years of flying, you don't even notice them. We found Norton Sound easily and followed the southern coast of the Seward peninsula west to Nome. We looked for seals and walrus along the coast but didn't see any. Majestic Rocky Point Bay drew breathless exclamations from everyone.

As Nome came into sight, I was struck that the town was about the same size as the airport, which was also not very large. It was a pretty small place, and the most isolated village I had ever seen.

By 3:30 p.m., we were walking into town, and it wasn't a very long walk. But we needed a little exercise. Only about 3,000 people lived in the Nome area. Everybody knew everybody. The main street looked like something from an old movie. Sitting by the side of the road was a big sign on a wooden sled marking the end of the Iditarod dog sled race. Every winter, much heartier souls than I, and their faithful dog teams would spend 10 to 17 days covering some 1,150 miles of pretty much the same route we had just covered in a few hours.

We enjoyed a substantial second lunch of more cheeseburgers and fries and apple pie at the Golden Nugget. I didn't think there was another place to eat or stay. This was it. We wanted a good meal in case the Russians didn't feed us dinner that evening. Or perhaps I should say the next evening, as Provideniya was across the international dateline.

By 4:30 p.m., we were back at the airport, making some final preparations. I asked the others to find all the water bottles in the cabin and cargo hold and fill them up with water. Water quality in Provideniya was yet another unknown.

Jim Cook, the briefer in the Flight Service Station, was very professional and incredibly helpful. Few aircraft were flying into Provideniya. Fortunately, most diligently reported back to the Nome Flight Service Station on the conditions they found. Jim had the latest information on the runway conditions at Provideniya. He told me about a big hole in the middle of the gravel runway. He cautioned me to avoid it, as if he needed to. He suggested I land beyond that point, as we wouldn't need much runway anyway. I expected the airplane to stop very quickly on gravel, based on everything I had heard from other pilots who had done it.

Jim also reviewed the double Non-Directional Beacon (NDB) instrument approach with me. This was going to be the most challenging instrument approach of the entire trip. He gave me more details on the Valda waypoint crossing time, and the various radio frequencies I'd need. I had already accumulated much of the information he provided. He added some crucial technical details I didn't have. More importantly, the opportunity to discuss the plan with a knowledgeable professional boosted my confidence in my mission readiness.

As we walked out of the Flight Service Station, we ran into the then US Secretary of the Interior, Bob Udall. Tom and I both recognized him and stopped to chat with him for a few minutes. He was on an aerial tour of Alaska. He was amazed to learn what we were up to. Tom gave him one of our souvenir stamped envelopes with our mission logo and signatures on it. He wished us well.

Don and Ann from the airport FBO wrote in Ed's book "California Kamchatka Crew—Siberia the Last Frontier—Provideniya is now only 230 miles!"

We sat at the end of Runway 21, facing southwest toward the ocean as I completed my final checks. The engines sang. The sky was mostly clear. The wind was out of the southwest, straight down the runway. The airplane was working perfectly. The fuel gauge read 2,550 pounds. We were at 10,325 pounds maximum gross weight. We had plenty of fuel to take off, fly to Provideniya, land, take off with two additional passengers at or below max gross weight with the fuel remaining, and either fly on to Anadyr or fly back to Nome. We had options.

I checked the time and my calculations for crossing Valda at the appointed time. It was all so confusing. Time zone changes, crossing the International Date Line, Zulu time versus local time. Today, with internet access, cells phones, and a full GPS constellation overhead, there's no reason to screw it up. In 1992 it was a very different story. It was all a worry. I sweated bullets, not wanting to get this wrong.

It was 5:20 p.m. (05:20 Zulu). Time to launch. I pressed down on the toe brakes on the upper end of the rudder pedals my feet rested on, and pushed my rear end into the back of the seat, creating maximum hydraulic pressure on the brake pads. I smoothly advanced the throttles as the needles on the two shaft horsepower gauges moved up to meet the red line, indicating 715. I sat there for three or four seconds, looking at the engine gauges to satisfy myself that we were ready. I slowly released the pressure on the brakes and the airplane lurched forward as if launched from a catapult.

"Let's go to Russia!" I exclaimed.

There was an answering cheer. We were all totally up for it.

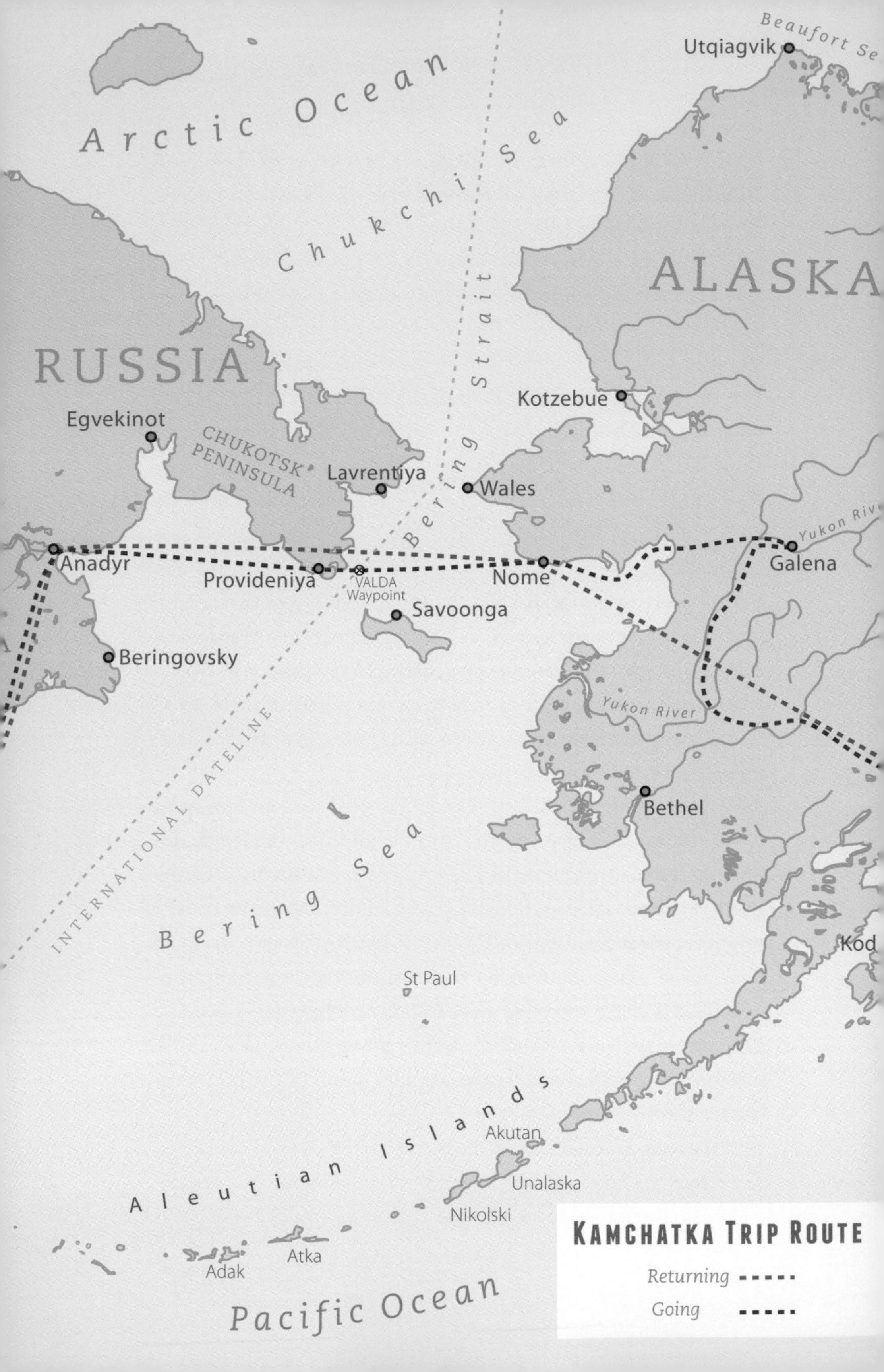

Arctic Ocean

Beaufort Se

Utqiagvik

Chukchi Sea

RUSSIA

ALASKA

Egvekinot

CHUKOTSK
PENINSULA

Lavrentiya

Kotzebue

Wales

Yukon Riv

Anadyr

Providentiya

VALDA
Waypoint

Nome

Galena

Savoonga

Beringovsky

Yukon River

Bethel

Bering Sea

Kod

St Paul

INTERNATIONAL DATELINE

Aleutian Islands

Akutan

Unalaska

Nikolski

Adak   Atka

Pacific Ocean

KAMCHATKA TRIP ROUTE

Returning - - - - -

Going ▪▪▪▪▪

6

ADVENTURE OF A LIFETIME

As we popped in and out of broken clouds, we saw dozens
of small, mountainous islands. Ahead was a rugged, craggy
mainland with a large bay that looked alien and unfamiliar.

These were very treacherous waters. Icebergs everywhere, with suggestions of white faces and odd shapes floating in the deep, dark blue ocean below. The swells and whitecaps signaled a great deal of wind blowing over strong currents. The sky to the north looked very different than any I had seen before. The vast panorama was a painted mural of vivid purples and blues mixed with clouds in patterns that made them appear unearthly and a beautiful image to behold. We were indeed strangers entering a strange land. Our team of five was excited, committed, and completely in the moment.

The flight time was less than an hour from Nome to Provideniya, 230 nautical miles. But in that hour were three time-zone changes, an International Date Line, and no end of potential unknowns to contend with. We needed to cross the Valda waypoint at the exact time we were expected, 06:00 Zulu, forty minutes after our takeoff from Nome at 5:20 p.m. local time, 05:20 Zulu. The Valda waypoint was located just across the International Date Line. Getting the math right shouldn't have been particularly difficult, especially after all of the preparation I had gone through. But there were too many silly ways to screw it all up. I'd soon know if I had it right.

While everyone was having a great time, there was much less banter than usual. Mike took pictures and video. Ed made drawings and notes. Julie listened to everyone intently. I communicated with Anchorage center, and periodically discussed with Tom our position and altitude, while he made position marks on the aeronautical chart on his lap. I glanced at my watch and did the math in my head. We were doing 240 knots across the water or four miles a minute. We were forty miles from Valda. We'd cross in ten minutes. It was 05:50 Zulu. Math is a beautiful thing!

The receiver suddenly came alive with a call from Anchorage center: "Turbine Commander 42 Mike Sierra, Anchorage center, go to Provideniya Radio on 119.2. Good luck to you."

"Anchorage, 42 Mike Sierra going to 119.2. Thanks for your help. We'll see you on the return trip."

I jotted down the Anchorage center frequency on my notepad and circled it. That was one frequency I didn't want to forget. I might need it for no end of reasons.

I dialed 119.2 into the second of the two radio transceivers.

I looked over at Tom with a half-smile. "Well, Tom, we're about to find out if all those negotiations with the Russians amounted to anything. We can always do a quick 180 and enjoy the evening in Nome."

"It'll be fine, Steve. Don't worry," Tom replied. He wasn't at all convincing.

I hesitated for a moment, then pressed the transmit button on the airplane control yoke just below my left index finger.

"Provideniya Radio, this is Turbine Commander 42 Mike Sierra, ten miles east of Valda, at 5,000 meters inbound. Landing Provideniya. Over."

I held my breath.

"Mike Sierra xxxxxxxxxxxxxxxxx. I read you xxxxxxxxxxxxxxx."

There was a great deal of static mixed in with the communication. I didn't understand a word of it. I tried it again.

Tom commented, "Two minutes to Valda."

More static. Finally, the Russian controller began communicating again in a way that sounded much shriller and less confident than I had expected, in a heavy Russian accent.

"Roger, 42 Mike Sierra, I read you. Plan landing at Provideniya. Begin descent to 2,400 meters."

"Forty-two Mike Sierra, understand. Beginning descent to 2,400 meters."

I referred to my homemade meters-to-feet conversion table: 2,400 meters was 7,900 feet. I commented over the intercom, "Okay, everybody. It looks like we're in business!"

"Forty-two Mike Sierra, do you understand about how to enter from the United States?" More static.

"What kind of a trick question is that?" I wondered out loud. I looked at the double NDB approach plate clipped to the yoke in front of me. The briefer in Nome had gone over it with me in detail. It was the strangest-looking approach plate I had ever seen.

"Forty-two Mike Sierra, negative."

I thought I should play it safe. I wouldn't get in trouble for asking directions.

"Xxxxxxxxxxxxxxxx. Report 4,000 meters, then make a right turn, descend to 1,500 meters and xxxxxxxxxxxxxxxxx."

"Are you kidding me? Tom? What is he saying?"

Tom just shook his head.

"Xxxxx descend to xxxxxx from 1,000 meters, then make a left turn at xxxxxxx."

I didn't know what else to do than just say, "Roger."

I had the airport coordinates in my GPS receiver. It said that we were twenty minutes out. But I was slowing as we descended. I was in no big hurry to get anywhere.

I continued studying the approach plate and tried to compare what I saw with what I had scribbled down. A non-directional beacon (NBD), identified as BC, was critical to executing the approach. I selected the BC NDB frequency on my automatic direction finder (ADF) receiver and watched as the bearing pointer on the radio magnetic indicator (RMI) instrument swung to a heading 10 degrees to our left. I adjusted our course to the left to fly directly over the beacon.

Trying to reconcile the fragments of communication deciphered from the Russian controller with the chart in front of me was maddening. The basic idea was to fly over the BC NDB and then start right-hand descending spiral turns to an altitude of 400 meters (1,312 feet), from which the spiral turns would be exited with a turn north to the runway. It seemed simple enough except that the Russians had complicated it with many seemingly unnecessary additional instructions.

I later learned that the Russian tendency toward over-instruction had to do with their cultural assumption that anything not explicitly directed would almost certainly get screwed up. In the weeks and years to come, as I learned about Russia, its culture, and its people, I came to understand and fully embrace this assumption enthusiastically.

As we took in our first images of the Russian coastline, it looked beautiful. I was somehow surprised. Perhaps I had seen too many Hollywood black-and-white movies about Russia. The pictures in my head were of a dark and scary place. Popping in and out of broken clouds, we saw dozens of small, rugged, mountainous islands. Ahead was a craggy mainland with a large bay extending to the south that looked alien and unfamiliar.

We entered yet another cloud bank as we continued to descend. We were in clouds as we passed over the BC beacon.

I reported entering right turns over Bravo Charlie and was instructed to continue descending to 1,500 meters (4,800 feet). It was 06:35 Zulu. We hadn't been shot at yet. Presumably, I had done everything right or right enough. Or maybe they just didn't care.

"Provideniya Radio, do we circle at Bravo Charlie until 400 meters?" I asked.

"Xxxxxxxxxxxxxxxx I see you in my radar. xxxxxxxxxxxxx. Descend to 800 meters."

We were in and out of broken clouds as we continued spiraling down. There were numerous radio exchanges with the Russian controller. Way more than necessary. He was giving me too much information. I could not process most of what he was saying. I decided that the best course of action was to do the intent of what he was saying, as long as it was consistent with what was on the chart. The chart was a better bet than a controller who might, or might not, know what he was saying in English.

The good news was that the BC NDB was on an island in a bay to the south of the airport, called Komsomolskaya Bay. I didn't have any high elevation terrain to worry about as we spiraled down.

Tom suddenly announced, "Steve, I see the runway."

I looked up from the instruments and saw the runway ahead and to the left, as the aircraft continued turning to the right. I disengaged the autopilot, stopped the turn, and began turning to the left to align the airplane with the runway.

"Steve, he said to turn right."

"No way, Tom—the runway is to the left, and our altitude is perfect for a straight in, visual approach."

It was time to stop the fooling around and get this thing on the ground!

I transmitted enthusiastically and with conviction, "Provideniya Radio, 42 Mike Sierra has the runway. Beginning visual approach."

The response from the Russian controller seemed anticlimactic as if suggesting I was an idiot if I wasn't beginning a visual approach. After all, he had brilliantly directed me to this point on his radar screen.

I put the landing gear down and lowered the flaps to approach. I saw the gravel covering the runway extending to the north. I was still two miles away. I could not see the hole that I was warned about in Nome.

I continued slowing the airplane as we descended. I set the power to maintain a very slow 85 knots as we descended closer and closer to the runway and set the flaps to full. I couldn't fly this slowly with a jet, but using a propjet, I was able to "hang" the airplane on the propellers just a few knots above stall and make a very stable, slow descent to the runway.

"Oh, yeah, we're good," I commented to the others. I felt comfortable with the way things were looking. But what I was really planning was to do a low flyby and then go around before landing unless I was sure it was safe to land. It was too early to tell.

I had never landed on gravel before. As the gravel runway came closer and closer, I thought about what the experts had advised me. I should expect the airplane to stop much quicker than usual. I couldn't stop quickly enough. In aviation, there is no substitute for hands-on experience.

I saw the hole to my left as I stopped my descent and skimmed only a few feet above the gravel, hugging the right side of the runway.

"Look at the size of that hole, Tom. It would just ruin your whole day!"

I couldn't believe the Russians would let such a hazard to aircraft operations go unrepaired. After passing the huge hole, I eased back on the power, and the airplane descended the last few feet onto the gravel, just a little harder than I had expected. The airplane immediately began sliding to the left of its own accord. I had to take very aggressive action on the brakes and rudder while putting the propellers into beta mode (reverse) to maintain control. The airplane could quickly have gone off the left side of the runway and into the adjacent ditch if my actions hadn't been immediate. It all happened so fast my actions were automatic. There was no time to think, only to react. It felt like I was watching my automatic measures in slow motion. It was a scary moment. It was also the shortest landing I had ever made!

We came to a complete stop in only a few hundred feet. For a moment, I just sat there, trying to catch my breath. I'm sure the others thought nothing of it. Tom congratulated me on how "smoothly" I had moved to the center of the gravel runway and stopped. Perhaps it was best not to share with them my version of what had just happened. Better to keep the details to myself.

"Touchdown Russia!" I exclaimed, and everyone applauded and yelped. It felt good to be there. And we were still in one piece!

The Russian controller directed us to park in front of the main terminal building. To my right, I saw a small grey structure with an old fire truck sitting in front of it. We slowly taxied off the gravel runway and onto a gravel taxiway. Several people were waiting for us as we approached the building, including our friend, Viktor Kerzhanovich, a most encouraging sight. A couple of men in dark blue overalls that had seen better days directed me to park. I shut the engines down and just sat there for a moment, taking it all in.

I was the last one out as the others excitedly exited the airplane to meet Viktor and our greeting party. Viktor was all smiles as he introduced the airport director. I extended my hand to a portly, middle-aged man with a big thick mustache, wearing a uniform with a bunch of badges and medals from the Soviet era. I soon learned that anyone who was anyone habitually wore a uniform. It was going to be a while before they got new uniforms, especially out here in the boondocks.

We were quickly invited into the office of the airport director where there were more people in uniforms, lots of paperwork to complete and instructions about what we could do, and what we could not do. Viktor translated for us. We were told that only a few American private planes had come this far. They only came occasionally and always returned to Nome. The airport director said that no aircraft had ever gone on from there before. Viktor added that the local officials were all very impressed with us and the people we must know in Moscow to be permitted to go where we were going. Then the airport director did something odd. He opened a drawer and pulled out a bunch of metal parts and threw them onto the table. "Americanski propellers!" was all he said, with a big grin. I guess it was his way of congratulating me for not contributing to his collection.

The airport director invited us to tea at his club, which of course, we graciously accepted. Viktor K. said that all the arrangements were made for our lodging. Our navigator was on the way and should be there in the next couple of hours. We would remain in Provideniya until he arrived. We were not permitted to continue without him.

We went back out to the airplane to unload the stuff we'd need while there. I took a moment to look around and take some pictures. To the west was a very stark, steep range of mountains running north and south that disappeared into the clouds. It looked a little like the Front Range in Colorado, but with none of the charm. There were no trees. To the north were several large Russian military transport aircraft parked on a long ramp. They were all propjet aircraft, much larger than mine.

To the east and north, I could see part of the town. It looked like the place had been bombed the day before. Rubble was everywhere. The terminal building itself was a mess. It looked like it might have been strafed by machine-gun fire, with holes everywhere and wires hanging off the side of the building. I had never seen a place in such a state.

I began inspecting the Aero Commander. The propellers were severely nicked on landing. One of the mechanics came over to see what I was looking at and said something to one of the other guys hanging around. The next thing I knew, one of them had a file out and was going to work on the propeller blades. I started to object but could see very quickly he was an expert at repairing propellers. I realized that he must do this every day. He smoothed the propellers out in no time at all; there were a few minor nicks on the faces, but nothing significant.

There were more dings from flying gravel on the right propeller than on the left. I thought about why that was. Then it came to me. *When the aircraft touched down on the gravel runway, it was the combination of differential braking and asymmetric reverse thrust on a low friction runway surface that had caused the rapid slide to the left.*

Imagine driving down a gravel road and making an emergency stop. You have to work hard to keep the vehicle from skidding and sliding off the road. Why? The lower tire friction on the gravel, and the tires and brakes on each wheel, are not identical. The tire wear, brake lining, and pads are different. Your reactions to the skidding and sliding by those differences creates driver-induced oscillations, which also have to be dampened. It can be very disconcerting.

Now, imagine all of that happening while landing an aircraft. Unlike a car, aircraft have independent wheel braking because it allows for better directional control. But, it also creates the potential for greater pilot-induced oscillations. The largest contributor is reverse engine thrust. During landing, the pitch angles on the propeller blades on each engine are reversed, causing the thrust from each engine to be directed forward, slowing the aircraft. There's enough thrust available to stop the aircraft and actually move it backwards. But no two engines spool up, spool down, or change propeller pitch at exactly the same rates. These variations create pilot-induced oscillations. It's just one more thing a pilot learns to cope with.

On the gravel runway at Provideniya, the slightly more rapid deceleration of the left engine, in combination with the other factors described above, produced the very exciting yaw to the left that we experienced. The control inputs required to cope with the yaw to the left explains the larger number of gravel nicks on the right propellers. Fortunately, my muscle memory had been working well that day. I made a note to tell Jim Cooke, the Nome FSS briefer, about what had happened on our return.

The airport director and Viktor K. drove up to the airplane in a Jeep-like military vehicle, with another just like it following behind. We loaded our stuff into the second Jeep, jumped into the first, and headed for town.

To this day, Provideniya was the most depressing place I have ever seen. It looked like a war zone. Debris was everywhere. Every single building was damaged and in an advanced state of disrepair. The streets were mostly dirt roads. Nothing had any paint on it. The color palette was grey, dark grey, very dark grey, and charcoal. Groups of poorly dressed kids, in desperate need of baths, ran along the streets, playing and yelling at one another with dogs chasing after them. Adults, poorly dressed, moved slowly along dilapidated sidewalks.

We drove up to a building. To the right of the entrance door was a dark emblem with a picture of Lenin on it. It was an emblem for the Communist Party's local headquarters building. Viktor K. said that this was a club restricted to party members only. The Soviet Union may have ended, but, he assured me, no one who had not been allowed in before would dare to enter now.

Inside, we found a stark room with worn curtains and long tables with very worn, thick, dark green covers, similar to poker tables. We were invited to sit. Tea was scrved. We asked polite questions about Provideniya and how long our host had been there.

The area, called Chukotka, was to the east of Siberia and the last stop in the Russian Far East. It had the distinction of being the second-most uninhabited region of the former USSR. I assumed that the most uninhabited place must have been Kazakhstan, which has one of the lowest population densities in the world.

Provideniya was very difficult to supply. It could only be reached by airplane. The nearest base was Anadyr, several hundred miles to the southwest. With the end of the Cold War, Provideniya had become irrelevant. They had no idea what would become of them. Their only hope was American tourism, and they were making every effort to be hospitable. But they had very little to offer.

While we were talking, one of the officers from the airport came in with a young man in civilian clothes who was all smiles. "Hi, I'm Viktor Shlyaev. I'm your navigator. I have been assigned to fly with you while you are here in Russia." His English was excellent. Viktor #2, as I came to call him, was a handsome guy with light brown hair and dark brown eyes. He looked very fit.

He was taller than me by a couple of inches. The last thing we needed with us was a very large person, and his accompanying weight to further strain our range limits.

Viktor Kerzhanovich, whom I dubbed Viktor #1, had warned us that whoever was assigned as navigator was probably KGB, now FSB, and to be careful. I thought he was a bit melodramatic, but I took his point. Viktor #2 seemed like a nice enough guy. He turned out to be a great guy and a lot of fun. He would be with us the entire time we were in Russia. He became our interpreter, navigator, companion, and, of course, the eyes of the State. I liked him instantly.

After the introductions and chit chat, Viktor #2 asked me to take him over the airplane and brief him on its operational capabilities. He was a man after my own heart.

First, we all went with Viktor #1 to take a quick look at the "hotel," which was more reminiscent of a military barracks than anything else. Upstairs were three rooms with four cots in each room. It was the barest of interiors. Two water closets were down the hall, with a toilet and sink in each, but no shower. There was a central kitchen on the first floor with a stove and a small refrigerator, two sinks, eight spoons, two forks, two plates, ten saucers, six glasses, and one frying pan.

Tom went shopping with Viktor #1 and found some brown bread, eggs, juice, and canned goods that we'd have for breakfast the next morning. Mike, Ed, and Julie went exploring. Viktor #2 and I went back to the airport.

I unlocked the Aero Commander door and jumped into the left seat of the cockpit after Viktor #2 got in the right seat. I asked about his flying background. He had some flight time but was not certified as a pilot. I gave him the cockpit tour, showing him how the radios worked and the various navigational features. It was mostly all very familiar to him until I got to the GPS unit.

"What is that?" he asked.

Viktor #2 was more than a little excited to learn about the NorthStar GPS unit. He had heard vague stories about the US GPS program, but he had never seen any of the equipment. I turned on the unit and showed him how it worked, and how to program in waypoints based on latitude and longitude information. I explained how I had spent several hours in the weeks before departure programming the unit with dozens of useful waypoints. When he asked where I got the lat/long data from, I showed him one of the NOAA geodetic survey charts. He was very impressed with both the technology and my ingenuity.

I went through some of the waypoints I assumed we'd use the next day for our flight to Korf. I was surprised when he opined that the data for the waypoint was not quite right.

"Well, yes," I said. "The information is only approximate because of the map scale."

He said, "No, that is not what I mean. Some of the map points are wrong."

I said, "How can they be wrong? I took them right off the charts."

I pulled out the chart with Korf on it to show him how I had computed the location. He studied the chart for a moment.

"Yes, well, the chart is wrong."

We looked at some other waypoints. Again, he said they were wrong.

"You mean to tell me the US Geodetic Survey charts are wrong?" I said incredulously.

It didn't make any sense. The US had spy satellites in orbit, like the KH-11, able to very accurately determine the positions of any target of interest. True, the digital technology had not come together yet to automatically convert the imaging data into highly accurate maps, at least not for public consumption. Could the charts of Russia that the NGS produced for civilian use be deliberately inaccurate? Why? To not reveal our military capabilities? True, the Air Force had already announced that the GPS system would be significantly degraded for civilian use

By the way, a few years later, President Clinton, in what I think was one of the best decisions of his administration, directed that the GPS signal degradation be turned off, except for specific exceptions, such as war zones. The entire world was given access to the highest level of GPS accuracy.

I was still incredulous. But this did explain why during our landing at Provideniya, the GPS unit showed the runway half a mile away from where it actually was. It hadn't mattered, because I was high enough and far enough away to see the runway when we broke out of the clouds. If I had needed to make an instrument approach to minimums (the lowest altitude I could descend without seeing the runway), it could have been a serious issue. I simply couldn't risk using the GPS as a reference during instrument approaches in Russia, without much more accurate runway lat/long coordinates.

Viktor #2 pulled a notebook out of his bag and opened it to pages filled with handwritten information. "Ah, he's a real navigator!" I said to myself. We sat there for an hour reprogramming all of the waypoints we'd need for the remainder of the trip with his lat/long data. This also gave us an opportunity to discuss the plan. We'd overfly Anadyr on our way to Korf, at the north end of the Kamchatka peninsula, the next morning. We'd stay there overnight before flying to Petropavlovsk the following day. He promised me that the scenery on our flights would be breathtaking. I think he was looking forward to the flying as much as I was.

We now had current instrument approach plates and charts for our routes of flight. Sitting together in the cockpit reprogramming the GPS unit and going over the plan together, we bonded. We had charts, plates, data, communications, and working GPS. He was easy to work with, a great guy, and instantly my crewmate. In my mind, the risk factors for our mission had been reduced dramatically.

The positive impact Viktor #2 had on my psychology at that moment is indescribable. For the first time in many hours, I realized that my heart rate had returned to normal. I could now focus on having a good time and enjoy the adventure!

That evening we walked through the town to a small, surprisingly nice cafe that Viktor #1 had arranged. We ate a simple Russian dinner and chatted with the two Viktors about their backgrounds and our travels to get there. Everyone was very excited about the prospects for what lay ahead.

Later in the evening, we walked back to the hotel. It was still dusk. We had gained three hours of time zone changes, crossing the International Date Line on a one-hour flight that we had begun the day before. With two glasses of vodka under my belt, I no longer knew for sure what time it was, or what day it was. I needed to get some sleep.

Before going to bed, I wanted to call home with an update. Out in the hall was something akin to a circa 1920 crank phone. Viktor #1 tried to determine if it was feasible. After a brief conversation, he hung up, looked at me, and simply said, "Hopeless!"

"This is such an interesting trip," I thought to myself shortly after that, in bed, as I closed my eyes.

7

IT FELT LIKE LINDBERGH
LANDING IN PARIS

Out of nowhere, several hundred very excited people, screaming and yelling, appeared on the ramp and surrounded the airplane.

Early morning in Provideniya brought light rain and low-hanging clouds. The ceiling was less than 200 feet, which meant that the instrument-approach minimum descent altitude was above the cloud base. We could take off, but couldn't come back and land if we had an issue. This was fine with me. If we had a problem, such as an engine failure, I had no intention of coming back. We were either going to Korf or back to Nome.

We loaded the airplane and completed a very thorough pre-flight. Viktor #2 picked up our clearance at the headquarters building. At 9:44 a.m., we taxied out onto the north end of the gravel runway, facing south so that we would climb out over the bay. There were now seven people in the airplane and it felt a bit crowded. We were also at the airplane's 10,350-pounds maximum gross takeoff weight limit.

Before I began the takeoff roll, I turned to Viktor #2, sitting in the right seat, and asked if he had his passport with him. He said, "Yes, of course. Why do you ask?"

I looked at him and said unemotionally, "If we have an engine failure before the wheels leave the ground, I will abort the take-off. However, if we have an engine failure after the main wheels have left the ground, I will retract the landing gear, increase airspeed, raise the flaps, and direct you to declare an emergency. You will inform the controller that we have had an engine failure and are diverting to Nome. Any questions?"

"Can the plane fly to Nome on one engine at max gross weight?"

I nodded and said, "Oh, yeah."

He looked at me and said, "Impressive," and just smiled.

While my first gravel landing in an Aero Commander had been the day before, I had quite a bit of short-field landing and takeoff experience. A short-field takeoff procedure is a useful technique for minimizing the amount of runway needed to get the airplane into the air. First, I set the elevator trim to a rearward takeoff position to make the airplane want to pitch up during the takeoff roll. Second, I set the flaps to "approach" to increase wing lift. Third, using the back of my seat for leverage, I pushed my feet down onto the brake pedals as hard as possible, while advancing the power levers until the white needles matched the red lines on the shaft horsepower gauges. This would cause the airplane to accelerate more quickly when the brakes were released.

The airplane began sliding forward and to the left. As on landing, the sliding was because of the lack of tire traction on the gravel runway and differential engine thrust. But now the yaw to the left was being caused by the left engine thrust spooling up slightly slower than the right engine. I continued holding the brakes while adjusting the throttles and rudder pedals to stay centered on the gravel runway. I pulled the yoke all the way back into my lap to keep the propeller tips as far away from the gravel as possible. Then, I slowly released the pressure on the brakes.

We begin accelerating down the gravel runway, and the nose almost immediately lifted into the air. I could feel the elevator pressure increasing on the yoke. I adjusted the yoke pressure to hold the nose off the ground as the combination of increasing lift on the wings and propeller thurst pulled the airplane into the air in less than a thousand feet, well short of the now infamous hole on the right side of the runway ahead. As soon as the main wheels were off the ground, I retracted the landing gear and lowered the nose to skim above the runway to build up airspeed. By the time we were passing the end of the runway, we were already accelerating through 150 knots. I retracted the flaps, pulled back on the yoke, set our climb rate for 2,000 feet per minute, adjusted the trim, and activated the heading mode on the autopilot. I then selected the next waypoint in the GPS unit and engaged the lateral navigational mode on the autopilot. The GPS unit calculated our distance to Korf as 691 nautical miles and our time en route as three hours.

I finally sat back and took a deep breath. I looked at Viktor #2. He was all smiles. Even now, more than twenty-five years later, I can feel the pure joy of perfectly executing the most dramatic takeoff of my aviation career. As we climbed through the layers of heavy cloud cover, Viktor #2 looked at me and said, "We are at maximum gross weight?"

"Yes," I said.

The expression on his face showed he was clearly impressed. He shook his head and said with some astonishment, "This is quite an airplane."

Viktor #2 had made his first significant contribution to our mission the prior evening. He had provided me with the means to have the fuel range I needed for our return to Nome, at the end of the trip, without having to refuel at Provideniya. His home base was a military installation north of Korf called Anadyr. He had arranged permission for us to land there, as our "alternate." An alternate is required whenever the forecasted weather at the destination airport requires an instrument approach due to weather. Said another way, we had enough fuel to fly to Korf, make a missed approach for landing there, and fly back north to Anadyr, if necessary.

From my entrepreneurial perspective (anything not forbidden is permitted), this permission implied that we'd likely be able to get permission to land and fuel at Anadyr on the return leg from Petropavlovsk! The Aero Commander could easily fly directly to Nome from Anadyr. No way did I want to go back to Providenya. I didn't want to tell Viktor #2 what I had in mind yet. We just got here. He might misinterpret my motive as a lack of interest in what we were there to do. I'd save this conversation for later.

We continued our climb up to 19,000 feet. Julie and Ed were busy putting the wildflowers they had collected the previous day into a press they had brought with them. The cabin service was pretty good too. Tom and Viktor #1 distributed slices of apple from the hotel in Seattle, jams from the hotel in Anchorage, and brown bread that Viktor #1 had found the previous evening. Tasty stuff.

We broke out of the clouds over Anadyrskiy Zaliv (Anadyr Bay) with good ground visibility. I persuaded Viktor #2 to ask the Russian controllers to authorize as low an altitude as feasible so that we could check out the terrain. He quickly negotiated 6,000 feet.

We flew over the top of the Anadyr military base and turned southwest. From their shapes, I recognized at least a hundred MIG fighter aircraft lined up adjacent to the north-south runway. I didn't ask Viktor #2 about them; no reason to ask awkward questions he might consider sensitive.

I noticed that Viktor # 2 was looking down at the base too. I asked him if his family was based there with him and about his wife and children. He began telling me about his plan to have us spend the night at Anadyr on the way back. He wanted us to visit his home for dinner and meet his family before departing for Nome. I loved this guy. Could he actually read my mind? I didn't even have to ask about flying into Anadyr; he offered it up on his own. Perfect! I asked if he could perhaps arrange for us to look at some of the MIG fighters while we were there. He just laughed, but he didn't say no, either.

We arrived over Korf at 12:30 p.m. and began an NDB instrument approach into the airport. Korf was now solid overcast with cloud bases reported at the minimum descent altitude for our approach. Viktor and I reviewed the approach procedure. We broke out at the minimum descent altitude with the airport about two miles directly in front of us. It was a very short runway—no way to land a jet there. The town appeared to be a much more substantial and colorful place than Provideniya. Strangely though, I couldn't see any people. The town appeared deserted.

After landing, we taxied into the large ramp area. There were a few other aircraft there, but still no people. I picked a convenient place to park in the middle of the ramp and shut the engines down. As soon as the propellers stopped spinning, the sound of a large crowd hit my ears. Out of nowhere, several hundred screaming and yelling people appeared on the ramp and surrounded the airplane. I heard Ed exclaim, "Oh, my goodness—there are hundreds of people out there to greet us!"

We were the first non-Russian aircraft to ever land in Korf! They had never seen an American aircraft before and, with very few exceptions, had never seen Americans either. People congregated all over the ramp: men, women, kids, and their pets. Some of the men were in uniforms. It was a wild scene. I imagine

Lindbergh felt like this after he landed at Le Bourget. There were a hundred children or more running around the ramp. Everyone wanted to get close to this amazing thing that had come from another world. They all wanted to look inside. They pressed their faces to the windows so they could peer into the cockpit at the strange-looking instruments.

We spent the next couple of hours visiting with everyone, shaking hands, answering questions, and having our pictures taken with them. Viktor #2 introduced me to the chief navigator for the region. As Viktor #2 translated my description of our journey in some detail to him, the chief navigator began asking many questions. Upon hearing the story, the chief navigator took off his wings, pinned them on my jacket, and offered a smart salute. I was deeply moved. These were serious people, and this was a very meaningful gesture. It was one of the proudest moments of my fifty years in aviation.

Eventually, the crowd subsided. We then took a tour of the town with Vladimir Kvacof, the director of flight operations for the region. He began by taking us to a converted World War II barracks where we would be spending a couple of nights. Korf was initially constructed as a military base. All the buildings were wood construction. This was a significant improvement over Provideniya concrete. At least the buildings were colorfully painted. The women had placed curtains in the windows and added other homey touches.

As we walked around the town, everyone we came across had already met us at the airport. They were incredibly friendly. The children and teenagers all wore similar American-style clothes, jackets, and shoes. I wondered if someone had gone shopping for the town and brought a load back to distribute to everyone. Or perhaps an entrepreneur had just shown up with a load of stuff and sold the lot. People living in these remote areas were no different than people living in the remote areas of Alaska and northern Canada. They needed everything. Stuff was hard to come by. They'd take what they could get.

We eventually made our way to the beach area adjacent to the town. The shoreline was an astonishing sight to behold. Covering the beach before us was what looked like a massive field of battlefield debris. It looked like the Normandy Invasion without the cleanup. Rusted vehicle bodies, machinery, engines, refrigerators, and every kind of junk imaginable extended as far as we could see. We looked at each other in disbelief. We couldn't make any sense of it, and neither could the two Viktors.

We asked one of the locals to explain what had happened to the beach, and they said that the beach was where they dumped their refuse. "What? Why?" we asked. They had no concept of environmental consideration, nor did they even consider the aesthetic impact of their dumping on the beach. Indeed, it had been going on since World War II.

What a sobering and useful lesson. Foolish, selfish, and ignorant people have been polluting the land, air, and waters since the dawn of man. People who knew better got involved eventually and rallied the needed resources to clean up the mess. In a remote place like this, it was likely going to be a very long time before a mess of this scale could be cleaned up.

After our tour, we joined Vlad for a light lunch of apple juice, fried salmon, fish soup, pickles, and conversation. He was a fascinating guy. His family had come from western Russia. He had been flying for more than thirty years and directed all flight operations in the northern Kamchatka region.

We asked what people did there for a living. Their primary economic resource was a fish cannery. The area also offered excellent hunting and fishing. They were hoping that we would promote tourism when we returned home. They had large MI-8 helicopters he hoped that they could use to take people into the mountains to the south. Their biggest obstacle to tourism was the short summers in this part of the world. They have very long, heavy-snow winters with short days, with the temperature dropping to below -50°C.

We went back to the airport after lunch. Viktor #2, Tom, and I had a meeting with the pilots and navigators based there. We asked each other countless questions. They were quite intrigued by my geodetic survey charts and swapped some of their charts for some of mine. I liked these guys. I thought this must be what aviation was like before World War II. They were a very proud group, with strong personal bonds and a very professional approach. They worked in an aviation environment where every day they had to assume that nothing was going to work right and still had to get the job done.

Each of them knew or was learning how to do everything the hard way. Each understood old school basics and practiced all the time. Each knew every air route and instrument approach in the region by memory. Each had his own personal notebook carefully constructed, just like Viktor #2's, that contained critical information needed to fly their routes in horrendous weather with little more than a wristwatch, a compass, and an altimeter. It harkened back how Lindbergh did things when flying the mail in the Midwest more than sixty-five years earlier!

Vlad asked if he and some of the other pilots could go for a ride in the Aero Commander and maybe handle the controls. I was happy to oblige. But then, they asked me to first fly one of their workhorse airplanes, the Antonov 28, so I could brief them on the differences in the two aircraft. I enthusiastically agreed.

The An-28 is a twin-engine propjet similar to mine, but with larger payload capacity. Aeroflot used it as a short-range airliner. It could take a real beating. A fleet of them shuttled between the many villages and towns in the region. Slower and less maneuverable in the air than my Aero Commander, it could land on the rough roads, grass, and gravel fields that dotted the Russian landscape.

After our discussions, Viktor #2 and I were led out to an An-28 that had just been fueled. I climbed excitedly into the pilot's seat through the port access door to the cockpit. Vlad climbed in through the starboard cockpit access door. We both casually began strapping ourselves into our seats with the five-point seatbelt system very much like the one in my airplane. Viktor #2 strapped himself into the small jump seat between us.

Meanwhile, a dozen or so passengers, including Tom, Julie, Ed, Mike, Viktor #1, and a few of the pilots were escorted by a cabin attendant to the rear of the aircraft and entered through the open clamshell access door. I looked back at their grinning faces to see if everyone was okay with this or if they felt pressured to come along. Everyone wanted to go for a ride.

The Anatov cockpit instrument panel looked surprisingly familiar, a typical multi-engine turbine aircraft cockpit layout. The Russian markings weren't an issue for me. I knew what the gauges were for and how to read them. I asked Vlad what the typical operating numbers were, such as the airspeeds, and what the most important limitations were. Viktor #2 translated as Vlad gave me instructions on the numbers and talked about normal and emergency procedures. I listened intently, took notes, and asked pertinent questions.

After a twenty-minute briefing, I could hardly control my grin. It was time to start the engines and go flying! Vlad barked some orders into the back, and someone closed the hydrauli-cally-activated rear-entry clamshell doors. I had no difficulty interpreting Vlad's instructions. He knew what he was doing.

I started the engines without difficulty, completed the required checks, and then maneuvered the airplane to the runway.

I felt very comfortable as I pushed the power levers forward and accelerated down the runway to the south. After a very short takeoff roll, I turned left and passed over the beach we had been walking on only a couple of hours earlier. The beach wreckage was even more prominent from the air. I could see large dark masses in the shallow water, but couldn't tell what they were. Perhaps they were sunken boats. It really did look like the Normandy Invasion.

We spent the better part of an hour doing takeoffs and landings while flying a rectangular pattern around the airport that took us out over the bay after each takeoff. I was having an awesome time. I was worried that everyone in the back might be getting sick. Every time I landed, they thought we had finished. I'd raise the flaps, advance the power levers, and take off again. Everyone in the back would start laughing and giggling. They had no idea when the roller coaster ride was going to end. Frankly, I was having too much fun to stop. After the fifth landing, I decided that everyone had had enough. They were definitely starting to sound a bit giddy.

After we landed, Vlad and I spent about half an hour discussing my impressions of their workhorse aircraft. He was looking forward to flying the Aero Commander the next morning. But first, we needed to rest. It had been a very long day, and it wasn't over yet. With the sun out for twenty-three hours a day, it was so easy to lose track of time.

I met the others back at our rooms and took the opportunity to nap for an hour before cleaning up for dinner. The accommodations were far better than Provideniya. We had beds, and a bathroom. Water was another matter. Sometimes it worked, and sometimes it didn't. We left the tap open when we were there, so we'd know to leap up and use whatever decided to come through. In the meantime, we used some of the bottled water we had brought with us.

We met Vlad and his wife at their home for dinner in one of the barracks' buildings. Vlad's wife was a lovely woman who appeared to be Central Asian. We presented them with a bottle of Cuvaison wine Ed and Julie brought from California, along with a couple of souvenirs of our trip. The menu for the evening was an assortment of salami, salads made up of eggs with radishes, peas, and cucumbers, deep-fried salmon, potatoes with pork and lamb, and, of course, vodka. It was a wonderful meal, organized out of the simplest of ingredients.

Vlad and his wife could not ask enough questions about life in the US, and we could not ask enough questions about them and how they had come to be in Korf. They were the first Russian family I had ever spent an evening with. We spent hours interviewing each other. These were hardworking, humble, decent people with young children, trying to get by as best they could. We strolled back to our rooms late in the evening in full daylight. We were all so exhausted, none of us even remembered getting into bed.

For breakfast the following morning, we drank strong coffee and ate bread, dried fruit, and two cans of black caviar Viktor #1 had procured at the Moscow Airport that had come straight from the Caspian Sea. After breakfast, everyone had something they wanted to do. We all planned to meet up in a couple of hours.

Viktor #2 and I walked over to flight operations to meet Vlad and the other pilots. A casual glance at the sky during our walk over to the terminal building told me everything I needed to know about the weather. Thick, overcast conditions. Just the way I like it!

In the operations room, we talked with Vlad and the lucky pilots who were going flying with us about what would be most useful for them. Vlad suggested we make the same instrument approaches I had done the day before in the An-28. This would allow them to see how my airplane compared to theirs when executing the same procedures. Viktor #2 and I knew they were in for a treat. My Aero Commander could fly circles around an An-28.

I wanted to keep the fuel load down to stay well under max gross weight. There were eight of us for this flight, and some of these guys were bigger than any of my team. But leaving 1,000 pounds of fuel on the ground boosted the airplane's performance capability significantly. At 9,700 pounds, it was a rocket. We had five of Vlad's pilots in the back, while Viktor #2 knelt between the two cockpit seats.

Vlad didn't mind sitting in the right seat because he spent most of his time instructing other pilots. I needed to be able to access critical switches best reached from the left seat. Vlad did most of the flying and was an excellent pilot. My primary concern was that he did not inadvertently break something. Almost everything in the Aero Commander cockpit required more delicate handling than the An-28.

In retrospect, flying one of Vlad's airplanes the previous afternoon was a shrewd move on his part. It had allowed him to gauge my piloting skills and get comfortable with me before flying a Western aircraft he knew nothing about. This was a very professional approach. Vlad had been flying for a very long time, and it showed. The pilots in the back were like kids with a new toy. They just loved it. I wanted to give them each a turn at the controls, but Vlad wanted to keep flying. We executed the same procedures we had used the afternoon before. The only differences were that it was my turn to instruct, and we were flying actual instrument departures and arrivals.

After we finished, I asked Vlad what he thought of my Aero Commander. He said it was what he imagined driving a race car would be like, and then added, "It is not the sort of machine I would allow most Russian pilots to fly in any event." He thought it was too elegant. Most of his pilots would certainly break something very quickly. Some days later, in Petropavlovsk, Vlad's prescient observations saved me from near calamity.

8

KAMCHATKA: A PLACE OF WONDER

I wasn't sure what they had in mind, but would soon find out.
We were about to become the news in the Russian Far East.

By 10:20 a.m., we had refueled for Petropavlovsk, picked up our clearance, and were saying goodbye to our new friends. We hoped to see them again on our return north. The Russians were very friendly and warm. What they lacked in creature comforts, they more than made up for in hospitality.

We climbed quickly through the heavy overcast into a beautiful, deep-blue, sunny sky. Petropavlovsk lay 536 nautical miles to the south. We adjusted our course to join one of the Russian airways running along the east coast of the Kamchatka peninsula.

The terrain below changed dramatically, as we flew south. Huge mountains to our west stretched far to the south. Snowdrifts reached downward like fingers from many of their peaks. Viktor #1 observed over the intercom that many of the mountains were still active volcanoes. Occasional puffs of clouds in an otherwise clear blue sky provided dramatic backdrops for scenic photography. Mike shot video and stills nonstop.

Three bodies of water wash the coastlines of the Kamchatka peninsula: the Sea of Okhotsk to the west, the Pacific Ocean to the south, and the Bering Sea to the east, from where we had just come. Two parallel mountain ranges extend north and south along the entire length of the peninsula, one running down the center, and the other running down the eastern side.

The Koryaksky Plateau, sometimes called the Kamchatka River Valley, runs south between the two ranges. All but one of the twenty-nine volcanoes in the eastern mountain range we flew along were active. Below us, along the east coast, was an endless array of the most beautiful bays, gulfs, and rivers with crystal-clear water. It was spectacularly beautiful.

Viktor #1 gave us an impromptu lecture on some of the wildlife of the peninsula. The coastal waters were rich in fish, dolphins, white whales, and majestic whales. Hundreds of thousands of sea birds populated the coast. Steller's sea eagles, with huge beaks and monstrous claws, lived on a staple of salmon. Large numbers of birds and seals populated the many small islands further to the east.

Viktor #2 received permission from air traffic control to fly lower and into the interior of the peninsula so that we could fly down the Kamchatka central valley. The valley formed a very long, green expanse between the two mountain ranges, with the Kamchatka River, rich in salmon, zigzagging its way south to reach the open ocean.

As the valley turned east, another unusually large, dramatic-looking volcano came into view. Less than 10,000 years old, Klyuchevskaya, the volcanic queen of all Russia, stood proudly at 15,584 feet. Nearby Bezymyannaya, or "No-Name," had exploded in 1956 in a monstrous mess rivaling the 1980 eruption of Mount St. Helens.

In the distance, Petropavlovsk looked like a substantial city. Vitus Bering named the settlement after his two ships, the *St. Peter* and the *St. Paul*, in 1740. As we flew south over the city and east over Avacha Bay, we observed how very substantial this deep-water bay was. It reminded me of Sydney Harbor or San Francisco Bay. The terrain around the city was very green and hilly. To the north were two massive snowcapped volcanos, Avachinsky and Koryaksky. We learned later that Koryaksky had great potential as a year-round ski resort.

We made a long, straight approach from the east over the bay to Elizovo airport, visible beyond the west end of the bay. We flew past the former Soviet, and now Russian, Pacific submarine fleet, tucked into an inlet on the south side of the bay. Quite a few submarines were visible in their berths. Farther to the south, beyond the submarine base, was a small village with smaller mountains.

We touched down at 12:26 p.m. It was a smooth landing on a long runway in desperate need of refurbishment.

"We're here. I can't believe it!" I exclaimed over the intercom.

We were the first Americans to fly an aircraft down the Kamchatka peninsula and land at Petropavlovsk. Viktor #1 and Viktor #2 shared our excitement. We couldn't have done it without both of them.

It was a long taxi to the headquarters building on the south side of the airport. Having spent so much of my career as a "Cold Warrior," taxiing past rows of MIG-31 fighters and Backfire bombers that I had only seen in intelligence photos felt very strange.

The large delegation of officials waiting to greet us was impressive. Some wore deep-blue uniforms adorned with badges and pins displaying their senior commercial aviation status.

Others wore dark-green uniforms with many badges, ribbons, and insignias of senior military flight officers. They were all very excited to meet us, with a great deal of handshaking and smiles all around. We posed for pictures with everyone. Of course, we had no idea who these people were or what they were saying. I smiled and said, *"Zdravstvuyte"* or *"Dobriy den"* ("hello" and "good afternoon" in Russian). The two Viktors were too busy hugging and shaking hands with everyone to do any interpreting.

A very distinguished, pink-faced gentleman with a large mane of white hair combed back, and a big grin, began vigorously shaking my hand. "Amazing!" he kept saying. He was so excited and wouldn't let go of my hand. Finally, Viktor #1 introduced me to Viacheslav Balabanov, the deputy director of IKI, the Space Research Institute of the Russian Academy of Sciences—and the primary motivator on the Russian side for making our adventure a reality. Slava, short for Viacheslav, had flown out from Moscow with Viktor #1's wife, Sveta, to be with us. Slava's blue-grey eyes bulged out of their sockets intently as he continued to smile at me and vigorously shake my hand. After a moment, he stopped, looked at me, and started shaking again, while repeating his refrain, "Amazing!"

In that moment, I realized how significant this event was for everyone, but particularly for Slava and his boss, Yuri Osipov. They had taken what seemed like an absurd idea to their leadership only five months earlier. The mission had come off pretty much as Tom and I had envisioned it on day one. I was only now beginning to understand the enormous risk that they had taken and the boost in credibility our pulling it off had given them in the eyes of their superiors. The bottom line was that IKI needed money to keep their space program going. Slava was going to make as big a deal out of this event as he possibly could to support their goals. It had been about politics and economics for them from the beginning. I wasn't sure what they had in mind, but would soon find out. We were about to become the news in the Russian Far East.

After the excitement settled down, we unloaded our gear and equipment from the Aero Commander into a converted all-terrain, military personnel carrier that had driven onto the ramp and parked next to the plane. It had plenty of seating, with good exterior visibility and a lot of storage capacity. This vehicle was going to be our primary ground transportation during our stay in Kamchatka. It was ideal.

Viktor #2 and I went with one of the officials to complete the inevitably tedious paperwork before joining Tom, Julie, Ed, Mike, Viktor #1, and Slava at the office of the airport direc-tor, Aleksey Tverdokhleb. Meanwhile, our driver, Volodya, and Viktor #1's wife, Sveta, moved the personnel carrier off the ramp to the front of the airport building and waited.

Aleksey had a spacious, corner-view office located on the second floor of the headquarters building. The building and its dark wood furniture were old and worn, but still vastly better than anything we had seen thus far. The conference room adjacent to Aleksey's office had a long conference table with seating for fifteen to twenty people. Along the interior wall was a red velvet curtain covering a large map of the Kamchatka peninsula. With the cur-tain drawn, it wasn't clear if we were permitted to look at the map.

Our team sat on the window side of the conference table with the Russian officials on the interior side. Aleksey began by introducing his staff. Viktor #1 did the translating, while a sec-retary brought in tea and cookies. Aleksey said how excited they were to receive us, and that our coming was both a significant aviation achievement and an opportunity for us to learn about Kamchatka. They hoped we would choose to become involved with them in business ventures.

Tom and I had decided that it would be best if he did the talking as my representative. It was all about stature with the Russians. I commented only occasionally to add some color. Tom described our journey, how excited we were to be with them, and how we were looking forward to learning about Kamchatka.

Viktor #1 went on to outline the plans for our visit. We were to spend three days or so in Petropavlovsk seeing the city, visiting some of the key historical sites, and meeting with local officials. We planned to meet with the director of the Institute of Volcanology. We were to be interviewed by the local television news anchor during the evening news. We needed to provision for a land trip north through the interior of the peninsula to Kozyrevsk on the Kamchatka River, and then on to the Mars Rover testing site located on the slopes of the Tolbachik volcano.

On the way back south, we planned to visit Geyser Valley, considered to be Russia's most beautiful national park. The trip would allow us to see up close what Kamchatka had to offer as a tourist destination and its potential for agricultural and industrial development.

Finally, after our return from the trip north, a meeting was scheduled with the governor. Viktor #1 believed that we could do all we came to do in about ten days. Aleksey was quite impressed with our plan and offered his staff's every assistance. He asked if we would brief him and his staff on our findings when we returned, perhaps after we had met with the governor. We assured him we would.

My impression of the Russian managers we met was quite positive. They were serious people operating in challenging circumstances, desperate to get something done. It was clear they wanted our help. They just did not know what to do. Whatever we wanted to do at this point seemed entirely fine by them. It was only a matter of time before we would run into the other types, the ones who didn't care, or worse, the ones who only knew how to say nyet.

I was very concerned about the security of the Aero Commander on their ramp. Viktor #2 inquired about what security measures were being taken to ensure that no one approached the airplane. The airport authorities considered the facility very secure. They were not particularly concerned. I asked if it would be possible to pay for "special" security around the airplane. Viktor #2 reported back after some investigation that it could be easily arranged. I asked for how much and who the guards would be. Two soldiers from the local militia would be on duty at all times on the ramp, and $100 would cover it for our entire stay. "Sold!" I told him. He went off to make it happen.

The Russians had a vested interest in our success, and the last thing they wanted to happen was for our trip to go off the rails because some fool broke into the airplane and did damage on their watch. Investing this trivial amount in guards gave me much-added peace of mind.

I assumed Viktor #2 had been directed by the authorities to report on our movements and activities in addition to his navigation support duties. It just didn't matter to me. He was an intelligent, competent, and affable companion, who loved flying. After talking with Tom about it, we agreed to ask Viktor #2 if he'd be willing to accompany us for the entire time we were in Russia. He was thrilled at the invitation and happy to oblige. He made a call and quickly arranged permission from his superiors to do so. We didn't talk about payment, but I certainly intended to compensate him well for his continuing assistance.

It was mid-afternoon by the time we left the airport and began a leisurely orientation drive around the city. There were no suitable hotels. Viktor #1 had arranged for us to use a couple of apartments he had access to when he was in town. We quickly settled into a hectic routine of sightseeing, meeting with business and government people, and meals together in our little apartment. Our cook, Ludmilla, was terrific. She could make a meal out of anything. Julie and Ed also loved to cook. Between the three of them, we were well fed.

We had a TV with only one working channel, TV Kamchatka (TVK). The most popular TV show in the Russian Far East was an American soap opera I had never heard of, called *Santa Barbara*, dubbed in Russian. They couldn't get enough of it. I had no idea what the show was about, but from what little I saw, translation wasn't necessary. It was all sex, power, money, and of course, drama and more drama. I wondered what impact these images of an arrogant, wealthy US society had on the psyche of Russian viewers. I feared that they believed this was how all Americans lived.

On the Russian Far East evening news, the anchor wore sunglasses. On our return from touring the peninsula, he interviewed us on his evening newscast. He sent a camera crew to film us as we trekked around the peninsula. Film clips of us were featured every evening on the news for a week leading up to our interview. In short, we were the news in the Russian Far East!

Two cities make up Petropavlovsk. The old city is everything pre-1917. It's a beautiful, charming, old European-style city adjacent to the harbor docks on the northwest side of the bay.

The new city is everything built since Stalin: large, unimaginative, poorly constructed concrete buildings and blocks of concrete housing projects that look grotesque. Stalin introduced this style of construction, and it was common throughout the Soviet Union. Some years later, while touring Poland, I saw a Polish State documentary called *Man of Marble*, about the construction of Nova Huta, a town near Krakow. The film was satirical in appearing to memorialize, while denigrating, mass-construction techniques. It wasn't a pretty picture.

Just as in Provideniya and Korf, disrepair was everywhere, but on a vastly larger scale. Those were small towns; this was a city of more than two hundred thousand people. Every building was old and worn, with a great deal of unrepaired damage. Trash hadn't been collected in a very long time. Junk was scattered everywhere. Old broken-down cars moved on bumpy, broken pavement, or dirt.

People walked in the streets, as there were limited sidewalks. Their clothes looked old and tired, and their faces appeared weathered. Regardless, people still moved with purpose. They were going somewhere. People were so accustomed to the lack of aesthetics that they acted as if they didn't notice. If it bothered them, they didn't show it. They had vastly more important issues to deal with, like where they were going to get food and money. Money was the real issue. There wasn't enough money in circulation. Even if there had been, there was little to buy in government stores.

Meanwhile, all over the city, including in the government stores' parking lots, kiosks and street vendors were selling food, clothing, and other essential supplies. With the collapse of the Soviet Union, no one had an immediate understanding of why or how anything still worked. What did people use for money to purchase goods? It had been many months since Moscow had sent any money their way. The bus drivers still drove their buses, the stores were still open, utilities still worked. Why? How?

There were about half a million people in the Kamchatka region. People on the street didn't look like people I saw the following winter on the streets of Moscow, who generally looked central European. The people here had a mixed Eurasian look to them. Many of the indigenous peoples were of Mongolian origin. Others were the offspring of Ukrainians sent to the gulags during the Stalin era. Still others were the offspring of military personnel and civilians sent during the Cold War to staff Soviet military bases and ports.

In new Petropavlovsk, we visited a classic Soviet-era grocery store. It was a dark, drab place with an old, tired exterior and missing letters on the sign over the door. Only essential items were sold. Loaves of brown bread, with no wrappings, were stacked up on shelves. Cans of beans were in plentiful supply. Jars of many pickled things were lined up behind humorless clerks, with bins of flour and sugar in front of them. Equally drab, tired-looking women came into the store with containers they had brought to fill. Another clerk slowly calculated the amount owed on an abacus. It was a tedious, energy-draining process to get anything done. The place sucked the life out of you.

In old Petropavlovsk, we visited something called the Holkam Supermarket. A few months earlier, a remarkable Dutch entrepreneur named Holkam had shown up at the port with a small ship containing several cargo containers. He paid some "fees" for permission to unload his containers and open a grocery store. He quickly found a suitable empty warehouse, hired some local workers to help him, and proceeded to unpack his containers. The containers contained market shelves, cash registers, shopping carts, signs, painting supplies, tools, and all the goods he wanted to sell. The workers cleaned up and painted the building, and painted a big colorful sign on the front. In under a month, he opened his doors for business. For opening day, everyone in town showed up. He was now bringing in regular shipments of supplies for sale. I loved this guy, even though I never met him. It's a wonderful story of brilliant entrepreneurship.

On the day we went shopping at Holkam's it was hard to get near the place. The line to get in wrapped around the block. Viktor #1, Sveta, and Ludmilla waited in line for a couple of hours to get in, while the rest of us walked around the area. Later, when we finally got inside, it was a madhouse, filled with energy and excitement. Eight registers were going full tilt with long lines of people waiting to pay. It could have been anywhere in Europe. For Petropavlovsk, this was a very big deal and a very hopeful sign.

Julie picked up a frozen package of chicken legs with both English and Russian writing on the package. The package was from Mississippi, complete with USDA inspection stamps. The Russians called them "*nozhki Busha*," or "Bush legs." President Bush in 1990 signed a trade agreement with Gorbachev to provide frozen chicken quarters as part of a food aid program to help the USSR. We wondered how they got to Petropavlovsk—the world's most well-traveled package of chicken legs for sure! We also loaded up on orange juice from the Netherlands, and a variety of other food products to sustain us for the remainder of our trip.

Early on the morning of our fifth day in Kamchatka, we loaded up our personnel carrier for the 400-mile drive north to Kozyrevsk, a tiny hamlet on the banks of the Kamchatka River, halfway up the length of the Kamchatka peninsula. Our group had considerably grown since we had arrived in Russia. We now numbered a baker's dozen: five Californians, two Viktors, Slava, Sveta, Ludmilla, driver Volodya, and our guide, also named Volodya, who was the assistant director of volcanology at the institute in Petropavlovsk.

The sun was just coming up as Volodya drove us west past the airport. I took my usual seat at the back of the carrier on the right side. The two-lane road was little more than blacktop with very little traffic. Less than a half-hour out of Petropavlovsk, the blacktop turned into a dirt road with virtually no traffic and no inhabitants to be seen.

We stopped at a recreational area, called Paratunka, for a rest break. There was a hot spring some of the locals were enjoying.

We all spontaneously decided not to miss our first chance for a bath in five days. The warm water was wonderful. Viktor #1 said that the minerals in the water were supposed to be therapeutic.

Refreshed and clean, we turned north up the central valley of the peninsula. The terrain remained fairly flat for hours, with wild growth and thick stands of trees on either side of the road. We couldn't see very much because the trees blocked most of the views. It was very much like driving in Alaska. Eventually, the ubiquitous stands of trees became monotonous, and I fell asleep.

Midday, our dirt road came to a stop at the Kamchatka River. No dock, no nothing. We stood around patiently, waiting for the small barge to make its way across the river to take us to the other side. My first clue that something was amiss came when I realized the barge was not slowing down as it approached us. The ramp at the front end of the barge was already down. I watched in amazement as the barge's ramp rammed into the mound of earth at the river's edge. Like a backhoe, it picked up several hundred pounds of dirt in the process. "What a novel technique for docking a barge," I said, with a tinge of sarcasm.

We then patiently waited as the two barge deckhands proceeded to shovel several hundred pounds of dirt into the river. When they finally finished, Volodya drove our personnel carrier onto the barge while our group walked on and enjoyed being in the outdoors on this beautiful, sunny afternoon in the countryside.

We were halfway across the river when Tom, Ed, and I realized that the barge was just slowly spinning in circles and not going anywhere. We walked up to the cockpit to see what was going on and found Ludmilla having an attitude adjustment session with the pilot. He was, quite literally, drunker than anyone I had ever seen still vertical! The cockpit smelled like a mix of vodka and many unpleasant things. He and his crew had been drinking all day out of a large jug.

I have no idea what Ludmilla said to the pilot, but the image of fire in her eyes, and terror in his, remains in my memory to this day. I was about to ask Ludmilla if I should take the wheel. But her inspirational encouragement had temporarily roused the pilot enough to get the barge to shore. Sure enough, he plowed the ramp into the riverbank. So, we waited once again while the crew shoveled another load of earth into the river.

By the time we arrived in Kozyrevsk that evening, we were exhausted. The Department of Volcanology owned our cabin. It had hot water delivered by a wood-burning water heater. Somehow, in less than an hour, Ludmilla organized a meal of borscht, salmon patties, salmon eggs on bread, radishes, hard-boiled eggs, and other goodies. There was also the re-cooked liver from the night before. Every meal was a mix of new things and whatever we had not finished from prior meals. The liver kept showing up at every meal. I thought about slipping a couple of pieces into my pocket for disposal later, but I was afraid Ludmilla might catch me. After the ferry pilot episode, there was no way I wanted to get on the wrong side of her!

After dinner, Tom and I took a late-night walk around the village. It was a throwback to the nineteenth century. The snow-capped mountains to the east looked foreboding against the full moon. Even at 1:00 a.m., there was still some daylight. Small kids were still out playing. A few came up to us to see who we were.

One unique feature of this hamlet was hard to ignore—the mosquitoes! They were the largest I've ever seen. Their numbers were endless, and they took particular pleasure in torturing us. Our insect repellent seemed to have some effect against the small ones, but the big ones didn't care.

During the night, a couple of local guys came into our cabin and started rummaging through our stuff. Julie woke up and began screaming at them, which woke up some of our team, who proceeded to chase the hooligans off. I slept through the whole thing.

When I awoke in the morning, my left eye was swollen completely shut. Mosquito bites were all over me. I was miserable. The three-hour ride on bumpy roads into the mountains to the IKI Mars Rover testing facility near the Tolbachik volcano didn't help. I had too little to distract me and too much time to scratch. All I could think about was cortisone cream, which none of us had thought to bring.

When we finally reached the IKI testing facility, there was little more than a shack to be found. Beautiful deep azurite and canary flowers grew between outcroppings of dark rock, with snow-capped mountains in the background. We drove on to a higher elevation and finally stopped in a barren, but striking, valley. The terrain had a very grainy texture and a reddish caramel color. The ground-up lava looked very much like Jet Propulsion Laboratory (JPL) images of the surface of Mars.

By lunchtime, we were all famished. We were going to need our strength for the climb up a steep cinder cone in front of us. Ed and Julie went to work organizing yet another incredible meal out of whatever ingredients were at hand. Julie broke out a couple of avocados from the stash she had been saving for just such an occasion. They sliced them up and mixed them with sliced hard-boiled eggs, tomato slices, some greens, a few secret ingredients, and some bread. Over lunch, Volodya, our guide, briefed us on the coming climb. In 1975, the desolate, barren valley we were sitting in was flat and heavily forested. It didn't seem possible.

The hike up the side of the cinder cone was strenuous, but the view from the top made the hike well worth doing. We were above 5,000 feet. It was windy and cold. The gravel beneath our feet was warm to the touch. From the top, we peered into a hellish scene. Glowing orange and red-hot lava flowed everywhere.

Steam plumes rose into the air. The rocks beneath our feet were hot to the touch and yet were extremely light. Each was a mix of different colors, with yellows, greens, blues, reds, oranges, grays, blacks, and everything in between on display. The overall scene formed an unearthly image.

It was 9:00 p.m. by the time we arrived back in Kozyrevsk. With the sun still high in the sky, it felt more like midafternoon. Endless eighteen-hour days and pet mosquitoes were getting the better of me. I was exhausted. While we washed up for dinner, guide Volodya walked down to the river with his fishing pole to get some fresh fish for dinner. He quickly returned with two large salmon that Ludmilla immediately went to work on. The salmon tasted wonderfully fresh, and we had salmon patties for the remainder of the trip. The liver continued to remain on the table, untouched and looking just a little the worse for wear at every meal.

When I awoke the next morning, I could see better out of my left eye, but my upper lip was swollen. Ed and Mike didn't look much better. The mosquitoes were eating us alive. Viktor #1 had some good news to cheer me up. He had been down to the local post office, where he discovered a telephone switchboard. He arranged for me to call home. The switchboard equipment was something out of the 1920s. Two older women served as both postal clerks and switchboard operators for every telephone for hundreds of miles in any direction. I was shown to a small room where a very old-style telephone sat on a table. I wasn't sure what to do. I sat down on the chair next to the table and picked up the telephone. I heard a low hiss in the background. After a moment, I said hello. My wife, Paula immediately responded, "Hey Steve, how are you?"

It was great to hear her voice. She had been waiting on the telephone for twenty minutes. She had received a call from

Moscow saying that a call was being relayed and to stand by. This call was taking the long way around the world. It was late in the afternoon in California. She was excited to hear my voice and know that I was in good spirits, the mosquitoes notwithstanding. We spent the next thirty minutes catching up. She wanted to know what Kamchatka was like and what we were eating. Things were fine at home. The kids were all doing well and looking forward to our planned vacation when I returned. I gave her messages to relay to Ed's wife, Suzie. The biggest news back in the US was that Bill Clinton had picked Al Gore to be his running mate.

In the switchboard room, the two ladies began speaking in very excited voices with Viktor #1. I interrupted my call to ask if everything was okay. Viktor #1 said they were very concerned because the call had gone on for so long. It would be very costly. No one had ever made a call to the US from there before. A few minutes after I finished my call, one of the ladies received a call from Moscow informing her I owed 1,100 rubles, about $5.00.

That afternoon we took a leisurely cruise down the Kamchatka River on an old Soviet patrol boat. The weather was warm and sunny. We were all exhausted and enjoyed a rare opportunity for some relaxation. Occasionally, we'd stop along the riverbank so Ed and Julie could pick flowers or look for berries. The Kamchatka flora and fauna were truly exceptional. We came across many large fields of orange lilies and many other kinds of colorful flowers. During this and our various other excursions, we saw a large variety of animals and birds, including rabbits, squirrels, deer, sable, fox, snow sheep, many different kinds of birds, and many bears.

Back in Kozyrevsk that evening, we took turns being interviewed by the camera crew the TV station in Petropavlovsk had sent along with us. They wanted our impressions of what we had seen.

It was Sveta's birthday. Tom, Julie, and Ed organized a little birthday party for her. I have no clue how they came up with invitation cards. Ludmilla made a cake out of bread and fish. Another bottle of wine mysteriously emerged from Ed and Julie's secret stash. It was our last dinner in Kozyrevsk. More fresh salmon—and anything not already eaten previously—reappeared on the table for the last time. The liver continued to sit there.

In the morning, we were greatly relieved to learn that we would not have to drive the ten to twelve hours back to Petropavlovsk. Viktor #1 had been successful in making the arrangements for us to use a Mi-8 helicopter courtesy of our new best friend, airport director Aleksey Tverdokhleb. He sent Vladimir Samarski, the commander of the helicopter wing, with the Mi-8 up to meet us, take us to Geyser Valley for an over-nighter, and then back to Petropavlovsk.

Volodya drove our group to a clearing where we were to meet the Mi-8 and Vlad. The huge helicopter suddenly appeared 100 feet overhead, with Vlad hanging halfway out of the pilot seat door waving to us while he landed the helicopter in the clearing. He had quite a colorful personality.

We all were a little startled when Vlad asked if I wanted to fly the helicopter. My local reputation as an aviator, now inflated beyond reason, required he show me this courtesy. In truth, I had very little helicopter time. It had never been my thing. But I could hardly say no. I was familiar with the theory of how helicopters worked and had enough flight time in small ones to know how to fly one under adult supervision. The convention for airplanes is that the pilot sits in the left seat. It is the opposite in helicopters; the pilot always sits on the right. Vlad spent twenty minutes briefing me on the details of the large, complicated cockpit instrument panel and controls while Viktor #2 translated. The more he talked, the more comfortable I became. Vlad sat in the left seat, and Viktor #2 sat on the jump seat between us. A flight engineer sat behind us and handled most of the electrical switches too far over our heads to reach.

While we were getting prepared up front, Ed, Tom, Julie, Mike, Viktor #1, Sveta, Slava, and our TV station camera crew piled into the back. The two Volodyas bid us good-bye. They were driving the personnel carrier back south with most of our gear and would meet us at the helicopter drop off point outside Petropavlovsk the following day.

Julie was a little nervous. She had high confidence in my flying ability, but she wasn't so sure I could really fly a Soviet helicopter. But I knew it was going to be fine. Vlad was a great coach, and Viktor #2 was an excellent translator. Vlad easily coached me through the finer points of helicopter flying. Without undue delay, I started the engines, completed the preflight checks, and lifted off for Geyser Valley. To the surprise of some aboard, I had no difficulty handling the helicopter. It was much larger and heavier than any helicopter I had flown, but also, much more stable. Flying is flying. The controls were very responsive. I liked flying this helicopter.

I flew a couple of hundred feet above a dark-green canopy of trees, beautiful lakes, rivers, and streams. In the distance, to the east, were towering volcanic mountains we'd catch glimpses of through broken, low-hanging clouds. The helicopter was loud and vibrated to a rhythm created by the rotating blades above our heads. It was difficult to hear anything without a headset. The flight engineer opened a bottom hatch so Mike could shoot video of the terrain below. The side door was also open. Everyone was shooting video and taking pictures out of every opening they could find. It was a gorgeous day for flying.

After an hour or so, we cleared a ridge marking the east boundary of Geyser Valley and descended for landing in an open field on the valley floor, where our guides were waiting. I expected Vlad to take the controls at some point, but he never did. My natural flying instincts just worked. I flew the helicopter to a hover and then just landed it. Viktor #2 was as surprised as I was. He said, "Steve, I didn't know you knew how to fly helicopters." I replied, "Neither did I." All Vlad said was, "Nice job!" I wasn't sure what he really thought, but I was very relieved to have made a respectable job of it.

The Valley of Geysers looked like a miniature Yellowstone National Park, a small valley filled with wonders. The ice-covered slopes of the dark hills around the valley combined with the lush fields of colorful flowers, green grasses, and trees on the valley floor to create a beautiful spectacle. Columns of steam and fountains of boiling water bubbled up from the many geysers surrounding the valley.

There were more than twenty geysers of significance. Some gushed forth every ten to twelve minutes, while others erupted once every four or five hours. Local guides led our group on a hike to one of the many hot springs for a swim. The water was 108 degrees Fahrenheit. It was wonderful. We spent the afternoon hiking and exploring in the valley before finally settling in at our campsite for a delightful evening of campfire bonding, eating, storytelling, and, oh yes, vodka!

On the afternoon of day nine of our visit, I flew the Mi-8 helicopter back to Petropavlovsk from Geyser Valley. Flying low and relatively slowly created the opportunity to see Kamchatka in a way that would otherwise have not been possible. We flew south from Geyser Valley through the mountains and explored some of the lower-lying volcanoes. We hovered over a small lake in the middle of one volcano where the teal-colored, mineral-rich water appeared in stark contrast to the dark volcanic formations surrounding it. Heading farther south and west, we passed over lakes, rivers, and forests. Finally, we came to a place by the side of the road east of Elizovo, where Volodya waited patiently with the personnel carrier. With another successful landing under my belt, I thanked Vlad for his great hospitality and pilot mentoring.

After settling back in our apartment in Petropavlovsk, we enjoyed a segment about our group on the evening news before dinner. The footage was from the day before and earlier that day. TVK had been running segments on us on the evening news every night since we had arrived the week before. Our Kozyrevsk interviews were one of the topics of the evening's segment. Everyone laughed at how funny I looked with one swollen, half-closed eye and a swollen upper lip from all the mosquito bites. Viktor #1 was even more entertaining. An unusually large mosquito harassed him through his entire interview, while he desperately tried to focus on what he was saying. Occasionally he'd take a swipe at the mosquito while continuing to intently look at the camera, all the time pretending it was not happening. Just as the interview ended, he caught the mosquito. The gratification on his face was adorable. We all laughed hysterically.

PHOTOGRAPHS

The Kamchatka Travel Team: Julie & Tom Heinsheimer, Steve Myers, Ed Beall, and Mike Stoner.

July 4, 1992—The Travel Team launches for the Kamchatka Peninsula.

Extraordinary glaciers and terrain in Canada and Alaska

Flying through the Wrangell Mountains to Anchorage.

Following the Kuskokwim River west.

Passing Anviko following the Yukon River north to Galena.

Cheeseburgers at the Nugget Inn in Nome were an absolute must!

Launching for Provideniya from Nome, the sky had an unearthly hue.

Steve and Tom In the cockpit at Valda waypoint.

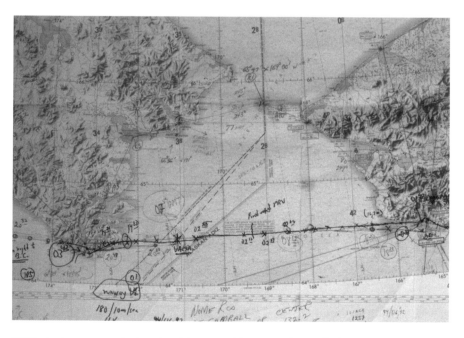

WAC charts were marked up to plot our position, note key radio frequencies, and other useful info.

Our first look at Russia revealed a harsh and desolate landscape.

On the ground in Provideniya, one of the most isolated places in all of Russia.

Provideniya looked like a war zone lost in time.

The scope of infrastructure damage was shocking, with no way out for its people.

Steve and Viktor Shlyaev (Viktor #2), our Russian navigator and travel companion.

Preparing for takeoff from Provideniya on a short, gravel runway, into low, overcast skies.

Viktor #2 proved an excellent professional flight officer and was easy to work with.

Hundreds gathered to witness the first-ever landing of a Western aircraft in Korf, at the north end of the Kamchatka peninsula.

Viktor Kerzanovich (Viktor #1) interprets as Steve describes the journey from California to Kort for local officials

A proud moment for Steve as the Chief Navigator of the Kamchatka region decorates him on learning the details of the journey and required airmanship.

Walking the "invasion" beaches at Korf. Debris as far as the eye could see.

Young girls are the same everywhere.

Vladimir Kvacof, Korf Director of Flight Operations, with his lovely wife.

Julie and Ed check out gardens fashioned out of former runway materials.

Flying over one of Kamchatka's 28 active volcanoes.

Klyuchevskaya, the largest active volcano in Northern Hemisphere, 15,584 ft.

Looking east over Old Petropavlovsk and Avacha Bay.

Taxing past rows of MIG-31 fighters at Elizovo.

The Deputy Director of Elizovo greets Steve and congratulates our team on being the first Westerners to fly down to Kamchatka and land in Petropavlovsk.

Unloading at Elizovo for an indefinite stay.

Our first meeting with the Elizovo Airport Managers. It's been a long day!

Street vendors selling stuff in front of the Elizovo Airport Headquarters building.

"New" Petropavlovsk built during Stalin era looking north.

Cruising around "Old" and "New" Petropavlovsk.

Shopping in "New" Petropavlovsk...Soviet style.

In "New" Petropavlovsk, first you pay, then shop. Don't forget your own containers.

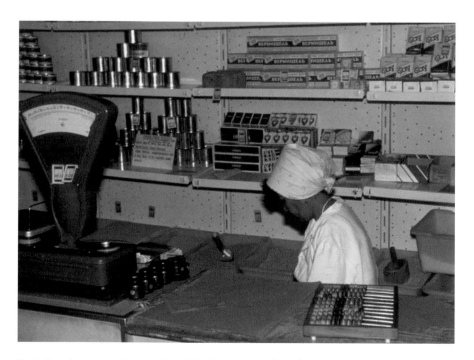

Note the abacus on the counter. At the bank, the tellers also used abacuses.

In "Old" Petropavlovsk, waiting in line to get into Holkam Supermarket.

Note the red, white and blue colors used for Holkam Supermarket. The store only accepted US dollars. Everyone seemed to have them. We wondered where they came from.

Our distinguished host, Viacheslav (Slava) Balabanov, Deputy Director of IKI and the most important member of our expanding group, Ludmilla the cook!

Our transportation across the Kamchatka River heading north for the grand tour.

Kozyrevsk on the Kamchatka River—Mosquito heaven!

Midnight sun on the Kamchatka River.

The IKI Rover Testing Facility on the slopes of Tolbachik Volcano.

Beautiful outcroppings of summer flowers adorn the slopes.

Lunch on Tolbachik Volcano with our personnel carrier in the background.

Julie and Ed used the last of their avocado stash on our delicious lunch before climbing the Tolbachik cinder-cone.

Spectacular view of "Mars terrain" as we climb a cinder cone near Tolbachik.

Peering into the magma flow at the top of a cinder cone at Tolbachik.

Ludmilla, our excellent cook, could make a meal out of anything.

We all wanted to make the liver vanish but were afraid Ludmilla would catch us.

Cruising down the Kamchatka River in a patrol boat.

Preparing to fly to Geyser Valley in an Mi-8 helicopter.

Geyser Valley—the Russians considered it their most beautiful national park before its destruction by volcanic activity in 2007.

After a rugged tour of Kamchatka's interior, the wear was starting to show. But we were a hearty group of adventurers eager for more.

Entrepreneurial inspiration begins to take hold on the ramp at Elizovo.

The Travel Team with the Governor of Kamchatka, Vladimir Birjukov.

Our last evening in Petropavlovsk was one of joy and great sadness.

Steve exchanging gifts with the Elizovo managers prior to departure.

Ominous weather at Anadyr, with dozens of MIG fighters and military transports lining the runway to witness an extremely difficult crosswind landing.

The weather was deteriorating rapidly. It was time to leave. Next stop, Alaska. We could smell the cheeseburgers!

Happy to be home, Tom, Steve, and Ed smile for the waiting crowd of reporters, family, friends, and well-wishers.

Steve answers reporters' questions with happy daughter Megan in his arms.

Ken Colbaugh, SM&A COO (on Viktor's right) joins Steve for "Exclusivity" negotiations with Kamchatka Vice Governor, Vladimir Sinchenko.

Congressmen Chris Cox (later Chairman of the SEC) and Dana Rohrabacher join Vice Governor Sinchenko for a reception and dinner at Steve's home in Irvine.

Boris Gurevich (center) and Viktor Kerzhanovich join Steve for Moscow negotiations crucial to Russian Parliament approving the CKC Joint Venture.

Steve, Boris and two members of the Russian negotiating team at "vodka dinner."

Dennis Crosby, CKC Chief Operating Officer (second from left) on one of his endless trips to Petropavlovsk for meetings with Elizovo Airport managers.

Chuck DeVore in Petropavlovsk, visiting the memorial site of the Russian victory over the Anglo-French expedition during the Crimean War in 1854.

It's all hands on deck at NBAA in Atlanta to persuade the aviation community to use our "gas station" on the great circle path to Asia. Dennis is very persuasive.

Evergreen 747 taxing out after fueling. Winters are long in Kamchatka.

9

ENTREPRENEURIAL INSPIRATION

I began pacing quickly down the runway, lost in thought.
"Kamchatka is California before the Gold Rush!"

On the evening of the tenth day, our team of five Americans, plus Viktor #1, appeared on TVK in Petropavlovsk for a two-hour live special. Vladimir Efimov, the chief editor of TVK, personally conducted the interview. He was a delightful personality, even if he did wear sunglasses on the set. After the initial introductions, Vlad asked me to explain why we had come to Kamchatka and what we hoped to accomplish during our visit. Viktor #1, as usual, assisted with the translation.

Our trip had three primary objectives: first, to be the first Americans to fly into the Kamchatka peninsula and demonstrate that it could be done safely; second, to learn all we could about Kamchatka and share what we learned with the people of the United States; third, to understand the potential for tourism and commercial opportunities in the region.

Vlad eventually turned the discussion to our impressions of Kamchatka. We all had very positive things to say about our experiences. None of our group, except for Tom, had ever been to Kamchatka. We had no preconceived ideas of what we would find. We found the region beautiful, the people warm and hospitable, and the opportunities for development innumerable.

Then I said something that piqued Vlad's interest, that Kamchatka reminded me very much of California. He wanted to hear much more about that. Remembering that Santa Barbara was the number one TV program in the Russian Far East, I explained how the general topography of the peninsula was very similar to many of the features of California.

For example, Kamchatka's eastern mountain range is much like the Sierra Nevadas, and Kamchatka's central range is very much like the coastal mountain range of California. The central Kamchatka River Valley is much like the San Joaquin Valley, but much more forested, perhaps as the San Joaquin Valley might have been in the distant past. Kamchatka's eastern shoreline resembles California's Pacific coastline. The birds and sea life along the Kamchatka coastline are amazing to behold. Avacha Bay looked similar to how San Francisco Bay would have looked before being developed and dredged.

Some of Kamchatka's other features reminded me of other parts of the western US. The Kamchatka River, which has some of the best salmon fishing in the world, is similar to the Columbia River, which divides Oregon and Washington states. Geyser Valley is reminiscent of places I had visited in Yellowstone. I also had to confess to the TV audience that, in this case, it was a limited comparison. Geyser Valley is quite beautiful but covers only a tiny fraction of the vast area Yellowstone National Park covers. Vlad reacted very positively to my comparative descriptions. He hoped such visual comparisons might help attract visitors.

Vlad was a most gracious host and the program a mutual love fest. He could not have been more positive and supportive.

Tom was already having discussions with him about a deal for a taped SM&A segment to appear weekly on TVK.

After the show finished, Vlad took us out for drinks. He was an avid skier and was very interested in skiing in the US, especially Aspen. Ed talked about the architectural work he had done in Vail and how great the skiing was there. Mike and I told him about our experiences in Colorado and helicopter skiing in the Canadian Rockies. Vlad begged us to take the short trip to the ski camp on one of the volcanoes just north of the city and to try out the glacier skiing. I thought about it for ten personally painful seconds before explaining how I needed to be able to fly us all home. We just couldn't take the chance that I might get injured.

But Mike and Ed were all smiles and ready to go. When they returned the following day, Ed said that Vlad was a former member of the Russian Ski Team, and the team trained at the ski camp there year-round.

"Yes, but how was the actual snow?" I asked.

"Nothing you'd want to ski on," was all Mike had to say about it.

We were convinced Vlad and TVK would be critical for any development effort we hoped to launch in the region. Our instant notoriety, high profile, and growing credibility in the Russian Far East created the opportunity for us to get any message out we chose. The hard question I put to Tom was, "What do we want to sell them?"

We had two days left in Petropavlovsk before beginning the long trip home. Viktor #2 and I went to the airport to make sure that all was in order and to fuel the airplane for demonstration flights scheduled the following day. We had promised to take the airport director and some of the other airport officials for rides after our return from touring the peninsula.

I wanted to show up at the airport unannounced to be sure that the militia was really guarding the airplane. I paid $100 for 24/7 guard duty during the entire time we were there. I was relieved to find two guards on duty, properly uniformed, armed, and showing some military bearing. They could not have been more respectful to us.

Viktor #2 arranged for a fuel truck so that we could supervise the fueling. We carefully inspected the exterior and interior to ensure that everything was in order. There was no reason to think otherwise. We checked anyway.

A young Russian Air Force officer saw us on the ramp and came over to say hello. He was a handsome, square-jawed, Russian fighter pilot, resplendent in his flight suit. He told Viktor #2 he was bored and looking for some company. There was no fuel available for flying before the following month, and there wasn't much for him to do.

Viktor #2 asked if he would give us a tour of his MiG-31. To my astonishment, he eagerly agreed. He came back a few minutes later in a Jeep and took us over to the bunkers where the fighters and bombers sat. It was extraordinary. I was a former Cold Warrior being escorted around a former Soviet military airbase, looking at Backfire Bombers, MiG-29s, and MiG-31s. The big red star on each of the Soviet aircraft tails made the hair on the back of my neck stand up. It felt unsettling and downright spooky.

It was also an incredible opportunity to take a close look at the latest in Soviet aircraft technology. So much could be learned about the Russian people and their engineering methodology from examining their technology.

In the US, we generally design for effectiveness and efficiency. We're technology-driven, anxious to incorporate the latest ideas into the next generation of everything. This primary mission drives aircraft design. The most important considerations in achieving that mission are some combination of speed, range, payload, weight, fuel capacity, cost, and reliability. There may also be a host of other secondary considerations. Finding the optimal balance for the mission intended is usually challenging. The role of "systems engineering" is to find that optimal balance. This topic is one of the core interests that dominated my professional career, most of which was spent in the aerospace and defense industry, working on the development of new systems. I spent a great deal of time in many of our nation's best engineering and manufacturing facilities.

One of my fondest accomplishments is the work we did in support of Lockheed Martin on the Joint Strike Fighter, the F-35 program. The F-35 is the most elegant aircraft the world has ever produced. It is a fantastic accumulation of a vast number of technologies and sits at the pinnacle of US manufacturing capability. SM&A worked on that program for more than ten years, from a paper concept to the end-to-end manufacturing processes. I visited the Fort Worth F-35 engineering and manufacturing facility many times and walked the two-mile assembly line as the first aircraft were coming together.

The Soviets' engineering, and manufacturing methodology viewed aircraft design from an entirely different perspective. They started with "rugged" in mind. They assumed that anything that *could* break *would* break, and probably at the worst possible time. Russian weather is vastly harsher than the US weather, and their infrastructure less accommodating. Their operators and maintenance technicians are less educated but not necessarily less skilled. They had some excellent technical people, but also a much larger supply of weak and unreliable performers. Their design methodology assumed the worst: poorly trained pilots flying poorly maintained aircraft, in terrible weather, with inadequate technical infrastructure, and insufficient ground-support infrastructure. Everything had to be designed for ease of assembly and disassembly, over and over again.

Soviet access to technology was generally limited, and always years behind the West. They tried to keep up by reverse-engineering designs obtained by KGB agents in the West. For example, their Space Shuttle program, many of their aircraft programs, and their ICBM program all tried to take advantage of US designs. But only in limited ways.

Examining Soviet-era aircraft close up, the differences in manufacturing capabilities were readily evident. By comparison, the MiG-31 was anything but elegant. The limitations in the precision and the quality of the manufacturing processes used to create it were evident. These limitations translated into significantly higher weight and lower fuel efficiency, and consequently, shorter range. But it was also evident that it could take a real beating.

Soviet fighters also needed much more maintenance, particularly for their engines. The typical time between overhaul (TBO) for a Soviet fighter engine was half of a comparable US fighter engine. Their avionics, radar, and weapons systems were not as light nor as elegant and didn't perform as well. All that being said, the Soviet aircraft were also much cheaper to build and generally easier to maintain.

The Soviet's military strategy was to compensate for inferior technology with higher numbers. In aerial combat, it's all about exchange ratios. If x number of US fighters engage y number of Soviet fighters, what happens? The outcome depends on several factors. It can't be assumed that superior technology will win the day. This is why US military pilots train so hard. We're counting on winning with fewer numbers of more capable aircraft, flown by superbly trained pilots using better tactics.

After we finished our tour, I asked the Russian fighter pilot if he would take us out to the runway. I wanted to check the condition of the runway for foreign object damage (FOD), debris that might damage aircraft on takeoff or landing.

As we inspected the runway, something occurred to me in the blink of an eye. Call it a moment of entrepreneurial inspiration. I heard myself say out loud, "Oh my, I have gone back in time a hundred and fifty years!"

Viktor #2 looked quizzically in my direction; my words made no sense to him.

I ignored him, and our fighter pilot escort as I began pacing quickly down the runway, lost in thought. "Kamchatka is California before the Gold Rush!" I started thinking about the gold mines of the Sierra foothills, the Sacramento River with stacks of rocks left over from placer mining, Yosemite Valley, and San Francisco Bay. My thoughts focused on a time in California before the Gold Rush. My pulse raced, and blood rushed to my head as I desperately tried to recall every detail of that period.

Fortunately, I knew something about the topic. Paula's father, Ray Mathis, lived in Grass Valley, a small town in the Sierra foothills, not far from the Empire Mine, one of the iconic gold mines of the gold rush. My family had visited the area frequently and visited the mine. We had also spent one of the hottest summers of our lives living near Folsom Lake and the Sacramento River. The rivers of the area are all about summer fun, boating, and rafting in the rapids. But during the gold rush, every grain of gravel and rock in those riverbeds had been turned over by rabid gold hunters. Endless giant stacks of boulders still line the rivers where long-ago machines had deposited them as gold hunting became industrial.

I asked myself, "What would have been the most valuable thing to own before the Gold Rush?" The answer to this question had profound consequences. I thought about it this way: If I arrived in California before the Gold Rush, where would I have gone, and what would I have wanted to own? I wondered if I could take my knowledge of the history of that period and apply it in a practical way to a prospective enterprise in Kamchatka. An obvious answer would be to own a gold mine. But gold mining is a risky business. I couldn't know in advance exactly where any particular mine was. I couldn't be sure that any specific gold mining enterprise would succeed in the long run.

But what if I could control access? Then I could make money on everybody else's enterprises. The Ottoman Turks understood this concept very well. They controlled the Bosporus, one of the greatest access points in the history of the world. This natural border between Europe and Asia allowed the Ottomans to charge everyone coming and going in every direction for a thousand years.

I thought back to the California Gold Rush. The owners of the Empire Mine made a fortune, but most gold miners didn't make much, if anything. Who made the most money with the least risk? The answer was obvious to me as soon as I thought about it. The railroad and the Port of San Francisco! The money was in the logistics and handling of all the people coming and going!

What was the equivalent of the Port of San Francisco in Kamchatka in 1992? It was the piece of ground I was standing on at that very moment—Kamchatka's only potential international port of entry, Elizovo.

I was very excited. I took Tom aside, as soon as we found him, and began briefing him on my vision. He got it right away. Tom, Viktor #1, and I went back out to the airport for an impromptu meeting with the airport director and his staff to try out some ideas on them. Without their support, we had no chance of succeeding, no matter what we hoped to accomplish.

Their reaction was supportive of our every idea. They liked the idea of tourism. They readily acknowledged that a new terminal was required, and were anxious to have an American partner who would bring much-needed investment capital.

But it was not up to the airport director and his staff who the partner would be or what the limits of the agreement would be. That was the prerogative of the governor, Vladimir Birjukov. Our timing couldn't have been better. We had a meeting scheduled with the governor the following afternoon!

We then went with some of the airport staff to have a much closer look at their facilities and infrastructure. It was like putting on a pair of different-colored glasses. Now we were focused on how to make things work, not just make do. The runway was in desperate need of repair. The fuel tanks were old and rusted, and the ground-support equipment were relics. The terminal was an ugly, dilapidated, grey building. We could never process Western passengers through such an unsightly place, and it couldn't possibly meet International Civil Aviation Organization (ICAO) standards.

Then it hit me. I needed to think bigger. These people had nothing, and they needed everything. Everything was going to have to be reconstructed. I was the first person to fly here, which gave me visibility and clout. If only I had the creativity and courage to take advantage of it. The entrepreneurial spark had lit a fire within me, and the fire was crackling!

BE CAREFUL WHAT YOU ASK FOR

We needed exclusive rights to operate international flights in and out of Elizovo. We also needed exclusive rights to develop the area for tourism.

During our last full day in Petropavlovsk, Tom, Viktor #1, and I met with the governor of Kamchatka, Vladimir Birjukov. The governor's offices were located in a fairly modern-looking government building built in the old city, near the port. The building and the grounds around it were well kept. A large granite pedestal stood in front of the building that had recently been the base for a large statue of Lenin. Some months earlier, the statue had quietly been removed. The only bank in the city was up the street. We had visited the bank earlier. The bank tellers, like the clerks in the government stores, used abacuses for calculating.

Governor Birjukov was an old-guard communist trying to find his bearings in the new order, like everyone else. We began our discussion describing our impressions of the Kamchatka peninsula and its people. We went on to say that we were prepared to invest millions of dollars in the development of Kamchatka and to bring incredible resources to the region. We had his attention.

We explained that, before we could do any of this, we needed exclusive development rights. We needed exclusive rights to operate international flights in and out of the airport. We also needed exclusive rights to develop the area for tourism. We asked the governor if he was willing to grant us those rights in a joint-venture agreement.

He looked me straight in the eye and said, "Yes, of course." Just like that.

In that instant, the old adage came to mind: "Be careful what you ask for . . . you just might get it!"

After much discussion, we agreed to prepare a proposal for the governor over the following three months, describing the details of our exclusivity rights and our plans for moving forward. Before we could legally proceed, a formal joint-venture agreement would have to be ratified by the Russian Parliament.

Holkam's supermarket experiment had been instructive. Holkam had shown up only three months before us on a small cargo ship and thrown together his supermarket in a matter of weeks. He had demonstrated that the biggest problem with the Russian economy at the local level was a lack of product. There wasn't much to buy. Basic food and clothing needs were being met. But there was little availability of the stuff that consumers wanted.

A fundamental rule of capitalism is that consumer spending drives gross domestic product (GDP). No product means no spending. But lack of spending doesn't necessarily mean no demand. It all starts with investment. No investment, no production. No production, no jobs, and no product. No jobs, no money for spending. Growth stimulates investment, to be sure, but how do you kick-start a dead economy?

In Kamchatka, after the fall of the USSR, the people had quickly adapted to barter trading. They lived in old apartment buildings built in the 1950s and 1960s, sparsely furnished with tattered pieces of furniture. They lived in perpetual poverty. It was a very sad thing to see. Still, when Holkam opened his supermarket, people flooded in to buy everything he offered. Holkam didn't take rubles. Where did all the hard currency come from? I concluded that the locals had become trapped in a system of forced hard currency accumulation through bartering. They had little to spend their rubles on that had any real value. Anyone who had something of real value to sell didn't want rubles for it. They demanded a hard currency. The locals also knew that if they didn't spend their rubles, the rubles would become worth less and less because of the inevitable inflation sure to come. So, they traded rubles for whatever they could turn into hard currency as fast as they could.

I wondered how to create a sustainable level of hard currency, i.e., dollars, and provide the needed products on which the local people would be able to spend hard currency. The answer had to start with jobs that paid in hard currency. I also wondered what they wanted to buy most with hard currency if they had it. The people of Kamchatka needed everything and at low prices.

Home Depot and Walmart came to mind.

For example, I thought the availability of construction materials would stimulate the creation of jobs, starting with tradespeople to build things. I imagined loading cargo containers onto barges in Seattle and opening up a mix of a Home Depot/Walmart-style shopping facility. Once an ambitious project like this began to spool up, no end of opportunities might emerge. It could take on a life of its own. There were so many possibilities. We just needed to find the right catalyst to start an economic chain reaction.

Whatever the catalyst, this kind of enterprise would need staff and infrastructure to implement. There were no decent hotels for visitors. Who would build a hotel? If we constructed a hotel, we'd have to worry about how to attract customers. To attract customers, we needed to bring commercial flights into Petropavlovsk. ICAO would require a passenger terminal that met its standards to allow international flights. Who was going to build the terminal, and how were we going to finance it? These and so many other ideas swirled around in my head nonstop. Tom and I had a constant dialogue about the possibilities. I made lists, and lists of lists.

Our last evening in Petropavlovsk was a mix of celebration and sadness. Ludmilla, Sveta, Julie, and Ed had worked all afternoon preparing a wonderful farewell dinner for the group. Some twenty of us jammed into our tiny apartment. We sat around a long table made up of two doors covered with tablecloths made from curtains. Julie and Ed brought out everything left in their secret stash of food supplies. The meal was accompanied by many, many toasts given by all. The consumption of vodka was unending. Everyone was in a happy, festive mood. The liver was nowhere in sight! Julie had finally taken care of the matter. I didn't ask how.

At about 11:00 p.m., the telephone rang. The call was for Viktor #2. Viktor's tone changed considerably as the call went on for several minutes. We didn't need to speak Russian to know that it was bad news. Someone heard him say "nightmare!" into the phone.

Viktor #1 said, "Something very bad has happened. I don't know what."

After the call, Viktor #2 came back to the table with tears in his eyes. His closest friend had been killed a few hours earlier in a plane crash. He was heartbroken. We all felt so sad for him.

For the next couple of hours, Viktor #2 talked about his friend. There were many toasts offered in his friend's memory.

He was relieved to be returning to Anadyr in the next couple of days. He needed to be with his family and with the family of his lost friend.

Our final morning in Petropavlovsk began early for me and Viktor #2. At breakfast, the agony on Viktor's face was readily apparent to me. He was also a professional with a job to do. I knew he would perform to the best of his ability. It had been a long trip, and we were both anxious to begin the process of getting home.

Before leaving, we had promised to take some of the airport management people for a joyride flight around the area. The rest of the travel team planned to meet us at the airport later in the morning after we had finished.

We met up at the airport with the lucky six airport managers. They looked impressive in their dark blue uniforms as they piled into the Aero Commander. Viktor #2 instructed them on airplane procedures and made sure that they were all strapped in. The deputy director sat in the right seat, with a huge smile on his face as I strapped him in with the five-point harness. He was a particularly distinguished-looking, middle-aged fellow, tall and thin, with deep, blue eyes. He could hardly wait for us to get going. He seemed not to notice Viktor # 2's dark mood as he knelt between the two cockpit seats.

The preflight checks, engine starts, and taxi out to the runway went very smoothly, and the launch was particularly exciting. We only carried about ninety minutes of fuel, no cargo, and had a long runway roll. The extra speed on takeoff allowed me to show off a bit with a very high rate of climb to 2,000 feet. In less than thirty seconds, we leveled off with a steep right turn back toward the bay to the east. It was another beautiful day for flying. My passengers' smiling faces pressed against the windows like little kids.

I asked my new co-pilot if he'd like to fly the plane. But before I could say another word, he eagerly grabbed the controls. "Oh boy!" I said under my breath as I realized that I should have asked if he knew how to fly. Fortunately, I hadn't taken my hands off the controls, or Viktor #2 would have been on the ceiling. The deputy director had grabbed the controls with both hands, a big no-no in flying, and, worse, was holding on with a death grip. The tactical situation went from a beautiful day for flying, to a problem of the first order in the blink of an eye!

I struggled mightily to keep the airplane from reacting violently to his control inputs. I turned to Viktor #2. "Tell him to let go of the controls, Viktor!" Viktor #2 began speaking to him, but he didn't let go. It was taking all of my strength to keep him from causing the plane to react violently and perhaps kill us all. I feared we could break something in the flight control system if this went on much longer. I spoke to Viktor again, this time much more forcefully, "Viktor, tell him to let go of the controls, now!" I was about two seconds away from punching the guy in the mouth when he just let go. What a relief! There is an old adage about flying being hours of boredom punctuated by moments of sheer terror.

I'm certain the guy had no idea what was going on. He was just having a grand old time of it. He might have actually thought he was flying the airplane, not realizing that I was preventing him from killing us. Fortunately, none of the passengers in the back had a clue what had just happened. None of them spoke English. We tried it again. Only this time, I asked Viktor to instruct him to touch the controls only very lightly and with one hand. He complied with the delicate touch of a blacksmith. Some people just needed to leave the flying to others.

We spent an hour flying around the bay, sightseeing, and making various instrument approaches into the airport from both the east and west. I wanted a better understanding of what to expect if I encountered poor weather on my next visit. For example, I wanted to avoid having to overfly the airport from the bay to the east, and then circle west of the airport to line up for the approach heading east. Mountains on both the north and south sides of the approach from the west made executing such turns more hazardous than I'd be comfortable with in actual instrument conditions.

After we landed, there were smiles all round, handshakes, and picture-taking in a farewell ceremony in the office of the airport director. Gifts of books, pins, hats, and souvenirs were exchanged, and more picture-taking. The conversation was all about everyone's many hopes for a bright future.

By 11:00 a.m., we were back on the ramp, fueled up, and ready to go. We said our goodbyes to Viktor #1, Sveta, and Slava, who were leaving on the commercial flight for Moscow later in the day. We looked forward to seeing everyone again very soon.

The three-hour flight north to Korf was quiet and uneventful. The spectacular terrain seemed much more familiar than it had two weeks earlier. We sat quietly, enjoying the scenery, each of us lost in our thoughts. Viktor #2 sat in the right seat, remaining quiet unless he was required to say or do something. I let him be.

Between the two cockpit seats and below the dashboard, there is a pedestal where the throttles and propeller pitch controls are located, along with several switches. One is an intercom switch that the crew can use to prevent the passengers from hearing what is being said. Viktor #2 slowly moved his left hand over to the switch and flipped it to the cockpit-only mode.

"Steve, there's something I'd like to ask you."

"What's on your mind, Viktor?"

"Would you consider dropping me off at Anadyr this afternoon instead of tomorrow? I need to be with my friend's widow and help with the funeral arrangements."

My response was immediate. "Of course. What exactly do you have in mind?"

"We can fuel up in Korf, have a rest and lunch break, and then fly to Anadyr this afternoon instead of tomorrow. You can spend the night at the base and then leave from there for Nome in the morning."

"It's a good plan, Viktor. Except I think we'll want to keep going. I'm feeling the need for a cheeseburger in Nome. Can we refuel in Anadyr and fly directly for Nome this evening and bypass Provideniya? You'll need to tend to your friend's affairs. You won't have time for us. Better we should just keep going."

"Yes, I think it can be done. How do you think the others will feel about this?"

I flipped the intercom switch so that the others could hear us. I briefed the plan. Everyone enthusiastically agreed. They shared my renewed sense of excitement at this unexpected opportunity to keep going. We all had seen enough. We were all emotionally exhausted. We wanted some American food. I needed to call home. I desperately wanted to sleep in an American hotel room.

Viktor spent the next hour on a secondary radio frequency talking with Russian air traffic control to sort out the new arrangements. Alignment of interests is a beautiful thing. He wanted to go home, and so did we.

On the ground in Korf, we felt like old friends were there to greet us as we taxied into the now-familiar ramp area. We knew everyone. Vlad Kvacof took us to what passed for a small diner for some tea, light food, and conversation, while the airplane was refueled for Anadyr.

The Korf city fathers joined us for an impromptu discussion about our impressions of Kamchatka. They were very excited about our concepts for promoting tourism in the region and hoped that some of this would come their way. They peppered us with suggestions about hunting and fishing opportunities. We were supportive and did what we could to encourage them. The truth is that our focus had to be on Petropavlovsk if we expected to have any hope of success. I didn't know how Korf and its people fit into our plans at this point. I hoped that we could help them if the opportunity presented itself.

By the time we got back to the Aero Commander, Viktor #2 was in a much lighter mood. He had worked his magic with the Russian air traffic control authorities. We had clearance to fly to Anadyr. Further, he had clearance for us to fly east from Anadyr direct to the Valda waypoint, where we would be handed off to Anchorage Center. He said that at first, ATC didn't want to allow it because they couldn't provide adequate radar coverage to Valda from Anadyr. I then remembered what the airport director in Provideniya had said about no western aircraft ever flying west from there before. No western aircraft had ever flown into Anadyr before either. This would be yet another first for us. He persuaded them that the magic GPS receiver in the cockpit would allow us to fly direct to Valda easily.

The only remaining unanswered question was what to do about customs service in Nome. If they weren't there when we arrived, I could face a $10,000 fine. Viktor #2 had made the request through channels but had not received an answer yet. He hoped to have approval by the time we got to Anadyr.

As we taxied out for the flight north to Anadyr at 4:00 p.m., the weather was deteriorating rapidly, with broken clouds, strong winds, and light rain. Two hours later, when we reached Anadyr, the weather was considerably worse, with fierce winds coming out of the west. It was not until I lined up with the runway for landing to the south that I understood how fierce the winds really were. I immediately realized that we were in trouble. Using the right rudder pedal, I had to yaw the airplane thirty degrees to the right of the runway to keep the airplane aligned with the runway, something called "crabbing." The rapid wind fluctuation made matters worse. I had to continuously change the crab to maintain runway alignment.

To appreciate this situation, imagine that you are steering a boat into a dock in a strong crosscurrent. You steer the boat into the current to keep moving in a straight line toward the dock, without being shoved downstream. The stronger the crosscurrent, the larger the crab angle, the boat needs to keep moving in a straight line toward the dock. The more you slow the boat as you approach the dock, the larger the crab angle, and the more difficult it is to keep from being moved down current. Now imagine that the speed of the current keeps changing. Everyone in the boat is getting whipsawed by the constant adjustments.

The same principle applies to flying. At my 90-knot approach speed, a thirty-degree angle from the runway into the wind meant that the crosswind component was 52 knots! There was no way to set the airplane down on the runway without sliding so severely to the left that I would lose control of the airplane. The airplane operating manual said that the maximum demonstrated crosswind in this type of aircraft was 35 knots. There was just no way.

Viktor #2 said that the control tower was reporting gusting and highly variable winds out of the west at 30 to 40 knots on the ground. He looked at me and asked my intentions. I said, "Viktor, I'm going to continue the approach and see what the wind is doing near the ground. Honestly, I don't think we can land. You'd better start thinking about where we're going on ninety minutes of fuel. We can easily make Provideniya with this tailwind." Viktor just shook his head as he looked to his left through my front window at the runway. It was a cockpit sight picture neither of us was used to.

I stopped the descent ten feet off the ground and flew down the 10,000-foot runway at 90 knots with the plane still pointed far to the right. I left the flaps in the approach position, assuming that I'd have to abort the landing. Along the sides of the runway sat dozens and dozens of MiG fighters. I was too busy to notice. I waited.

Viktor looked at me and said, "What are you doing?" I didn't reply. I just waited. 90 knots is 1.5 miles a minute. I had 45 seconds left to catch a break and still have enough runway to stop. Finally, my chance came. The plane began moving to the right of the side of the runway as the wind momentarily subsided. I adjusted the rudder and ailerons to stop the airplane's sideways movement. The airplane's nose began moving left. I still had a third of the runway left. It wasn't going to get any better. It was good enough. I chopped the throttles and aligned the airplane's nose with the runway. In only a second, the main wheels firmly connected with the runway. I simultaneously pushed the yoke forward to force the nose wheel onto the runway, and with a roll to the right using my left hand, began maximal breaking with my feet while dancing on the rudder. I moved the propellers into maximum reverse, beta mode, with my right hand.

To this day, it is by far the most difficult landing I've ever made. I was shocked at how quickly we stopped. We sat on the runway for a moment, the wind severely shaking the airplane and beating fiercely against the control surfaces. I was barely able to keep the aileron, elevator, and rudder controls from moving about wildly. I looked over at Viktor #2 and back at the others. To say that we were all very relieved to be on the ground was an understatement.

There was no way to taxi the airplane and manage the flight controls at the same time. I attached the mechanical control locks to the yoke and rudder. I had to steer using the tops of the rudder pedals for braking, without being able to move the rudders.

We taxied slowly to the end of the runway and into a ramp area where a fuel truck was waiting for us. I asked Viktor #2 to have the tanks filled to the caps, all the fuel we could carry.

Although we didn't need that much fuel to reach Nome, I had something in mind that I wasn't ready to share with the others yet. We didn't have a gross weight issue. There were now five of us again. Over the prior two weeks, we had used most of our expendable provisions and given out a lot of gifts and souvenirs. But we had also collected a lot of gifts and souvenirs to take home. There was no way to be sure what our exact weight was. But I estimated we'd be at max gross weight again as we had been for almost every flight.

I had no intention of trying a landing here at Anadyr on one engine in these wind conditions, based on what we had just experienced with two. If we lost an engine on takeoff, I had the fuel to fly northeast to Provideniya, and land, or just keep going to Nome, depending on the facts at the time. We had options.

The walk over to the operations shack was miserable. It was very cold, windy, and rainy, and getting worse by the minute. We were fortunate to have been able to land. We needed to get out of there as fast as we could. Viktor #2 worked on our clearance and customs request, while we relaxed in a waiting room with some hot tea and cookies. A few minutes later, he came in and said that it was all fixed. He wanted to take us over to his home to meet his wife and kids, but he was worried that there would not be sufficient time to get back before our clearance takeoff time voided out. I could see the pain in his eyes. He didn't want us to leave.

"Viktor, it is okay. You need to go be with your wife and kids. It's time for us to go. We'll be back," I said.

There were hugs all around. It was an emotional farewell to our invaluable navigator, interpreter, travel companion, and friend. I hoped to see him again. I waited for the others to walk out of the waiting room and then shook his hand while I handed him an envelope containing a very generous gratuity and a personal note. I thanked him again for his enormous support and then gave him a big hug. There were tears in his eyes as I turned and walked out.

As we taxied out, my watch dial read 7:37 p.m. local time. The GPS receiver showed that Nome was five hundred nautical miles away. It also showed that Anchorage was 1,034 nautical miles due east, right over the top of Nome. I had three and a half hours of fuel and expected a huge tailwind. It was all about the wind. It was still too soon to let the others know what I was thinking. We needed to take this one step at a time. The Russians expected us to go to Nome. There was no reason to tell them otherwise.

Taking off into a severe crosswind is very difficult, but not as difficult as landing under the same conditions. Even at maximum gross weight, the Aero Commander seemed as anxious to get into the air as we were. It was one of my shortest takeoffs ever, and as soon as we were in the air, the wind helped turn the airplane east toward the Valda intersection. We climbed to our assigned altitude of 7,000 meters, or 22,966 feet. We needed to go high. The higher our altitude, the better the tailwind and the lower our fuel consumption.

We reached our assigned altitude in twelve minutes. The GPS receiver groundspeed readout showed 402 knots. We had a 142-knot tailwind! Wow! In less than forty minutes, we were over the Valda intersection. The Russian air traffic controller wished us good luck and directed us to contact Anchorage Air Traffic Control on 132.2. It was all so effortless.

"Good evening, Anchorage. Aero Commander November 42 Mike Sierra, flight level 230 over Valda."

"Good evening, Aero Commander 42 Mike Sierra. Welcome back to US Airspace. Squawk . . . ."

Thunderous applause and happy yells erupted in the cabin. I used the moment to share my secret plan with the team. We were on our way to Anchorage, not Nome. They were thrilled. I quickly negotiated a change in our flight plan with Anchorage Center and was cleared to fly directly to Anchorage, some six hundred miles to the east. With our increasing tailwind, the GPS receiver said that we'd be there in ninety minutes.

We passed over Nome at midnight. There was enough daylight to see the runway and the town five miles below. The cheeseburgers were out. We'd make do with ham and eggs, and a short stack of pancakes, in Anchorage.

There is only about thirty minutes of total nightly darkness in Anchorage during July. We managed to arrive right in the middle of it. Low, overcast skies with light rain showers greeted us, requiring a full-on, night instrument approach at the end of a very, very long day. This was not what I had in mind for our arrival back into the USA, but made a good job of it.

On the ground at Anchorage International, it felt incredible to be standing on US soil. The air smelled of America. The customs process took longer than usual. We had to unload everything out of the airplane and present it to customs for inspection. It had been a very long day. The team was pretty cranky at having to go through this process.

By 4:00 a.m., we were sitting in Denny's quietly eating a hearty breakfast and feeling quite a bit better. By 5:00 a.m., we were in our beds and out cold.

I woke at 11:00 a.m. and called home. I missed my family. I wanted to go home. We'd be there in a couple of days.

The team met up in the early afternoon for lunch to talk about our options for heading home. Much to my amazement, the group still had their sense of adventure intact. There was no end of wilderness to see on the way home. In retrospect, perhaps we needed a couple of days to process the experiences of the previous two weeks.

We spent the next two days in perfect weather flying around Alaska, Yukon, and the west coast of British Columbia down to Seattle. We flew low to take full advantage of the breathtaking terrain. We finally saw Mt. McKinley up close as we circled above it. It was magnificent. The many mountains, glaciers, and rivers along the way provided a beautiful end-of-trip transition for us.

We spent our final evening in Seattle enjoying a dinner filled with storytelling about all we had experienced, with many toasts to the wonderful people we had met.

On Sunday, July 19, 1992, we touched down at Orange County's John Wayne Airport at 2:25 p.m. On the ramp at Martin Aviation, a large crowd of reporters, news crews, friends, supporters, and family members had gathered for our triumphant arrival. As I stepped from the airplane into the waiting crowd, my youngest daughter, Megan, rushed into my arms. I proceeded to make a speech and do all the interviews while holding her.

One of the news photographers captured Megan in my arms. The picture was featured the following morning on the front page of the *Orange County Register's* "Metro Section." One of the national networks had a satellite feed set up to broadcast our remarks live on their Sunday evening news broadcast.

After the endless team interviews finally died down, we went through the extensive process of sharing long goodbyes with my fellow travelers.

That evening, it felt so good to be home with my family. After a long family catch-up session and a home-cooked meal, we sat together in our family room, relaxing and enjoying our favorite Sunday evening TV shows. I was physically and emotionally exhausted. But my mind couldn't help but drift into thoughts about all that had happened and what would happen next.

It had been the most incredible aviation adventure of my life, a fifteen-day trip that had felt more like a month—summertime in far northern latitudes made for long, active days. We had flown 8,500 miles in forty-five hours of flight time, made eleven instrument approaches, and thirty landings. We had encountered every imaginable flight condition. And we were the first Americans, in fact, the first non-Russians, in history to have flown into the Kamchatka peninsula.

It was the end of a great aviation adventure. But as I sat on the couch surrounded by my family, I felt that it was also the

beginning of what promised to be an incredible entrepreneurial adventure. There was an enormous economic opportunity waiting to be tapped in Kamchatka. The people there were anxious to move forward, if only they could be shown how. It was a place where a little creativity could go a long way.

11

THE CONCEPT TAKES FORM

We now had a baseline anchor business concept
that we all agreed on, and it was the Hudson
Bay Company of Kamchatka!

I couldn't wait to get started! But the concept had to percolate for another couple of weeks while I paid much-needed attention to my wife and children. I arrived home to discover that my wife and kids were packed for a two-week family flying vacation that I had promised before leaving on July 4th.

After flying the Aero Commander some forty-five hours into the Russian Far East and back, we left two days later, racking up another twenty-three hours of flight time. We flew a grand tour of the US, including Carlsbad Caverns, San Antonio, New Orleans, Walt Disney World, Charleston, Washington, DC, Mount Rushmore, Yellowstone, and Lake Tahoe. The family had a wonderful time. And the vacation gave me a much-needed opportunity to decompress, digest, reflect, and figure out how best to proceed.

Two days after returning from vacation, I scheduled an urgent meeting with my key staff, Ken Colbaugh, Tom Heinsheimer, and Chuck DeVore. From the excited looks on all of our faces as we met up in the conference room, it was clear that we all sensed we were on the brink of something big. Ken loved the idea immediately. Tom added a great deal of color. We had been talking about the concept almost every day since I had first suggested it to him three weeks earlier on the Elizovo airport ramp.

The strategic situation was clear: the Soviet Union was over. Kamchatka was at the bottom of the new Russia's financial priority list. No money was coming east any time soon. Kamchatka's financial situation was desperate. Other than some revenue from fish and timber, the region was heavily dependent on the military and the science programs for money, and both were collapsing.

The good news was that everyone was carrying on pretty much as before, and in the same roles that they had under Soviet authority, simply because no one knew what else to do. Bus drivers drove their buses, stores sold what they had to sell, and pilots flew their planes. Life went on while everyone waited to get paid.

The critical question I put to the group was this: "What could we do quickly to take advantage of this situation, develop the Kamchatka peninsula, support the people there, and make money in the process?" We considered many possibilities.

"What about light industry? Are there technically trained or trainable people there we could hire?"

"What about small motor manufacturing operations?"

"Too much initial capital needed for either of these and way too much risk."

At SM&A, our business strategy was to start new lines of business with modest capital investment, get profitable traction, then upgrade and reposition using profits of an ongoing operation to expand into the market space we were pursuing. I thought the same model should work here. We needed to build a little, do a little, prove a little to everyone involved, and then scale up incrementally.

As the hours passed, we discussed a long list of ideas. I listed each on the whiteboard along with its pros and cons.

"Tourism, guys, it's begging to be developed. Take visitors to explore the volcanoes, skiing, hiking, fishing—it's endless!"

"We do not have exclusive rights to fishing or skiing. The Japanese have pretty much got the fishing sewn up."

"Yeah, but we can still build a cold-storage unit and export salmon to the US."

While we kicked around a lot of ideas, my inner voice wasn't reacting. I was sure I would know "it" when I heard it. We each took on homework assignments and scheduled a second brainstorming session for a week later. We had much SM&A business to attend to in the meantime. And that business was on fire!

The following morning, Chuck and I were walking out to the Aero Commander, on the Martin Aviation ramp at SNA, to make one of our endless flights up to Lockheed. We ran into the general manager of Martin Aviation. I knew Rick Janisse casually. He had been very helpful with support for the news media.

Before going to work for General William Lyon, the owner of Martin Aviation, Rick had worked for World Airways, a very large airfreight company. Rick asked how things had been going since our return, and we began chatting about some of our ideas.

Rick then said something completely unexpected:

"Well, you know, that area over Kamchatka was always a blank for World Airways. It's right under the great circle path from Anchorage to Southwest Asia. World had to dog-leg east into the Pacific and take a less than optimum route, before stopping for fuel at Chitose, in northern Japan. All the carriers do. They have to spend a lot more money on fuel in Chitose because the Japanese have a monopoly, and they know it. They also charge an arm and a leg for landing fees and get away with it. As I recall, Chitose's landing fees were something like $20,000 for a 747."

Chuck and I were all ears at this point. My inner voice began screaming!

Rick continued, "If they could land in Petropavlovsk for refueling, it would save a significant amount of time and money. All the carriers could fly a straighter route and might even be able to cut out a refueling stop or possibly carry more cargo. If you could charge a smaller landing fee and offer lower fuel prices, the cargo carriers would be all over you. I can't imagine you not being able to make a great profit in the process."

"Bingo!" I thought. Rick had provided the critical enabling idea. This was an idea with real legs. He knew what he was talking about. And it matched perfectly with the exclusivity agreement we had with the governor of Kamchatka!

My mind went into overdrive. If the carriers flew up from Taipei, they'd have to stop at Chitose, then Anchorage, and then have the reach to get somewhere deep into the US, like FedEx's headquarters in Memphis, Tennessee. But if they could refuel at Petropavlovsk, they'd cut out one of the stops and just go Taipei, Petro, and Memphis.

"Rick, that is brilliant!"

"You should chat with a guy I knew at World, Dennis Crosby. He'll tell you a lot more."

"Thanks, Rick. Can you give me his contact info?"

"I'll do better than that. I'll call him, give him some background, and have him call you in the next couple of days."

Petropavlovsk was definitely the missing link in the Pacific Rim's flight routing. I had spent quite a lot of time staring at the globe and studying maps in preparation for our trip to Kamchatka. Petropavlovsk was right on the great circle path between the US and Asian destinations. As I was to discover many years later, it was the reason Pan Am Airlines asked Charles Lindbergh to explore the route back in 1931.

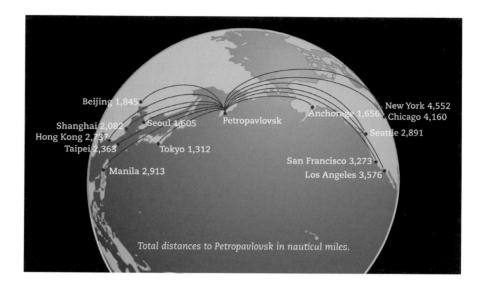

Beijing 1,845
Shanghai 2,082
Hong Kong 2,737
Taipei 2,363
Seoul 1,605
Petropavlovsk
Manila 2,913
Tokyo 1,312
Anchorage 1,656
New York 4,552
Chicago 4,160
Seattle 2,891
San Francisco 3,273
Los Angeles 3,576

Total distances to Petropavlovsk in nautical miles.

I've always believed that the key to success in any business is offering better value, and what great value this concept offered! This would be a cheaper place for cargo and transport aircraft to land than Japan, a shorter flight route using less fuel, and more capacity for cargo and/or people—thus producing more bottom-line profit per plane! Business aircraft, particularly larger cabin Gulfstream, Challenger, and Falcon business jets, could stop there too. And they'd pay more, and also bring wealthy tourists. Eureka!

I reconvened the brainstorming team ahead of schedule. Everyone got it right away. Our business strategy would begin with cargo and business jet aircraft refueling, and then expand, using the revenue to finance an endless daisy chain of ancillary developments.

Passenger aircraft and the development of tourism would inevitably follow. A cold-storage facility at the airport would facilitate exporting salmon to the Western Hemisphere and importing US fruits and vegetables. Warehouse facilities would store and distribute an endless array of stuff that the people of Kamchatka would need to build and expand their local economy.

It would be a win-win for everyone. The IKI scientists would make money to keep their space program alive, the locals would vastly improve their living conditions and lifestyles, and we'd make money on every element of the supply chain.

We now had a baseline anchor business concept that we all agreed on, and it was the Hudson Bay Company of Kamchatka! Exclusivity was a start, but the key to our grand plan was the viability of the Elizovo airport as our base of operations.

The good news was that Elizovo had storage tanks for seven million gallons of fuel, functional repair facilities, and a long runway. The bad news was that the fuel tanks and fueling system were primitive. The repair facilities were a mess. The runway needed substantial repair. Also, the instrument approach equipment was not good enough to pass muster with any of our prospective customers. Finally, the administrative infrastructure was decrepit. And these were the issues I knew about. But I also didn't think any of these issues were insurmountable.

What we needed, and needed immediately, was someone who knew the cargo aircraft business to validate our concept and lead the implementation effort. As promised, Rick had called Dennis Crosby. Talk about great timing! Dennis and Rick worked together in years past at American Airlines as subsidiary presidents. Dennis left American to be Senior VP of Sales & Marketing at World Airways.

Rick told Dennis about our adventure in Kamchatka and that we were looking at a ton of opportunities, one of them being the airport. We were still trying to figure out how to connect the dots and needed some help. Dennis was sure we had a very good idea. What interested Dennis the most was the 11,500-foot runway at Elizovo.

A few days later, Dennis sat in my office, at SM&A HQ in Newport Beach, presenting an operational concept in substantial detail. We hit it right off. I couldn't get enough of what he had to say. In his days at World Airways, one of their major freight platforms was the DC-10. They ran freighters full of Liz Claiborne clothes from Hong Kong to New York and Chicago. With 110,000 pounds of freight out of Hong Kong, they couldn't reach Anchorage. They had to refuel in Seoul or Chitose.

The biggest issues for all the cargo carriers were the slot controls, curfews, and landing fees. If they were late getting out of Hong Kong, they might miss their landing slot at Chitose. The flight could be delayed for hours. Delays cost more money.

Dennis had done his homework. The bottom line was that Petropavlovsk could be a viable alternative for Seoul or Chitose. Especially with no slot controls and cheap fuel. When we finished our discussion, he looked at me with a question in his eyes. I had already decided what we needed to do.

"We're definitely on to something very exciting," I said. "How quickly can you write the business plan?"

He stared at me thoughtfully, his eyes blinking. "Well, I'm working on this other project in Dallas. But I would be glad to help you guys out."

I had something else in mind entirely, and it involved commitment, not involvement. I gave Dennis a detailed description of what I thought we needed in the business plan. We needed a business plan that was practical, logistically implementable, financially supportable, and profitable.

Finally, I said to him, "I want you to write the plan here in Newport Beach, so we can talk about it all the time while you're conceiving it."

Dennis didn't know it then, but I had already begun thinking about him as an excellent COO for the new company. The plan would be his test. I'm an entrepreneur, and when I want something, I can make it difficult to say no to me. In this case, no was not an option. I had to have him. I took him to lunch at my club, and we spent the next couple of hours getting personally acquainted and socializing a great deal.

I proposed that Dennis fly to Orange County on Monday mornings and fly back to Dallas on Friday afternoons. I'd cover all of his expenses. I explained how I had done something very similar a decade earlier, shuttling between LAX and Philadelphia every week for six months to work on my first major consulting project. The project was a proposal for a highly competitive government satellite program General Electric Valley Forge was competing for. I took a Sunday night red-eye back east every week to Philadelphia to lead a 9 a.m. meeting every Monday morning and then flew back to LAX every Friday afternoon. It was brutal.

But SM&A would never have gotten off the ground without my commitment to doing what was needed to succeed. The proposal effort culminated in a contentious meeting with none other than Jack Welch, GE's famous CEO, and his staff. Talk about Daniel walking into the lion's den. I tried to persuade Mr. Welch to change a crucial decision he made that I believed would adversely impact our ability to win the program. He didn't change his mind. But I did come out of the meeting in one piece. Importantly, I earned the gratitude of the people I led, and the respect of the people I tried to persuade.

A few days later, my sponsor, a GE vice president, and a famous expert in radar design, Alan Horvath, came into my office and told me to start packing. He had just come back from a meeting with Lockheed in which they agreed to team on the largest competition in the aerospace industry during 1982 and 1983. The new DoD program was called MILSTAR, a secure communications satellite program, and a lynchpin of President Reagan's defense build-up.

Dr. Horvath had arranged for the Lockheed program manager, Sam Araki, to meet with me. I flew to the Bay Area, met with Sam, and then worked with him for the next eighteen months. The win that came out of that proposal effort cemented my reputation, which made SM&A possible, and my career as a CEO. By the way, Sam became president of Lockheed Missiles & Space Company.

Successful entrepreneurship requires courage and sacrifice. This was Dennis' moment to carve out a very lucrative future for himself. It was crunch time. He said yes. During the ensuing months, Dennis began to appreciate what a tremendous amount of work it was to create a business plan from scratch around such an audacious entrepreneurial concept. It also created the opportunity for us to get to know each other well and to validate that we were indeed the excellent match needed for this endeavor to succeed.

About halfway through the planning effort, while looking at the organizational design, I suggested that he put his name on the organizational chart as the COO of the new company. He was surprisingly reluctant at first. He wasn't all that excited about going to Russia. But my vision captured his imagination, and my enthusiasm pushed him over the top. My timing was right. By making him COO then, the business plan became his plan. He was the one who would have to make it happen.

Dennis's wife, Patti, was the key. She was very wary of the start-up airline he was working with at the time. She turned out to be right; they eventually went bust. She loved the idea of moving to Orange County. He brought her out the following week, and the three of us spent a few hours driving around looking for their new home. She loved the area.

A few days later, Dennis walked into my office and began pacing back and forth. I looked up, waiting for him to speak his mind. Finally, he said to me, "Steve, do you know what an enormous project this is?"

I smiled. "Yep. We can do this." He smiled and went back to work.

There was so much to do. It was hard to know where to begin. An opportunity like this was all about sweat equity for the participants. Very early in the process, I began consulting with my lawyers and accountants about how to create the needed corporate entities. A great deal of analysis was required to evaluate the tax consequences of various cash-flow strategies for each of the corporate structures we were considering.

One critical aspect of creating our corporate structure was deciding what to call it and what to have as our logo. Tom was in my office one day discussing various ideas for corporate names and began studying one of the trip decals sitting on my desk.

Suddenly, he said, "Why don't we call it that?"

"Call it what?" I asked.

"California Kamchatka Company."

I just stared at him with a big grin on my face. "Of course!"

The trip logo would be the logo of the venture, and the title on the logo would be the name of the company. Recall that Tom had designed a large logo for our flight with the title across the top, California Kamchatka, that we placed on both

sides of the Aero Commander fuselage. Tom also made a large quantity of smaller stick-on decals and baseball caps with the same logo that we had given out to everyone we encountered on the trip. He even made special envelopes preprinted with the logo and then collected exotic stamps during the trip, with cancellation marks from local post offices, and was still giving them out as special gifts.

We needed three separate entities for starters, so the overarching name became the California Kamchatka Companies. We needed a joint-venture company with our Russian partners, which we called CKC International. We needed a Russian company, which was called AKCORD, the Aviation Kamchatka California Organization for Reconstruction and Development. Finally, we needed an American company, which we called CKC Services, Inc. This would be the entity that customers around the world would contract with, and most importantly, to where the money would be wired!

A very complicated array of tax, business, and political issues needed to be resolved in arriving at the optimal legal structure. The flow of money had to make economic, contractual, and business sense. The structure needed to be compatible with US and Russian tax codes. The most critical factor driving all these decisions was my control of the cash flow for a host of reasons. The contracts with the customers were with the US company. The US company managed the customer relationships. So, it made sense that the US company control the cash flow.

But these were justifications, not the motive. Control provided me with the leverage I needed to keep our prospective Russian partners from running amok. It didn't take rocket science to grasp that people from a culture with zero experience in business and who had never handled any serious money needed to be kept on a short leash. Every parent knows what happens if you turn your children loose in a candy shop and ask them to behave while you're not watching.

This business was going to have no end of both parenting and governance challenges. Control of the cash flow was my one non-negotiable requirement. But if my instincts were right, I also didn't appreciate how much this issue would become the basis of endless wrangling with our Russian partners as the business spooled up.

There were no plans for Cayman Island or other exotic off-shore arrangements. We wanted to avoid any possible perception that we were doing anything other than setting up a 100 percent legitimate enterprise. We needed a scalable structure. We also needed a business model that we could morph into many different enterprises. We were going to need the cooperation of countless US and Russian government entities. The last thing we needed was to appear to be finaglers and tax dodgers.

We planned to be in business for a very long time. We needed to set up the business right from the get-go as a legitimate, high-integrity operation. We also needed to set an example for the Russians in how we approached all issues. Our policy was to create a win-win alignment of interests with every issue, no matter how small, showing consistency in our actions and reactions, and demonstrating every time that we operated with high integrity.

Between August 1992 and March 1993, we labored tirelessly to refine the concept, define the enterprise, and get buy-in from our Russian partners. There were endless numbers of conference calls and faxes. We asked for feedback on every idea of significance. While a seemingly simple concept to describe, this was an incredibly complicated enterprise to implement. With all the effort we put into transforming our vision into reality, and so many complex details to work through, it turned out to be one of the most innocuous of matters that nearly killed the deal.

As the business plan came together, our understanding of the details of the various working relationships between us, our clients, and our partners began to crystallize. A large number of insurance-related issues emerged. Our customers, and their customers, would have their insurances on the aircraft and the cargo. But what if something happened to an aircraft on the ground at Elizovo while being refueled? What if someone on the ground were injured while servicing an aircraft? What if someone associated with our enterprise was injured or killed, for any reason? What if there was property damage due to an accident caused by the negligence of our employees or subcontractors? The list was long. Many critical questions centered on a sound legal understanding of where the client's insurance ended, where ours began, how much protection we would need, and where we would get it.

Dennis gave Rick Janisse a draft copy of the business plan to review and comment on. Without checking in with Dennis or me first, Rick gave the draft business plan to an insurance agent to price the coverage. But we had never met with them, and they had no understanding of what the limits of liabilities were which they would assume. Without any discussion, they used the financials in the draft business plan to arrive at their premium quote.

The quote was outrageous and unaffordable. It was a nightmare. Worse, there was only one reinsurance market in the world for this kind of exotic coverage: Lloyd's of London. With Lloyd's having taken a position, there was little chance of changing it. I was furious. I had to resolve this before negotiating the final JV agreement with our Russian partners. Otherwise, there would be no reason to go! No insurance, no business. It was that simple.

Woody Allen famously said, "80 percent of success is showing up." I've always thought that the other 20 percent is about what happens when you arrive. If you don't prepare, don't do your homework, when the opportunity comes, you're very likely to blow what could be the chance of a lifetime.

The only way to fix the insurance disaster was to "sit in the box" at Lloyd's. This is what a meeting with an underwriter is called in the insurance game. I recruited a close friend in the aircraft insurance business, Bill Myers (no relation), to help me organize a presentation for the underwriters at Lloyd's and go with me to see them. In February 1993, we flew to London for the meeting. My strategy was to persuade the underwriters that they had misunderstood entirely and over-estimated their exposure. They needed to take a long-view approach to our relationship, or the enterprise would be dead before it was born. There would be no premium at all if they didn't reconsider.

One of the critical factors in the development of the modern world has been the availability of insurance. Imagine life without auto insurance, homeowner's insurance, or life insurance. How could businesses operate without insurance? Insurers cover individual risks for a premium. The insurer, in turn, may spread the risk by going to the reinsurance market, where they in turn spread the risk over a very large number of individuals through syndicates. By the time the risk gets spread around, the risk is acceptable to everyone involved, in consideration of the premium received. Their challenge in dealing with exotic risks is when there is little or no actuarial data, and/or the risks are hard to define. This was our problem.

Lloyd's, the largest reinsurer in the world, began by insuring ships and their cargo. Without this insurance, no business-man or shipowner could have ever accepted the considerable risks of seafaring in the 1800s. Lloyd's organized syndicates of "names," who received a share of the premium in exchange for the assumption of their shares of the risk. Before every voyage, someone representing the shipowner would go to Lloyd's and sit in the box with the underwriter and tell him what the ship was, who the captain was, where it was going, and what the cargo was. The meeting would rarely last more than a few minutes. The essential information was logged by hand into a huge book, the premium set, and the deal done.

The "box" was more like a small cubicle, where we met with the assigned lead syndicate underwriter. I was reminded by Bill before the start of the meeting that such encounters rarely lasted more than just a few minutes. He thought we were fortunate to get the meeting at all. It was a rocky start. The underwriter opened by saying that he didn't want to do the deal and was withdrawing their bid. We didn't leave. After further discussion, he wanted to charge so much that it would be impossible to proceed. We continued to sit there pushing back, trying to get him to understand there was confusion about what they were, and were not, insuring. He was thinking about a 747 blowing up on the ramp as their liability. It wasn't. That was covered by the aircraft insurance policy.

What we needed was something akin to workers' compensation liability insurance for the employees, hangar keeper's insurance for "damaging" aircraft parked on the ramp, third-party liability coverage for the nonemployees, and general business liability coverage for the company. These were all coverages he understood well. The conversation became calmer. Once we changed his perception of the risk, he began opening up about practical concerns and issues. He was very concerned about Russians laying hands on the aircraft. I explained that only Americans would be doing the actual servicing and fueling of the aircraft. The Russians would provide perimeter security, pump fuel from the remote tanks, and operate equipment around the aircraft, such as deicing equipment. They would not have any physical contact with any customer aircraft, such as hooking up the fuel lines to the aircraft.

We were there an hour. We reached an acceptable compromise on the limits of liability that would work for all concerned and a clear understanding of what the underwriters would and would not cover.

It was ironically fortunate that this meeting occurred before sitting down with the Russians or with any of our potential customers. Everyone had to be on the same page regarding coverage requirements and limitations. Insurance drove everything. What had started as a perceived insurance disaster was transformed into a sales feature and a competitive discriminator. It was a valuable learning experience for me. Persistence and tenacity are truly the most essential ingredients in success. While a myriad of other issues remained, after the insurance saga, I so much better appreciated the concept of viewing issues not as problems but as opportunities waiting to be discovered.

Dennis and I had the same success qualities in common. He was a great team player. My instincts had proved right about him from our very first meeting. I knew from the beginning that he'd be the perfect COO for this business. The business planning process created the opportunity to mentor him and infect him with the same enthusiasm for the business that I had. As time went on and the details began to take form, I watched Dennis' natural enthusiasm take hold. From then on, there was just no stopping him.

After a thorough analysis, we concluded that there was little useful infrastructure at Elizovo. There was no suitable ground-support equipment for servicing the aircraft once they landed. Just getting there was going to be a challenge. We had to work our way through the FAA approval process to allow

US-registered aircraft to fly to and land in Kamchatka. The creation of entirely new FAA-approved air routes from Alaska would be required. These would be published around the world. The Russian version of the FAA, their CAA, would have to approve these air routes as well.

We also needed approvals from the FAA and CAA for all the operational procedures that our clients were going to use and all the operational and safety equipment that we'd be using on the ground. In other words, not one but two massive bureaucracies had to get behind absolutely everything we were doing, and relatively quickly! Dennis had to put together the staff needed to get it all done in both the US and Russia. To say that he had a full plate is an understatement. But he was excited, passionate, committed, and incredibly competent.

One of our most valuable assets was a seemingly inexhaustible supply of capable Russians eager to work for us, starting with Viktor Kerzhanovich (Viktor #1). He was already in Moscow recruiting and greasing the skids for us on every front. Viktor's increasing sphere of contacts within the Russian government would prove critical to facilitating whatever we needed done. We simply couldn't succeed without him.

Meanwhile, our primary business (SM&A) also had to be run. Ken Colbaugh was the most capable COO that SM&A had in my twenty-five years of leading the company. And some of SM&A's profits were being used to finance CKC. Because Ken shared in SM&A's profits, making him a significant equity stakeholder in CKC was critical to ensuring that our interests remained aligned. The relationships that Dennis, Ken, and I formed during this period were some of the most rewarding of our professional careers. It was a privilege to have these two highly seasoned, mature, and intelligent senior executives work with me and provide the day-to-day leadership of these two very complex businesses.

12

NEGOTIATING WITH RUSSIANS

The process ironically worked to my advantage. It just took longer. Twelve-hour days of negotiations, then several hours of drinking, every night.

We left Petropavlovsk on July 18, 1992, with an agreement in principle for exclusive rights to Elizovo and many other ancillary opportunities. A great start to be sure. As with all agreements, the devil was in the details. We had agreed with the governor that we would go back to California and write our prospective Russian partners a proposal to perfect the agreement. Tom Heinsheimer successfully recruited Viktor Kerzhanovich (Viktor #1) to be our lead representative and negotiator in Moscow.

Viktor was essential if we were to have any chance of breaking through the Russian bureaucracy. He had made the trip to Kamchatka possible and had spent two weeks with us touring around the peninsula. He was a very intelligent, well-educated engineer and scientist. He was someone who had an extraordinary attention for detail, was fluent in English, and was an enthusiastic supporter. He also hoped to immigrate to the US. Our agreement was his ticket, and the equity stake I would provide would give him financial security.

I successfully recruited Dennis Crosby to write the business plan, and then assume more and more responsibility for the day-to-day process as CKC's COO. Financing was not an issue at this point. My cash investment mostly consisted of paying for Viktor and Dennis. SM&A was a very profitable, rapidly growing enterprise. We had the resources to pursue this high-risk, high-payoff opportunity.

Tom and I worked tirelessly through August and September, drafting a proposal to our prospective Russian partners: the governor and vice-governor of Kamchatka, the Elizovo airport director, the president of the local bank in Petropavlovsk, and some of their staffs. Over the subsequent year, a few other players elbowed their way to the table.

A joint venture implies two "equal" partners. The proposal was all about what we would do for our half, what they would do for their half, and what the limits of the agreement were. The devil really was in the details, and the Russians loved details.

Fax was our primary means of communication. We had Apple desktop computers at SM&A. There was no such technology in Russia. We went through several drafts of each communication in Newport Beach, then printed them out, and faxed them to Viktor in Moscow. He translated the faxes into Russian and distributed them to the appropriate parties. The same process worked in reverse. This approach ensured that we had consistent interpretation and that Viktor stayed in the loop.

Tom, Dennis, or I either prepared or reviewed every communication coming and going to doubly ensure that the process worked. As time went on, Dennis assumed more and more responsibility for handling the ever-increasing array of details that the Russians wanted to delve into.

With the evolving details of our JV proposal, the business plan came together in parallel. Every detail translated into responsibilities, which turned into costs for work and equipment. The costs had to be considered in the context of their impact on revenue and profitability. For every aspect of the plan, options had to be explored to arrive at practical means of getting the job done. Every proposed solution had to be agreed to by the JV partners. The process continued this way for more than six months.

By February 1993, we had a complete business plan in hand. We had a clear definition of the capital structure of the enterprise and the roles of each of the Russian and American entities involved. We had either resolved or had a plan in place to address the most critical issues moving forward. During the first week in March 1993, I received an urgent page to call Dennis.

"Steve, I think we have a deal."

I swallowed hard. "Really?" was all I could think to say.

"The Russians are on board, and they want to send a negotiating team to Moscow to meet with you to sort out the final details before they present the agreement to the CIS Parliament for approval. They also want you to meet directly with representatives of the Air Ministry to answer some of their questions and give them assurances on a number of technical matters. They need to know when you are coming to Moscow."

I swallowed again. After a long pause, I said, "Dennis, I'm feeling very uncomfortable about this."

"Are you afraid to go?"

"Yeah. I am. I don't know why. I feel very anxious."

"I totally get it," Dennis said.

"Give me a moment, Dennis. I'll call you right back," I said.

It was difficult for me to connect with what I felt so anxious about. I wasn't afraid of the Russians. I wondered if it was fear of failure or fear of success that I was feeling. Failure had little consequence. Success would dramatically affect my life and the lives of my family.

Entrepreneurs are driven. It is that simple. What drives an entrepreneur may be any number of unrecognized motivations. The bottom line is that once we have the bit in our teeth, the people around us quickly learn to get out of the way. We won't, or perhaps just can't, stop ourselves. To others, it may look like we're being driven by money or power. For me, it was never about the money. The money was always a means to an end. Something else drove me. Whatever it was, it was crunch time. I was back in the crevasse looking up at that wall. If ever courage was needed, it was right then and there. I wasn't going to back away from this opportunity. No way!

I put my anxiety aside, pulled out my calendar, and began looking at blocks of time I could create to fly to Moscow. I picked up the phone and called Dennis back.

In preparing for the negotiations, Dennis concluded that he should not come with me to Moscow. First, we didn't want to create any confusion in the minds of the Russian team as to who the decision-maker was. This would be particularly important later when he was dealing with these same people on a day-to-day basis. He needed to rely on me as the go-to policymaker, or the Russians would undoubtedly take advantage of him at every turn. He needed to be able to take the position with them that he was there to *implement* policy, not *make* policy. I was his air cover.

Dennis and I also agreed that we'd never be in Russia at the same time. If something happened to one of us, such as being detained, injured, or whatever, the other would lead the rescue and recovery effort.

On April 14, 1993, I flew to Moscow for a week. It felt like a month. I had the good sense to arrive a couple of days ahead of our scheduled negotiations. This allowed me to recover from jet lag, see some sights, and become comfortable with my environs.

I brought a Russian business consultant with me from Newport Beach. His name was Boris Gurevich. Boris had been living in the US for several years after getting out of Russia. He was charming, sophisticated, intelligent, and spoke English beautifully. Most importantly, he was very knowledgeable about Russian history, culture, and politics. We had met a few months earlier when he spoke at an Orange County World Affairs Council dinner. I was impressed with him. I had thought that it might be useful to have someone who could offer a different perspective than Viktor. I valued Viktor's perspective greatly. But I also had learned long ago that no one has a monopoly on the right answer. I wanted a second set of eyes and ears looking at everything.

It was still quite cold in Moscow in April. Snow was still on the ground in places. An overcoat, hat, and gloves were essential for going anywhere. Viktor had selected a brand-new hotel near the Air Ministry, called the Aerostar. A Canadian JV had only opened the Aerostar a few months earlier. It was modern and well-appointed, with excellent conference-room facilities. The buffet was good too.

In 1993, Moscow was like the Wild West. In addition to being my interpreter and handler, Boris had another critical duty. He was also my bodyguard. He was a strong, very fit guy. During our flight to Moscow, I had instructed him that he was never to let me out of his sight unless I was in my hotel room, or I specifically instructed him otherwise. It was a good policy.

On the afternoon of our first day in Moscow, I asked Boris to check with the concierge to see if we could get tickets to the Bolshoi Ballet that evening. I needed some fresh air, wanted to see a few sights, and, most importantly, needed to find any excuse to stay awake until later in the evening. This is the only way I knew to get over jet lag.

"Do you think there are any tickets, Boris? How much do you think they'll cost?" I asked.

Boris said, "Do not worry about it; only a couple of dollars."

"How can that be?" I asked.

I told Boris not to skimp and to get the best seats available. Half an hour later, he called my room and said that we had two tickets in the front row center for $40 US, but that he thought most of the price was the kickback to the concierge.

"Are you kidding me?" I said. I am sure whomever he got those tickets from thought that they were ripping us off. Front row seats at the Bolshoi for $40? Really?

Off we went to the ballet. I waited on the front steps of the Bolshoi while Boris retrieved the tickets. I was hardly there a minute when two extremely attractive women approached me and began speaking in perfect English. Let's just say they were very friendly. When Boris returned with the tickets, he quickly sent them on their way. He turned to me and said, "Steve, you have to be very, very careful of these women. There's no telling what they are up to."

As we walked into the ballet, an elderly woman was handing out programs. Boris had encouraged me to bring a large stack of $1 bills to Moscow, and not be shy about handing bills out to anyone who did anything for us. I handed $2 to the woman. She stared at the bills for a moment, then ran away, screaming something in Russian.

I turned to Boris and asked, "What just happened?"

He replied with a smile, "You just gave her a month's pay!" I looked at him in utter disbelief, trying to absorb and interpret what that meant.

Such were the conditions in Russia in 1993. It was how I imagined Brooklyn ˌwas in 1917. "Bleak" was the only word I could think of as Boris and I walked around Moscow during the first couple of days there. Elderly people were victimized the most by the extremely high rate of inflation of the ruble during 1993. Their pensions had become worthless. Alcohol consumption was off the charts. Many people had committed suicide. They had no hope. I began stuffing dollar bills into the hands of anyone who did anything at all for us. I could see the impact I had on them, and I felt joyful to do it.

The security around the hotel was extraordinary, and it took some considerable time for the Russian negotiating team to get through the front door on the first day of our negotiations. They weren't at all happy about it either. They seemed quite cranky. Viktor and I quickly decided that we should change the planned schedule to have an early lunch at the buffet before getting started. The Russian team needed some time to calm down and socialize a bit before getting down to business. It was a good move. They hadn't eaten anything that morning before arriving.

After lunch, Viktor led our group to a large conference room he had arranged for our use during the entire week. We needed plenty of wall space to tape easel paper onto, a drawing easel, markers, pads of paper, pens, pencils, etc., and, of course, plenty of coffee, water, and soft drinks.

The Russian negotiating team was made up of the Elizovo airport assistant director, two of his key staff, and an attorney. Our side consisted of Viktor, Boris, myself, and our Russian attorney.

The meeting almost immediately sank into a mind-boggling marathon of discussions around random details covering every conceivable aspect of the JV. After eight months of communications on every single point of the agreement, every point was again reviewed and subjected to extensive discussion and, of course, a desire for renegotiation. Their strategy became obvious to me. They hoped to disorient and confuse me into agreeing to innocuous matters without understanding their impact on the overall plan. They counted on my not being intimately familiar with all the details of the plan. I had done my homework. It wasn't going to happen.

Fortunately, none of the four members of the Russian negotiating team spoke English. Neither did the attorney Viktor had arranged to represent our interests. Viktor was there to interpret as well as give his perspective on all matters. Boris was there to offer his perspective. It seemed like a good idea at the time. But the immediate friction between Viktor and Boris was palpable from day one.

Viktor is an engineer and scientist. Boris is a non-technical, but highly-skilled, paralegal negotiator. It made for an interesting dynamic. They couldn't have been more different. I had not foreseen Viktor personally resenting anyone on our team disagreeing with his interpretation of the facts. He was very concerned about losing face with me, or with our Russian partners. Boris, I soon realized, had a vested interest in disagreeing with Viktor at every opportunity, to establish his credibility and his value to me.

My drama meter pinged at least twice an hour every day. I needed to intervene to keep Viktor, Boris, our lawyer, and our would-be Russian partners on track. It was a never-ending diplomatic challenge to keep the negotiations from running off the rails.

But the process also bought me valuable time. Translating what each side said and then discussing it amongst ourselves before replying made all the drama worth it. If Viktor and Boris disagreed, we'd have to discuss the matter until we were all on the same page, along with our Russian lawyer, before responding. The process slowed everything down to a crawl. In the end, it helped much more than the pain it caused.

Viktor and Boris argued all the time about everything. At . my insistence, they always argued in English. The Russians didn't know what to make of it. It was beautiful. In their arguing, I was able to understand the nuances of what the Russians were driving at. The process ironically worked to my advantage. It just took longer.

Our negotiation sessions began early every morning and continued until the evening, stopping only for lunch to partake of the buffet in the hotel restaurant. We went out every evening for a heavy dinner and then went drinking until midnight or two in the morning. To say these were hard-drinking guys seriously understates it.

Russians love to drink, and the more they drink, the more their personalities and feelings emerge. It was during the evenings that we really got to know each other, and I began to understand that these were much more sentimental and emotional people than I had expected. Just as importantly, they were able to become more comfortable with me. This process of drinking together as a means of getting to know one another is deeply ingrained in Russian culture.

In golf, we have a saying, "If you want to get to know someone, play eighteen holes with them." There never was a more valid statement. You learn a great deal about people by how they conduct themselves on a golf course. Are they humble? Do they cheat? Are they obnoxious? Is it all about them? How do they react when things go well? How do they react when things go badly, which they always do? Do they make bad situations worse? Are they focused, or are they sleepwalking? For the Russians, drinking is their version of eighteen holes.

Then we'd get up the next morning and do it all again. It was exhausting brain damage.

Our negotiations focused on three primary issues: How would the JV be organized? Who would be responsible for doing what? How would the money flow? It sounded simple. It was all in the details. There were many technical issues involved. Taxes, corporate law, aviation regulations, insurance, cash flow, contractual arrangements, fuel costs, landing fees, etc.

It all came down to the control of the money. If we did not have control of the money, it would have been impossible to enforce accountability and impossible to protect ourselves against getting ripped off. There was just no way that I was going to do a deal in which the Russians collected from the clients and then paid us. No possible way. Not going to happen!

It was all about leverage. The clients were only willing to contract with an American company and would only pay in US dollars to a US bank. Dennis made sure that this was the case in his negotiations with each client. In the end, the Russians agreed, because they had to. But as we came to understand later, every agreement was only provisional and temporary, subject to renegotiation. Who controlled the money was the subject of repeated conversations and attempts to renegotiate the deal at every opportunity.

In a surprising show of graciousness, on the last day of the negotiations, the Russians proposed that I serve as chairman of the JV, and the vice-governor of Kamchatka, Vladimir Senchenko, serve as vice-chairman. It was the only point that didn't require any discussion. The Memorandum of Agreement was finished.

Boris and I went back to Newport Beach, the Russians went back to Kamchatka, and Viktor went home for dinner. There was strong agreement among the new Russian leadership in 1992 that joint ventures were the way to go if they were to attract Western entrepreneurs and capital. We were one of the first joint ventures to go through the Russian JV approval process. No one could be sure what was and was not permissible. To our astonishment, the following month, the parliament, the foreign minister, and the prime minister of Russia ratified the agreement. We were in business!

We invited Senchenko, the director of airport operations at Elizovo, the assistant director, and two of the key managers critical to the operation to visit Newport Beach for a signing ceremony, impress them with our environs, and socialize the agreement. We also included two of the local air traffic control operators who were the most conversant in English as part of the delegation.

English is an ICAO requirement for air traffic controllers all over the world. We arranged for the two Russian controllers to spend time with the FAA controllers working at John Wayne Airport, and take a tour of the Los Angeles Air Traffic Control Center in Palmdale. Naturally, we picked up the tab for all their expenses.

We had a signing ceremony with the delegation at SM&A headquarters and a reception at my home in the nearby foothills. Two of our local congressmen, Chris Cox and Dana Rohrabacher, came to the reception, along with several prominent local business leaders. I gave a speech about what this agreement represented for the future of Kamchatka. Chris Cox, who spoke Russian fluently, delivered a short speech in Russian. I could feel the energy in the room; everyone was very excited about what we were doing.

Earlier in his career, Chris Cox had run a business with his father, producing a daily English version of Pravda that was used by US government agencies and academics. Later, he became a lawyer, a congressman, and in 2001 was appointed by President Bush to head the Securities and Exchange Commission.

Chuck DeVore, formerly a senior assistant to Congressman Cox, acted as our protocol officer. He took the vice-governor to Chapman University to give a speech, which was well-received by the students and faculty.

The funniest aspect of the delegation's visit involved Disneyland. You simply can't bring people from another country to Southern California without taking them to Disneyland. But when Dennis told the Russians about the planned outing, they objected: "No, no, no. Disneyland is for children; we're not going to Disneyland."

Dennis told them, "No, you don't understand. Disneyland is for everybody. We're going to take a day and take you there. Trust me. You're going to like it."

Dennis and Chuck later told me they had never seen adults act more like children than our Russian friends did. Bringing the Russians to California was an important exercise in confidence-building for all concerned. They could see that we were real and that we had the means to make this happen.

We held several meetings with the Russian delegation around a large, beautiful, granite table in our SM&A headquarters conference room. By this point, we had taken over most of the remaining space on the seventh floor of the office building the company operated out of on Dove St. in Newport Beach. We moved the CKC operation into its own set of offices with the space they would need, including an operations control center with computers and satellite links. The impression given by the physical arrangement was one of a fully functional, substantial operation. The Russians were very impressed.

We hammered out more details of our business arrangements. We came up with samples of different logos and wanted their reactions. The Russians thought that our preferred logo, which featured the outlines of California to the left and the Kamchatka peninsula to the right, looked like the balls of a bull hanging down. They laughed and joked about it. We weren't quite sure what to make of their reaction and wondered if we needed to do more research.

We never got to the bottom of what they really thought about the logo or many other things. The Russians tended to play their cards very close to their vests. There were just so many questions that we were never to know the answers to.

Our approach became one of assuming anything not objected to was agreed to. We did what we wanted most of the time. The Russians would occasionally object, and usually about the most ridiculous, inconsequential matters. Perhaps they just wanted us to know they were paying attention. Trust is very hard to earn in Russian culture.

CKC/AKCORD Business Structure

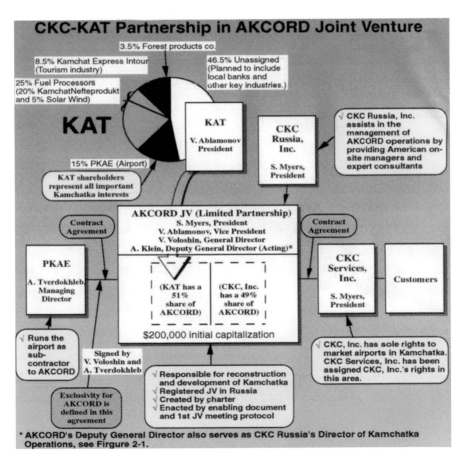

13

SPOOLING UP THE ENTERPRISE

It never occurred to any of us that the fuel supply could be a problem. The fuel supply chain should have been the first thing we analyzed.

Spring through early summer of 1993 focused on getting CKC up and running. In the US, our priority was sales and marketing. We needed to start signing up international cargo carriers. Publicity was critical. One of Chuck DeVore's primary responsibilities was publicity. He created many articles for all of the aviation industry trade magazines and journals. He persuaded editors to run editorials and write articles about what we were doing. The internet and email were nascent mediums for advertising. We did business the old-fashioned way: making phone calls, preparing and mailing out PR packages, and arranging exhibits for trade shows.

Our operations center in Newport Beach was up and running for scheduling and coordination. We expected to have a working satellite link with our operations hub at Elizovo in short order. Our operations team leaders were in place on both sides of the Pacific. The entire CKC team worked tirelessly toward the launch of the business, with our first refueling stop for a wide-body cargo customer at the earliest date practical.

Every day presented new challenges to overcome. In retrospect, it doesn't seem feasible for us to have accomplished as much as we did in so short a time. For starters, nothing worked to our requirements at Elizovo. Servicing aircraft, especially large aircraft like 747s and DC-10s, wasn't a simple matter of getting customers to drive into our gas station and load up. When things go wrong in aviation, they can go very wrong, very quickly, and with disastrous consequences. It was serious business: dozens of large fuel tanks loaded with jet fuel, fuel lines running everywhere, hundreds of millions of dollars in aircraft on the ramp loaded with fuel and cargo. A foolish mistake could produce a catastrophe.

That our reputation would be ruined was the least of it. Lives were on the line.

Our Russian support team was not permitted to touch the aircraft, as an explicit condition of our contracts with the cargo carriers, and most importantly, our insurance. This requirement alone had substantial implications for how we organized our operations and how many people we needed.

During the winter of 1993, Dennis made his first trip to Petropavlovsk to meet all of our Russian partners and support team members, survey Elizovo, and become familiar with the environs. He also needed to establish the baseline procedures for all ground operations and prepare the Russians for our conducting a detailed analysis of all the ground equipment, facilities, and infrastructure.

Unfortunately, to get there, he had to travel the hard way, on an Aeroflot flight out of Anchorage to Khabarovsk, on the Chinese border. The six-hour flight cruised right over the top of Petropavlovsk on its way southwest. In Khabarovsk, he connected with a flight to Petropavlovsk, three hours back the way he had come.

After some considerable delay in Khabarovsk, Dennis took his seat on the connecting flight and waited patiently for the cabin door to be closed and the engines to start. Instead, two uniformed Russian guards came onto the aircraft carrying a pair of shoes. They began speaking to each of the passengers. The guy next to Dennis said in broken English, "Those are pretty big shoes. Are those your shoes?"

Dennis, who is six-five, looked more closely and said, "Yeah, those are my shoes. They're from my suitcase!" During luggage transfer, somebody had grabbed his suitcase. They caught the guy who claimed it was his suitcase. The guards knew better. The shoes couldn't possibly have been his.

An ice-cold and dark winter in Kamchatka greeted Dennis on landing. He had been flying for most of his life and was generally relaxed about flying. But by the time he landed at Elizovo, he was a nervous wreck. He doubted the aircraft was airworthy. It was certainly decrepit.

The good news was that Viktor Kerzhanovich was waiting for him at the bottom of the stairs, along with several airport officials. Viktor's first words to Dennis were, "How are you?"

"Oh, Viktor, believe me, you don't want to know!"

Dennis spent the next two months in Petropavlovsk, leading the startup of CKC operations at Elizovo. He fought all the initial battles with Russian officials, got the necessary documents signed, and obtained required approvals from the local Russian authorities. His mantra became, "I'm not leaving until we get this thing done!"

Dennis stayed in a small "hotel" that I didn't know existed until our Russian partners arranged a room there for Dennis. We had heard nothing of it on our trip the prior summer. The way

Dennis described it, we wouldn't have been willing to stay there if had we known. "Pretty awful" was his most common descriptor. Dennis stayed in the same room every time he travelled there. We assumed the FSB had bugged the room.

When Dennis returned to Newport Beach from his first trip, he looked like he had lost weight. We had a lengthy meeting where I debriefed him on all that had happened. I began by asking him, "Dennis, what were your first impressions?"

"I was shocked, Steve. I expected Russia to be a place of great military might, culture, and education. Instead, it was more like Tijuana! I felt like I was in one of those old newsreels you see about WWII."

Dennis confirmed the need to send a technical team over to make a thorough survey of the state of the entire Elizovo ground support and equipment infrastructure. To lead the technical survey and be our operations manager on the ground there, we were very fortunate to recruit a retired US Air Force officer named Michael Rodzianko. He spoke excellent Russian, had strong technical skills and a knack for making things happen—a critical ability for operating in this kind of environment.

Michael offered another very important advantage. He was the grandson of the last non-communist prime minister of Russia, Mikhail Rodzianko, who had led the abdication of Czar Nicholas II. The Russians were very familiar with his last name, and there is no doubt it helped.

Michael had been working on the Partnership for Peace program, a cooperative threat-reduction program to help the Russians destroy their excess stockpile of nuclear weapons in the wake of the Cold War. The US was paying the Russians to disarm and secure both their nuclear and biological weapons. Michael knew a great deal about the Russian military and had traveled extensively in Russia. We were fortunate to have found him.

Michael helped us understand the capabilities and limitations of the equipment we had in place and compiled the list of equipment and other things we needed to purchase and send to Russia. His most interesting discovery was about the fuel tanks. They were contaminated, which was a showstopper for us and our clients. The contamination came in several forms, water being the most common. There were also issues with the deterioration of tank interiors, due to corrosion. The rusted metal was getting into the fuel, along with microbes and other foreign particulates.

The jet fuel had to be free from water and other contamination. It was absolutely critical. During flight, the temperature of the fuel in aircraft tanks decreases due to the low temperatures in the upper atmosphere. The outside temperature can be as low as -60°C. After several hours aloft, the fuel tanks become cold-soaked, causing any water to precipitate out of the fuel. It's impractical to remove all water from fuel, so jet aircraft use fuel heaters to prevent a limited amount of water in the fuel from freezing. Water is denser than fuel. A significant amount of water dropping to the bottom of the tanks and freezing would overwhelm the fuel heaters, eventually blocking the fuel inlet lines to the fuel pumps and engines. While rare, there have been accounts of business and commercial aircraft fuel contamination causing engines to shut down at altitude—several crashes resulting. Particulate contamination is even worse. These would clog fuel filters, pumps, and lines, and do significant damage to aircraft engines and other components.

The good news was that the contamination problem could be fixed. The bad news was, as with most things in Russia, it would be expensive. Our original thought was to refurbish the tanks, but we quickly gave up on this idea. We needed to ensure that we met the FAA's very stringent requirements every step of the way. We found experts who knew how to process the fuel and modify the Elizovo fuel-pumping system by adding our own processing, filtration, and testing equipment. Our people would carry out the testing and do the fueling.

Michael shared a great story with us about how one of the Russian technicians had said to him, "I don't know what's wrong with your airplanes. You must build weak airplanes. Russian airplanes are strong. We do not need any of these tests. We run engines hundreds of hours before we throw them away."

Michael tried to explain to the technician that the engines on jet aircraft built in the US and Europe usually operate for two or three thousand hours before having major inspections, then for another two or three thousand hours before being removed for overhaul. After overhauling, the engines are reinstalled, as essentially new. Avoiding contamination was the first key to long engine life. The Russian technician just stared at Michael in disbelief.

In the USSR, there had been no economic motive to keep things working. The only motive was to build things to create more jobs. The bureaucracy was not worried about profit—just creating jobs. There was simply no concept of producing a superior product more efficiently and more cheaply. It was all about jobs. Perhaps this is why they called it the Soviet Union. It functioned as a national labor union.

Dennis began flying over to Petropavlovsk frequently to make sure that our plans stayed on track and to deal with startup issues, Russian regulatory issues in particular. He would regularly show up at the office and be told, "We need to go down to the oblast office." An oblast is a political, administrative, and tax region in Russia. "We need to have a meeting with the Ministry of Transportation, and we are going to have to discuss a painful subject."

Dennis would ask, "What's the painful subject?"

"Well, we forgot to pay our taxes last month. They're going to shut us down at 3 p.m. today."

Our venture was clearly on their radar and very important to them. Everybody wanted in on the action. Dennis would take two interpreters with him just to be sure he didn't get the translation wrong. They'd troop down to the oblast for a meeting with some minister and a bunch of officials. There would be ten or more people in the meeting.

"You failed to pay your taxes, and there is a fine."

Dennis would patiently ask, "OK, how much do we need to pay to fix this problem?"

"You owe us 4,000,000 rubles."

"How much is this in US dollars?"

"Thirty-two dollars and thirty-three cents."

Dennis would keep a very straight, humble face and deal out forty dollars. "Please, apply the difference to our next payment due."

This kind of thing happened so many times we lost count. As soon as he paid the tax, the doors would swing open, and ladies who worked in the office would come in with ritual bandanas or carrying caviar and carafes of vodka. It was usually around 10:30 a.m.

"It's time to celebrate the resolution." Someone would make a toast, "Here is to Russian/American brotherhood, and here is to the success of our joint venture."

By noon Dennis was done for the day. He never drank so much vodka as he did in those few years. He had to drink with them, or they would have been offended. This routine scenario is not to suggest that everybody we had to deal with was dishonest—not at all. Most people we encountered were honest to a fault. The situation was not about dishonesty but survival. The government was so dysfunctional that managers had to become creative just to keep as many jobs in place as possible.

Rapid communication was a critical issue for us. We needed a way to ensure fast two-way voice and fax communications between our operations hub at Elizovo and our operations center in Newport Beach. Our ability to function day-to-day depended on this. We had flight plans and fuel orders to process that required quick action. If we used landlines, it could take a week for a call to get through.

We started with International Maritime Satellite System phones (INMARSAT), which cost more than ten dollars a minute, but did the job. Dennis took one of the new satellite telephones, which was the size of a briefcase, over to Elizovo, along with a satellite dish, cabling, and support equipment. Shortly after he arrived, he received word from the local police in Petropavlovsk that "people" were going to take our satellite equipment. Dennis was explicitly told to not activate the service. If he turned the system on, he could be executed as a spy.

"Are you kidding me?" was Dennis's reply.

The police chief came to his hotel, took the satellite phone and locked it up in the police station. Eventually, a "special engineer" flew out from Moscow to "certify" the system. We were certain that the FSB wanted to plant a bug in it.

We assumed that every conversation between Elizovo and Newport Beach was monitored, and not just by the FSB. We assumed the CIA and NSA were also listening. Frankly, we didn't care who listened. I made it very clear to everyone that our policy was never to say or do anything we wouldn't have wanted everyone to know about. It was not about being careful about how we kept secrets. It was about not having any secrets to keep, or at least as few as possible. Transparency was essential. We simply couldn't afford to have anyone on either side of the Pacific misinterpret our motives. Our communications protocols were designed to ensure not just that those listening would get it right, but rather that they wouldn't get it wrong!

Once the "special engineer" was finished and the INMARSAT connection operational, we needed to reimburse him for his fee and the cost of his roundtrip flight back to Moscow. Dennis tried to give him $314 in cash. But the technician didn't want cash. He wanted caviar to take back to Moscow. Caviar in Moscow is what we would call fish eggs—salmon eggs—not the fine caviar we pay a fortune for here in the US.

Dennis arranged for him to go home with a sack full of cans of fish eggs. He could sell it in Moscow for five times what we had paid in Petropavlovsk. We were impressed with the man's ingenuity. Everyone needed to take advantage of every opportunity they could to make money. They all had families to feed.

We set up our operations hub at Elizovo in a secure area that had been used as a children's daycare center. The Russians had been experiencing a negative birth rate for quite some time, and there weren't many kids there. Michael remodeled the center and paid to move the remaining kids over to one side of the building. Our satellite dish was secured inside the attic of the building, pointing up at the INMARSAT satellite in a geostationary orbit.

After the hub was up and running, a couple of random Russian "officials" showed up one day, claiming that they were worried about the kids in the daycare center being exposed to radiation from our satellite equipment. They pulled out a very primitive-looking RF meter to make sure that we weren't going to fry all the kids with radiation. Michael, of course, knew this was nonsense. He couldn't tell if it was the FSB making sure that their bug was in order, or it was just a couple of random guys pulling a scam. We paid their modest fee for conducting their tests. It was ridiculous.

CKC rapidly turned into a serious entrepreneurial venture. All of the new equipment, refurbishments, labor, security, and support financed by SM&A profits amounted to several million dollars by this point. As the JV partner, largest shareholder, and Chairman, I provided the financing in the form of loans against the enterprise on our balance sheet. Once aircraft started landing, our financial analyses showed that we'd have no difficulty continuing to finance this operation until it went cash-flow positive. All the other equity stockholders on both sides of the JV provided sweat equity.

I thought that this venture was well worth the financial risk. I was able to easily finance the operation out of SM&A profits, which was growing at 20 to 30 percent a year during the nineties. According to Dennis's very thorough business plan, our first profitable year was expected in 1996. However, cash-flow management is critical in any business. Setting up CKC's offices directly across the hall from SM&A's corporate headquarters, allowed CKC to share facility space, administrative, and accounting support from SM&A. We only needed to hire people for CKC who were critical to operations. Whenever possible, we would "lend" people from SM&A to carry out specific CKC tasks. It was an excellent cost-containment strategy. It kept the costs down and allowed us to take advantage of the exceptionally high-quality staff working at SM&A.

We had to recruit, train, and deploy people, and we had to move quickly. Spooling up was all about logistics. The process worked well. By June 1993, CKC was booking contracts and scheduling flights. Half a dozen people were working for CKC in Newport Beach, plus twenty or so Americans and about a hundred Russians working at Elizovo. Security was critical. We contracted with the militia to provide guards for our facilities and the ramp area set aside to receive and service the flights.

There were no stores anywhere in the Russian Far East to walk into to buy anything useful to us. Michael and his team prepared lists of a ton of equipment and stuff we needed to ship to Petropavlovsk on a barge out of Seattle, in July 1993. Two of the items were indispensable: medical supplies and vehicles.

If anyone became ill or injured over there, we had a real problem. I met with my concierge physician in Newport Beach and had him prepare a very substantial kit that a doctor or nurse could use to do anything up to, and including, surgery. My doctor asked what he should assume they had. I said, "Nothing useful!" He assembled a first-rate medical support and surgical kit fitted into a large, heavy-duty, green plastic container with appropriate markings, complete with instructions and inventory. It contained medicine, knives, syringes, tools, drugs, gowns, oxygen tanks, and more.

We needed reliable vehicles to get around in. My brother-in-law, Scott, was perfect for this task. I sent him to Seattle to find half a dozen used Chevy Suburban SUVs for sale by private owners, and have them at the Seattle docks in a week. We discussed criteria and budget. I wired him the money. He found, inspected, purchased, serviced, and transported the SUVs down to the docks, and loaded them onto the barge. One advantage of using a common vehicle was the use of common parts. Scott put together a maintenance kit with a host of spare parts and a substantial toolbox.

We had four significant issues to resolve before we could conduct flight operations: instrument landing procedures, air routes from Alaska and Southwest Asia, an alternate landing site, and overflight permits.

The Russian instrument procedures were very complex. We wanted to develop new instrument approaches that would be acceptable to the Russians, the FAA, and ICAO, and that were straightforward. I had the opportunity to experiment with Russian instrument approach procedures the prior July. We wanted to develop a straight-in ILS instrument approach from the east over the bay that would be used under all circumstances. Nothing to hit, and little to go wrong. If the winds were unfavorable, the aircraft could make a visual circle to land in the opposite direction after breaking out of instrument conditions. We also wanted a procedure for the missed approach that provided a 180-degree turn back out over the bay.

The second issue involved ICAO-approved air routes. The existing ICAO air routes, called "Nor-Pac tracks," from Alaska to Asia doglegged east, far out into the North Pacific. They were circuitous and required significantly more fuel than the new route we requested from the FAA over Kamchatka. The new route was called Green 583. The new route benefited air carriers no matter where they landed because it was shorter.

Frankly, we were just amazed at how cooperative the FAA was, right from the beginning. They embraced what we were trying to accomplish. I had never seen anything like it. But if the FAA and ICAO were on board, getting the Russian bureaucracy to agree to anything was another matter. Tom coordinated with Viktor in Moscow, who worked the Russian Air Ministry to open up the new air route. This was technically our Russian JV partners' responsibility to solve. But we needed speed, and we needed resolve. In this regard, Viktor was an anomaly, a Russian who wanted to get things done, and knew how to. He did not care whose side of the JV was supposed to be doing what. He pitched in and made it happen, no matter what task he was given. We succeeded in most of our wants. But we just couldn't get the Russians to agree to new instrument approaches. Their insistence on existing complex procedures was to come back and bite us later with severe consequences.

The third issue, which had an ironic impact on the second, was that flight crews are required to designate an alternate airport for landing on their flight plans whenever the forecasted weather at the destination airport is below visual flight rules (VFR) minimums. In other words, if the crew needs to make an instrument approach due to weather, and is unable to land (a missed approach), then they need to carry enough fuel to fly to the designated alternate airport and land, and still have thirty minutes of fuel on board.

Elizovo tends to become foggy because of its proximity to Avacha Bay and the open ocean to the east. In the winter, poor weather is the norm. There was another runway, less than thirty minutes flying time away, built as an alternate landing site for the Russian space shuttle. We wanted to designate the shuttle runway as our alternate, but the airport managers refused. The issue was that the shuttle runway was in disrepair. Moscow had been sending money to the airport managers to maintain the shuttle runway for years. The airport managers had routinely diverted the money for other purposes, and Moscow didn't know about it. This made any hope of returning the shuttle runway to serviceability infeasible without heads rolling over the prior misappropriation of funds.

Without a viable alternate, if the weather forecast for Elizovo was not VFR before a client aircraft's departure from wherever they were coming from in southwest Asia, they would probably use Chitose for their fuel stop.

Elizovo's closest alternate, Magadan, is 470 nautical miles to the northwest. But as an indication of how tight the margins are in the air freight business, carrying that extra hour of fuel to reach Magadan added enough cost to undermine the economic advantages of stopping at Elizovo instead of Chitose.

Because Elizovo is already at the outer range of either freighter's capabilities with full cargo, the carrier either had to reduce the cargo load to accommodate the extra fuel for the alternate, or go to Chitose, and pay the extra cost in fuel and landing fees.

I found this hard to believe at first. The tradeoff was the prevailing cargo rate of $1.25 a pound vs. the $0.68 difference in the cost of fuel plus the $25,000 landing fee at Chitose. For DC-10 or 747 freighters, adding one hour's flying time to Magadan, and the extra range added from Magadan to their next destination, easily translated into some 20,000 to 40,000 pounds of cargo that had to be left off the aircraft to accommodate the extra fuel required.

The irony was if the clients were only going to land in VFR conditions, the need for new instrument approach procedures wasn't as essential. They'd do fine with the existing ones. But it was going to cost us a great deal of money in lost revenue for the many flights we'd lose because of forecasted instrument conditions.

The fourth issue was developing procedures for routinely obtaining overflight and landing permission at Elizovo. As part of our services to our clients, we took responsibility for this and a host of other related activities. We wanted to offer one-stop shopping for route services into and over the region. We decided to offer this service not only for our clients refueling at Elizovo, but for all aircraft using G-583 and landing at Chitose. This strategy made sense for three reasons. First, situations could develop en route requiring our clients to overfly Elizovo and to continue to either Japan or Anchorage. Second, servicing Chitose aircraft offered an additional revenue stream for us. Third, the Russians liked the idea because it drastically simplified their job of collecting overflight fees from these carriers. We would take care of everything for them. All the Russians had to do was quickly provide the routine approvals we asked for.

With the final push coming from CKC, the international G-583 air route over Kamchatka opened by agreement between the US and Russia in May 1993. Even the FAA was amazed that we were able to get it done so quickly. We opened the G-583 air route six years ahead of when the FAA thought that it could happen. In just six months, we had completed an entirely new air route survey, had all the required documentation completed by the FAA, and had the required charts published for use. Of all of the incredible things accomplished by our fledgling enterprise, getting a new air route opened was by far the most difficult, and most enduring.

The key was, once again, an alignment of interests. We were not the only ones who cared. The regional FAA office in Anchorage cared as much as we did. What we were doing represented a tremendous opportunity for them too. Some of the airlines cared, particularly Alaska and American Airlines. They saw the passenger potential in the region. We even had friends we didn't know about.

Then, in June 1993, we obtained the first Western liability insurance policy for aviation operations in the Russian Far East. Of all the things I worried about, this had been the biggest. No insurance, no business!

It's so interesting to me that it's never the things we pay attention to in business, or in life for that matter, that get us into trouble. It's always the things we miss, or perhaps just take for granted. The one thing our JV partners were responsible for, and my side of the JV had no control over, was the delivery of fuel. They were swimming in fuel. We could manage everything else, but they had to deliver the fuel. It seems like such an obvious issue in retrospect. It never occurred to any of us that the fuel supply could be a problem. The fuel supply chain should have been the first thing we analyzed.

Our Russian JV partners were bullish but painfully naive about their ability to deliver the fuel. They had a fuel-supply system that they thought they controlled. After all, the system was there to fuel all their military and civilian aircraft at the base. They had a massive fuel tank farm. They had pipelines. They had an entire infrastructure system devoted to refining oil in Vladivostok, 1,200 miles away, piping it to the port, loading it onto barges, delivering it to the port near Petropavlovsk, and piping it to the fuel farm. Our survey had concluded that this was something they knew how to do very well.

As soon as people in the supply chain saw that there was serious money in this deal, and it was real, the haggling started. It was inevitable. Everybody wanted a cut. At the worst possible moment, there were inexplicable issues with fuel shipments. In retaliation, an audit by the local authorities of all fuel shipments for the prior year uncovered that 10 percent of the fuel supply vanished every month.

One of our Russian contacts reported confidentially to us they had heard, somewhere on the pipeline's twenty-five-mile route from the bay to the airport storage tanks, people had tapped into the pipe and were stealing fuel. It was safe to assume the same people trying to cut themselves into the deal were stealing the fuel and selling it.

Our Russian partners wanted to solve their difficulties by increasing the price we quoted to our clients. We pushed back, reminding them that our pricing strategy was to attract clients away from their current routes. If the Japanese were charging $1.35 a gallon, then we needed to charge $0.68 a gallon. Our competitive advantage was cheap fuel at a better location. "If it isn't cheap, they won't come." We would tell them this over and over again.

Our business plan hadn't considered the impact of potential fuel constraints or price increases. We assumed we were demand limited, not supply limited. As an entrepreneur, I accepted from the start that there would be no end of challenges. After all, if it wasn't hard, anybody could do it. And our Russian partners were a mess. The high barriers to entry that the situation created served my interests by keeping everyone else out.

But fuel had suddenly gone from being a no-risk to the highest-risk factor. We felt seriously blindsided. I was much concerned. While I still thought we could get through it, it was clear to me that the risk-reward ratio for this venture was changing. The Russians needed us as much as we needed them to make this work. I told my partners as clearly as I could that they needed to go to whoever was making all these waves and negotiate a better deal that everyone could live with, or we didn't have a business. Everyone would lose!

We began exhibiting at industry air shows and exhibitions like the National Business Aviation Association (NBAA) annual convention, which occurred that summer in Atlanta. Our sales pitch focused on six significant advantages: cheap gas, better location, the G-583 route, one-stop shopping for handling, US customer service, and the only airport in the Russian Far East with credible insurance. I'm quite sure that none of our anchor clients would have signed up with us if we hadn't provided all six of these advantages.

Dennis, like Ken, led in so many ways that senior executives should. Each would come to me with issues, and instead of expecting me to solve them, would say, "Steve, here's what I think we should do. What do you think?" Sometimes I had a better idea. Most of the time, I didn't. But it was never about who had the better idea. It was about communication, clarity, perspective, and validation. They were each empowered, and I was able to remain in the loop; it was a terrific management formula.

After spending so many months getting the air route open, getting critical equipment in place, and hiring people, we were finally ready to begin servicing aircraft.

FIRST REVENUE FLIGHT

*For the people of Kamchatka, these aircraft were
indeed a triumphant symbol of their hopes for
the future, over their experiences of the past. We,
too, shared their hopes, and their dreams.*

Against the backdrop of a dark blue, sunny, summer sky,
the white silhouette appeared as a gigantic, slow-moving
bird approaching Elizovo from over Avacha Bay to the east.
Nearly everyone in the city of Petropavlovsk stopped to watch in
amazement as the huge World Airways DC-10 slowly descended
over the bay with its landing gear and flaps extended.

For more than sixty years, World Airways had been a global
provider of long-range passenger and cargo air transportation
services. Their clients included the US Air Force, major international airlines, freight forwarders, international leisure tour operators, and cruise ship companies. They handled many military
and civilian passenger charters. They flew military personnel into
war zones. They even flew Muslim pilgrims to the Hajj. World
had nearly a dozen DC-10s at the time.

Before World Airways would agree to fly their DC-10s into
Petropavlovsk, they needed a team of experts to conduct a detailed
assessment of the Elizovo facility. After Dennis' experiences the

previous winter on Aeroflot, putting the World team on a Russian commercial aircraft out of Anchorage was a non-starter. This was no way to start a relationship with what we hoped would become our anchor client. We organized a series of charter flights to get Dennis and the World team to Petropavlovsk. World Airways took six people, all of whom Dennis knew, and two of our people.

We chartered a twin-engine propjet to get the travel team across the Bering Strait to Provideniya. Because it was such a dark, gloomy, and decrepit place, I feared the experience would put the World team off. Dennis sardonically reported on his return that I hadn't done the place justice. At least they didn't stay there very long. A YAK-40, three-engine commercial aircraft flew the team almost immediately from Provideniya to Petropavlovsk.

The YAK-40 was the workhorse for regional air transport all over Russia, but these aircraft also had a statistically alarming accident rate, particularly in the Far East. Bad weather, poor weather forecasting, few navigation aids, poor ground support, and inferior runway surfaces, if there were even runways to land on, made the Russian Far East a rough place for flying. It was common practice for these aircraft to land on dirt strips and roads. During the flight to Petropavlovsk, Dennis was invited to sit in the co-pilot's seat to better view the volcanoes erupting ahead in the distance. The pilot observed, "I do not know how this translates into English, but in Russia, we call this airplane the flying rock."

The World team spent nearly a week thoroughly examining every aspect of our refueling base and received the royal treatment from the Russians in the process. We had spent a great deal of time explaining to our Russian partners how critical it was to our joint success for our first customer to leave Petropavlovsk with a positive impression. Hoping to impress the World team, the Russians arranged for frequent breaks to take them on excursions to the most interesting landmarks in the area and introduce them to local leaders.

During one excursion, an unanticipated incident occurred that deeply moved the World team and gave them a new perspective on our broader strategic objectives. They were visiting Paratunka, the same resort and spa some forty miles west of Elizovo, that we had visited in July of 1992. It was initially constructed for use by Soviet military officers during the Cold War. By Western standards, the place was awful, but it was the only R&R facility the Russians had in the region, and they were very proud of it.

While touring Paratunka, another group of Russians was coincidently using the spa, including a young boy in a wheelchair. His legs and feet were severely deformed. It was heartbreaking to see for these men, most of whom had children of their own. Recognizing the team as Americans, an elderly Russian woman who spoke some English approached them, saying that her son loved Americans and wanted to meet them. The team was happy to oblige. When she asked why the Americans were there, Dennis told her what was going on. His explanation elicited highly emotional expressions of gratitude from the woman and her group. She exclaimed, "Thank you, God, for bringing these people here. Maybe now my little boy will be able to get the operation he needs, and maybe someday, things will be better here. We are so glad you're here."

The Russians spontaneously began hugging all the Americans, thanking them, shaking their hands, and wishing them all well. It was one thing to talk abstractly about helping people, and quite another to encounter prototypical examples of the very people whose lives you hoped to impact for the better. The encounter deeply moved the World team.

On their last day at Elizovo, the World team had another deeply moving emotional experience that affected them greatly.

One of our Russian partners, Yuri, said to Dennis, "We like your friends who have come from America to bring their airplane here. I would like to have lunch with them before they leave."

Dennis said to Yuri, "Of course. That would be very nice."

"But my apartment is very humble," Yuri added.

Dennis reassured him, "We do not care; we are just a bunch of guys. If you'd like to have us to your home, we would love to come."

Dennis and the team proceeded to Yuri's apartment building, not far from the airport. He lived on the fifth floor of an old walkup. I don't think that any of the housing in Russia had elevators. It was very primitive, with dark hallways that smelled of urine. The apartment was tiny. Between the World team, the Russian partners, Dennis, and Viktor, some fourteen men were squeezed in around a collection of small tables assembled in the living room.

Lunch was, naturally, accompanied by a lot of vodka. The Russians did a great job with what they had. It was very touching. As they were all getting pretty drunk, Dennis asked, "Yuri, how did you come to have this apartment?"

"It is a very sad story," Yuri responded. "My friend was Paul. He was my best friend in the whole world. Last year his heart exploded, and he died. This was his apartment." Yuri was a big bear of a guy and a former KGB agent. He became very emotional about losing his friend. There were tears in his eyes.

Dennis suggested, "You know what? Let's have a toast to Paul."

"No, no, no, you can't," Yuri responded.

"Why not?" Dennis asked, very surprised.

Yuri started to say, "In Russia, you don't . . . If you're going to toast someone . . ." He got up and left the room—he was in tears at this point. The vodka was working.

Viktor chimed in, "In order to make a toast properly, you would have to break bread and pour salt over it. We would have to have a picture of him in front of us while we toasted him."

Yuri came back into the room, wiping his eyes.

Dennis said, "We've got vodka, we've got bread, and we've got salt. Do we have a picture of Paul?"

Yuri found a photo, and they put it on the table. Then all the Americans toasted Paul. They toasted Yuri's friend. It turned into a very emotional event for the Russians that the Americans participated in this. Some of them were actually crying.

The Russians were astounded that we would do this, that we would care so much. Dennis looked over to his left to see that a World Airways VP he had known for years was also crying.

Dennis asked, "Hey, Jim, why are you crying?"

Jim said, "My dad died last year, and I'm just so sad, and this man, Paul, died, and it just all reminds me of what happened."

Dennis said, "I'm so sorry, Jim."

The experience brought out a lot of feelings in Jim. Dennis looked down the table, and there was another World guy named Mike, a very hard-hitting, tough guy, in tears too.

Dennis asked, "Mike, what's wrong with you?"

"I was just thinking about how not so long ago, we were fighting these guys. They were our enemies, and look at them—they're just like us."

Dennis then said, "This is an incredible experience. I cannot believe this. I mean, we have come together as a group of guys. We are not here as Russians, and we are not here as Americans; on the most basic level, we are just people sitting together having lunch and remembering lost ones. And, you know what? We are all the same—the same issues, the same worries, the same fears, the same joys, the same loves, the same everything."

People never forget this kind of bonding experience. By the time lunch was over and everyone had returned to the airport, they were all completely wasted. Dennis and the Russians somehow managed to pour the World guys onto the YAK-40 flight to Magadan, where they would make their connection back to Alaska. It was a tearful farewell with hugs all around.

The World team left totally committed to making things work. It was a business deal to be sure. It was also a poignant and very personal relationship-building experience. With the Russians, as in every country I ever did business in, there was no hope for a long-term business relationship without a personal relationship. Business is all about trust, not about contracts. You won't do business with people you don't trust, and you can't trust people you don't know. If you're not willing to invest the time to build personal relationships, you ultimately can't succeed—anywhere!

The arrival of the World Airways DC-10 was a most auspicious occasion and a seminal milestone for CKC. The entire city came out to Elizovo to witness this history-making event. Russian ladies were out on the ramp waving American and Russian flags. A band enthusiastically filled the air with Russian music. The arrival ceremony featured speeches by officials, including the governor, who broke bread and poured salt for all to taste. It was a proud occasion for everyone.

By the time the World aircraft arrived, Dennis had been in Petropavlovsk for several weeks. As soon as the mobile stairs had been put in place, he bounded up the stairs into the forward galley and cockpit to greet the crew. As he stepped into the galley, he stopped abruptly and exclaimed, "I smell America!" The captain—a good friend of Dennis and his wife, Patti—brought a box for Dennis that Patti had filled with special things for him and the other Americans. She knew that Dennis was desperate for tortilla chips and salsa. And there was one other very special item—a photo album.

Patti had given birth to their first child, Madison, three months earlier. She had been born prematurely and had been in the neonatal intensive care unit for most of the three weeks before Dennis left for Petropavlovsk. She was out of danger by the time he left, but he hadn't been able to see much of her. The photo album was filled with pictures of Madison, and the front cover read, "To Russia with Love." There he sat, exhausted and lonely in this far-away outpost, in the cargo bay of this huge aircraft, eating chips and salsa, and carefully going through every page of the album with tears in his eyes.

The next morning, as the crew was trying to get the DC-10 closed up and cleared for departure, a customs agent came onto the aircraft to complete the paperwork. The crew was anxious to get going because they had a time slot to make at their next stop. The customs agent was working very slowly and asking a lot of unnecessary questions. The captain then foolishly said to the customs agent, "Can we hurry this up? If you don't hurry up, we're going to miss our slot in Hong Kong."

The Russian agent looked at him and said, "You don't like the way I'm working? Well, let me tell you something: I'm going on break. I'll be gone now for eight hours, and we'll continue this process when I return." He then just left, and the plane sat there on the ramp for another eight hours.

After all of our hard work, with so much at stake for both the American and Russian sides, it came down to a lowly customs clerk with attitude and a busy pilot with a schedule. This one incident perfectly encapsulated the psychological challenges of clashing cultures all over the world. The Russian customs clerk didn't have a reason to care. If the captain had used a little tact, he would have taken out a few bucks, ten dollars would have been plenty, and asked if it would be sufficient to cover their "special handling" request to make their slot time. That's all the agent really wanted, a little something extra for his trouble.

He had nothing. From his vantage point, everyone else was getting something. What about him? It was really our team's mistake. We were being paid to handle the flight. We had missed it. This was just one of a thousand examples of the never-ending battle of psychologies that we had to deal with to get anything done. It's important to understand that this is not bribery the way we think of it in the US. It is simply compensating people for their services in a hopelessly broken system.

To help put this issue into context, in 1993, some 1,700 civilian employees were working at Elizovo. They provided ground support to some ten regional commercial flights and one flight arrival from and departure to Moscow every day—a ridiculous, inefficient use of labor. But in the USSR, the aim was not to create profit but to create jobs. Nothing had changed, except that in the new Russia, there was never-ending concern about actually getting paid.

When the World DC-10 finally took off into the distance late in the afternoon in the late summer of 1993, it was the culmination of the hard work of a great many people. For me, it was proof that, indeed, with imagination and courage, we really could do what most had thought to be impossible. Perhaps for me, this was what entrepreneurship was all about.

A month later, our first Tower Air Boeing 747 cargo aircraft arrived at Elizovo, heralding another huge milestone. By the summer of 1994, CKC was the largest service provider of non-Russian aircraft in the Russian Far East. Alaska Airlines confirmed our bullish projections of Kamchatka's tourist potential when they announced that they would begin a twice-weekly service to Petropavlovsk in the late spring of 1995.

It seemed like every time a flight came into Elizovo, hundreds and hundreds of people gathered to watch. Their faces were filled with joy and wonder as the giant airplane slowly taxied into the ramp area.

For the people of Kamchatka, these aircraft were indeed a triumphant symbol of their hopes for the future, over their experiences of the past. We, too, shared their hopes, and their dreams.

15

AGGRAVATION

*"The Russians took the money, took the cargo out of
the airplane, and then told the crew to get out!"*

B y the fall of 1994, we had been servicing wide-body cargo
airplanes and business jet airplanes for nearly eighteen
months. We had serviced about two hundred aircraft without
a serious mishap, which in and of itself was a remarkable
achievement. We had gained enough operating experience and
financial data to know what it took to run the business profitably.

Five issues dominated our attention. First, with rare exceptions, we could not rely on the Russians to reliably accomplish
anything. It usually came down to how much vodka had been
consumed the night before. Chronic alcoholism was so pervasive
that it significantly impacted each of the other issues. Second, we
were losing a significant number of flights every week because
the Russian weather services provided erroneous weather forecasts. Clients sometimes flew over Petropavlovsk, in perfectly
clear weather conditions, because of this issue. Third, we were
plagued with never-ending fuel supply-chain issues. Fourth, we
were losing about $50,000 a month in negative cash flow on the

US side of the operation. This negative cash flow was entirely attributable to the first three issues. Fifth, without proper deicing equipment, we could not service airplanes during the harsh winter unless weather conditions were right, which they rarely were, and we were struggling to get the leasing companies to provide the equipment.

Two incidents illustrate just how challenging it was to make a business function effectively in the Russian Far East. We were about to have our aggravation limits tested.

Every fall the heaviest air traffic came from Taipei and Hong Kong, in preparation for the Christmas shopping season in America. We had to have year-round operations to be economically viable. By the fall, it was already becoming icy in Kamchatka. Winter generally came early and stayed late.

Of all the companies we were eager to sign up for our services, FedEx was at the top of the list. FedEx was already a very successful company in 1994, operating a large number of flights between the US and southeast Asia. We were keen to win their business and have them become our bookend anchor client with World Airways. Dennis visited their headquarters in Memphis and met with their flight operation people. On bended knee, he asked, "Guys, please bring an airplane into Petropavlovsk. We will refuel it for you, you'll have a great tech stop, and here are the advantages: you are going to get cheap fuel, you're not going to have high landing fees, and you're not going to have slot controls if you're late. Let us do this. We'll do a great job for you."

After taking some time to consider the matter, they said, "Okay, we're going to bring an airplane up from Taipei or Manila en route to the US and see how you handle it."

The FedEx 747, like all of the cargo airplanes operating in this part of the world, used onboard inertial navigation system (INS) equipment to determine the exact position of the airplanes.

The INS was not nearly as accurate as GPS is today. The biggest limitation was that system accuracy decayed over several hours, which translated into several miles by the time it reached its destination. To address this limitation, for every flight, the aircraft route flown was designed for the airplanes to fly over known lat/long fixes of ground-based navigational aids (VORs and NDBs). The crew would use these to update the INS.

Early on a Sunday morning in the dead of winter, the FedEx 747 flight came up air route G-583. They flew over the waypoint called Malka, a point directly under G-583 and some thirty-two miles due west of Elizovo. At the Malka waypoint, there was allocated an NDB navigational aid the FedEx crew was planning to use to update their INS. The FedEx flight crossed over Malka, looking for the radio signal. But there was no signal. Later, we found out that the guy whose job it was to turn the transmitter on every day was drunk and hadn't woken up on time.

At this point, the FedEx 747 was committed to land at Petropavlovsk. They didn't have enough fuel to reach the nearest alternate, Magadan, nearly 500 nautical miles to the northwest and more than an hour away.

The weather had been forecasted for VFR conditions before they departed from Hong Kong but had deteriorated over the last several hours. They planned to fly the instrument approach to Elizovo from the east by first flying east from Malka over the top of the airport and Avacha Bay, then making a 180-degree turn and descending west straight into the runway. Easy.

But the Russians had a different plan. The crew was directed to make spiral descending turns over Malka before beginning their approach to the runway from the west. This meant that they would have to make a spiral descent in the valley west of the airport with three 12,000-foot volcanoes to the north and south of the valley.

The crew was extremely nervous about coming into an airport they had never seen, without the INS updates they had expected, using an instrument approach they had never flown, in heavy cloud cover, and with mountains on both sides of the valley. They were forced to make a continuous spiral descent with turns toward mountains with every turn to the north and south. They couldn't see the mountains or the high ground at any point. They sweated buckets all the way down. Miraculously, they finally broke through the clouds and landed without incident. The crew flight report we received later said it all: "There wasn't a dry seat in the cockpit." To say that they weren't happy was a vast understatement.

We refueled them and got them out of there as quickly as possible. The captain commented before leaving, "We really appreciate the fine tech stop. We appreciate the cheap fuel. We appreciate no slot curfews or curfews and slot controls. We are not coming back. There is no way we are going to do this again."

We had worked so hard to get FedEx in there. It was a trial run. We would have had hundreds of flights from FedEx had one guy not drunk too much vodka the night before, or if the Russian controllers had simply let FedEx land to the west from over the bay. This foolishness cost our joint venture many millions of dollars.

On learning the news, Dennis was so angry he immediately flew over to Petropavlovsk to read our Russian partners the riot act. On his flight to Anchorage, he decided to drop in to see the FAA during the layover.

"Guys, I need help. We've simply got to put another NDB into Petro and redesign the instrument approaches." He went on. "We've only got the one NDB at Malka for airplanes to use for INS updates, and if it's not working, they don't have anything else to reference. Their only safe option is to overfly the field and come in from the east, making spiral turns over the bay, not on the west side in the valley of doom. That's just nuts! We've got to give these carriers another reference point. Can you help?"

The FAA did help. They found a surplus NDB overnight and gave it to us! In Petropavlovsk, he explained to everyone that, "This fiasco has just cost our partnership a huge American customer and millions of dollars. We warned you that the approach from the west is a problem. We have to fix this, and I mean now! We need an alternative and reliable procedure that allows our airplane to stay east of the bay, lose altitude over the ocean, and come west up the bay to the runway. There's got to be a way to do that without overflying your submarine pens. We need to put an NDB out at the end of the bay by the ocean, on the east side of Petropavlovsk. The FAA is giving us an NDB for this purpose. Will you let us put it in?"

The Russian official responsible looked him straight in the eyes and said, "Oh, well, if that's what you need, we already have an NDB out there. We use it for military operations. But all our pilots know about it. When they want to use it, they just ask."

The blood drained out of Dennis' face at this revelation. He was speechless. They had never told us it was there. During my trip in 1992, I had experimented with all the instrument approaches at Elizovo, both from the west and east. The Russians never mentioned the existence of such an NDB, and it wasn't on the approach charts that Viktor #2 had brought with him. If Viktor #2 knew about it, he never mentioned it.

We weren't sure what was at the bottom of this nonsensical performance by the Russians. I began to wonder if this could have been a simple failure to communicate. My experience with Russian controllers was that it was better to over-communicate than to under-communicate. I began to wonder if the flight crew had not told the controllers that Malka was down and their INS couldn't be updated. Did they tell the controllers they couldn't land to the east because Malka was down and needed priority clearance to land to the west? Did they ask for priority radar vectors to the east because of navigation equipment issues?

We also began wondering if this had been done deliberately. Were people being bribed to slow us down? If so, why? Perhaps people were looking for their cuts and going to forget to do their jobs until they got paid? We did observe that the only time things changed was when the Russians recognized that their inaction or obstruction had cost them serious money. This was one of those times.

The Russians began cooperating to approve and distribute the improved instrument approach procedures we wanted. But our chance with FedEx had been blown. Even if my theory about the crew's failure to communicate was at the bottom of the incident, we could hardly go to FedEx and tell them that. We were confident that, eventually, we would get them back. We just needed to improve operational procedures and train the Russians to embrace that they were in the business of customer service.

Then, in late December, Dennis received a phone call from Emery Air Freight, one of the largest air carriers in the US. Emery told Dennis that they had a contract to send a DC-8 loaded with fruits and vegetables to Novosibirsk in Siberia.

"We were just wondering if you had any advice for us?" the Emery VP asked.

Dennis thought for a moment and said, "Yes, I do have some advice. It would be wise for you to bring your airplane to Petropavlovsk. We can refuel you and arrange all of your clearances into Russia. We can make sure you won't have any difficulties. You will probably have problems trying to fly directly into Novosibirsk."

The VP quickly replied, "Thanks, but we don't want to come to Petropavlovsk. It would add a couple of extra hours of flying. And we know you're just trying to sell a stop in Petropavlovsk."

Dennis sighed, "Well, not really. But I highly recommend you do it. It's not easy coming into Russia. There's no end to what can go wrong." Dennis couldn't convince the Emery VP of the value we provided.

Two days later, Dennis received another phone call from the Emery VP. This time he was in an absolute panic.

"We need your help. We're desperate!"

"What's wrong?" Dennis asked.

"Our DC-8 flew from Seattle to Novosibirsk. After they landed, the Russians surrounded the airplane with troops with machine guns. The authorities said we didn't have the proper permits, and the flight was illegal. They're confiscating the cargo, and there will be a fine. Our captain asked how much the fine was. The Russians asked how much cash he had. He replied he had $25,000 in cash for fuel. They demanded all of the money!"

He continued, "The Russians took the money, took the cargo out of the airplane, and then told the crew to get out. They took off, but they didn't have enough fuel to get back to Seattle, or even to Petropavlovsk. Their only option was Magadan."

Magadan is a horrid place, located some 470 nautical miles to the northwest of Petropavlovsk across the Sea of Okhotsk. Stalin established the city as a disbursal point for the gulags in 1930. Prisoners were brought to the town and from there sent out to the various work camps.

The Emery VP continued, "We're calling you because we can't restart the airplane engines in Magadan. We don't have an air-start unit on the airplane, and there isn't one at the airport there. We're dead in the water."

Most commercial and business jet airplanes have an auxiliary power unit (APU) to produce electricity, air conditioning, and heating while parked on the ground with the engines turned off. The APU is a small turbine engine located in the tail of the airplane. The APU is also used to start the engines of most airplanes, either by providing electricity to a starter or by providing a high-volume air to rotate the engine.

Alternatively, an external, ground power unit can be used the same way. For airplanes requiring a high-volume air, the ground unit is called an air-start unit. It looks like a big box on wheels and is moved around the ramp using a tug. The ground crew connects a large hose to an engine access port and pushes a high volume of air up into the engine so that it can rotate fast enough to be started.

The Emery DC-8 was an older airplane and didn't have an APU. Magadan did not have an external air-start unit. So, there was no way of starting the engines.

The VP then asked Dennis, "How do you get your airplanes started in Petropavlovsk?"

Dennis struggled to reply without being obnoxious, "We have an air-start unit. It's a Dev-Tech 250 that can start the Queen Mary."

"We need it in Magadan right away."

"You're not going to have it in Magadan right away!"

"Why not?"

"Because we need it in Petropavlovsk. No way can you have it. First, it's a valuable piece of equipment. It cost us more than $100,000. Second, to get it to Magadan, we'd have to load it on an air freighter we don't have and fly it 500 nautical miles. Third, there's no guarantee that the thing would ever get there or get back in one piece. The guys in Magadan might decide to keep it. Then what? No, I'm not sending it. No way!"

"What are we going to do then? We're dead in the water!"

Dennis then said, with a certain sense of satisfaction, "There's a barge once a month that leaves from Seattle and goes to Magadan. It takes about forty to fifty days to get there. I'd suggest you get your hands on an air-start unit in the US and put it on that next barge."

The VP clearly hated Dennis' answer. Emery had not thought through this mission before it started. And now they were paying a dear price for being penny wise and pound foolish. We genuinely could not help them.

The Emery VP called back the next day. He was even more frantic than the day before. It was getting close to the December rush, and they had a contract to fly mail for the US Postal Service. Their DC-8 was lost to them, and they desperately needed it back. They called Dennis every day for the next three days.

Finally, Dennis said, "Listen, I'm not going to give you our air-start unit. But I have come up with another idea. I haven't offered it up to you before because it's not safe, and I most certainly do not recommend this solution."

"There is a makeshift air-start unit that the Russians put together in Petropavlovsk before we set up our operation and brought over our own. Don't laugh, but it's a YAK-15 jet engine that the Russians mounted sideways in a panel van. A crew of three or four guys drives the van out to an airplane and parks it with the YAK-15 engine exhaust facing the intake of the airplane engine. Then they draw straws to decide who has to start the YAK-15 engine. They set up sandbags nearby. Then the short straw fires up the YAK engine. As soon as it starts to light off, short straw runs and dives behind the sandbags. They're worried the engine might rip away from the panel van at any moment. If that happens, you don't want to be there. This is not a piece of equipment that we would use, ever."

"Well, we're desperate. We'll take it. Can you get it to Magadan?"

Dennis said, "I don't want to profit out of your misery. Let me see what I can get done with our Russian partners. I'll get back to you."

Dennis talked to our guys in Petropavlovsk, and they spent some time figuring out how to get the YAK-15 panel van to Magadan. The Russians finally agreed to fly it to Magadan and do the air start, and then fly it back the same day.

Dennis asked, "How much?"

"$16,000!"

The YAK-15 jet engine fired up the Emery airplane, and they flew out of Magadan. It was probably the most expensive air start in the history of aviation. Emery learned a harsh lesson. You can't just wander into foreign lands without a plan. They assumed that because the USSR was no more, it was open season on doing whatever they wanted. They assumed that commerce was commerce, and no one would interfere. It was comforting to see that we were not the only people building a library of war stories to tell. The Emery story was a doozy.

An even more significant irritant was our Russian JV partners' never-ending efforts to renegotiate the JV agreement. In every meeting, letter, or fax, they would first bring up issues they were having, and then link those issues to the need to revisit the JV agreement. We, of course, recognized that once the Russians were able to establish the legitimacy of even a single change, the entire JV agreement would be up for grabs. At the end of the day, it was always about two things: the profit split and exclusivity.

Chuck, Dennis, and I had a lengthy meeting after they had returned from a particularly bitter cold few weeks in Petropavlovsk in the winter of 1994/1995. It had been so cold that I was sure they were still thawing out when the meeting started. Fatigue and frustration were written all over their faces. I listened patiently as they ranted about the tactical situation.

Chuck began, "They tried again. Two frustrating hours of trying to renegotiate the split." He looked out the window with tired eyes. "These people are so conditioned by communism that they think all capitalism is gangster capitalism." He got up and paced the floor agitatedly. Dennis and I exchanged glances. "They really believe you can only make a profit at someone else's expense."

Dennis cut in, "It seems like every two weeks we have to explain to them, "Look, you're making 51 percent of all the profits. You know 51 percent of this is a lot; 100 percent of nothing is nothing."

Chuck sat down. "Steve, we have to constantly remind them that we are not trying to rip them off. We can't seem to find a way to make them understand that we have no ulterior motive. We want them to succeed, and we have to make money. I just don't get why they can't get this one basic idea—if we make money, they make money. Which part of that don't they understand?"

I responded, "Guys, they're Russians. Look at their history. They don't think the way we think. It's going to take a lot more than one joint venture with a few Americans for them to learn to trust capitalism."

I changed the subject to a topic with a hopefully more upbeat answer. "What's going on with the erroneous weather forecasts? Did you get to the bottom of it?" I asked.

Dennis replied, "Steve, I can't prove it, but I think they're deliberately putting out those erroneous reports to create leverage to renegotiate. Every time they do this, it costs them money, too. But honestly, I don't think they care about that."

For our client cargo carriers to take advantage of Elizovo as a refueling base, the forecasted weather conditions had to be VFR when they fueled at their departure point. If the weather was good enough at Elizovo, they could they commit to a flight plan and load enough fuel to reach Elizovo, without having to carry enough fuel (an extra 45 minutes' worth) for the nearest alternate airport, Magadan, 470 nautical miles to the northwest. If the conditions were forecasted to be IFR, they probably wouldn't come unless there were other considerations.

The Russian weather reporting service put out reports in a format incompatible with ICAO standards. There was one phrase in particular that the Russians would occasionally insert in the remark section of their reports that meant one thing to the Russians, but something entirely different in ICAO weather reporting: "TEMPO." In ICAO-speak, this means that there is a significant adverse change in forecasted weather affecting half or more of the two hours following the time of issue.

Whenever TEMPO appeared in the weather forecast, our clients would assume that TEMPO meant deteriorating weather below VFR and cancel their scheduled servicing at Elizovo. This, even though the weather conditions were actually fine. We had dozens of flights fly over Petropavlovsk at 35,000 feet, look down, and see the field clearly. Every time this happened, we lost 50,000 gallons × 68 cents = $34,000, plus other services in revenue. It was maddening. Dennis reported that they said they were working on the problem and would have it sorted out in due course. He thought this was just their way of slow-rolling him.

The debate on fuel-pricing strategy was never ending with our JV partners. They just did not get it. The Japanese and Koreans were charging $1.00 to $1.25 per gallon. We wanted to sell fuel at half their price. They kept arguing that we should charge the same prices as the Japanese and the Koreans. We kept explaining that if we did that, no one would come. We had two things to sell, location and cheap gas. That was it.

Our strategy was to make the cargo carriers our regular customers. We had to do everything possible to make them comfortable with coming to Elizovo. It had to become their fuel stop of choice. Once they were used to us and appreciated our service, we would slowly increase our pricing.

Our Russian partners' thought processes were driven entirely by short-term gratification. Long-term client development to the Russians meant deciding where to take them for dinner. We knew that. We also understood that we had to be very careful about how we controlled and doled out the money. If we gave someone too much money, there was a very likely possibility of them disappearing to the four winds. They were all looking for the cash to get out.

Reconditioning our Russian partners to have faith and confidence in the future, something they had never known, was a long-term process. Based on their history, why should they have faith in the future? It was a never-ending struggle to prod them forward. Their instincts were all wired backward. Multigenerational conditioning had worked its way into their DNA. Change was coming very hard for them.

Their constant questioning of the deal that we had all worked so hard to create eventually began to work its way into our psyches. We had been so focused on changing the Russian's behavior. We hadn't considered the possibility they were deliberately trying to turn the tables on us by wearing us down.

Perhaps most troubling was the security situation. Dennis reported he was sure he was followed the entire time during his last trip. Neither he nor I had experienced this on any previous trip. "Steve, I don't know who was following me. I couldn't tell if it was the FSB, the CIA, the mafia."

We had received reports there were serious problems developing with mafia activity in the region, but nothing that had been actionable. We discussed ways and means of improving our security on the ground. Perhaps the most important action we took was to adopt a buddy system. All of our people on the ground were instructed not to go anywhere without someone they trusted accompanying them. It wasn't much. But it was all we had.

Success and money create options, and we had options that the Russians did not know anything about. While we had been working for the prior two and a half years on developing CKC, we had also had been working on the expansion of SM&A. That business was exploding.

One of the consequences of the end of the Cold War was the need for contraction and consolidation within the aerospace and defense industry. During the 1980s, there were about twenty-six A&D prime contractors doing business with the Department of Defense (DoD). By the end of 1999, that number was down to six. All of the others had been absorbed.

Another consequence of the end of the Cold War was that during the 1990s, the available funding from the DoD for the development and acquisition of new weapons systems dropped by half. The A&D industry didn't have a choice. They began laying off people in very significant numbers as they tried to right-size their businesses. Anyone who did not have a customer-paying project to work on was an endangered species. A mad scramble of musical chairs ensued while people tried to find their places in the new order.

An economic rationale for my interest in CKC had been the need for a hedge against things going sideways at SM&A. Conventional wisdom argued that the downturn occurring within the A&D industry meant that SM&A had no future. But conventional wisdom is usually the last to know when things have changed.

Two very significant, but unintended consequences of the A&D consolidation process greatly benefited SM&A. First, many more competent people approached SM&A for jobs than had ever before. Because of the nature of our consulting work, our business had always been supply, not demand, limited. It was very difficult to find people who could provide the kind of services we offered. We needed technically competent people, with excellent program management skills, who could work with people, and were effective leaders. We also needed these people to work ridiculously long hours, in remote locations, and for months at a time. The money made up for it. Almost everyone who worked at SM&A made more money than they had ever made before. Our strategy was to deliver better value by paying premium pay for premium services by our people. Our people's motivation was to work as hard as they could for a few years to squirrel away money into their 401k plans for retirement. We generally had to interview about a hundred people to find three who could pass muster.

By 1993 we were receiving resumes by the thousands, and from some amazingly qualified people. Some had retired. Some had been laid off. Some were afraid that they were going to be laid off. Some didn't like the new economics that consolidation had imposed on them. SM&A had a fantastic reputation. Our employees were our best recruiters. The ability to more easily recruit so many good people transformed our business. We were in the services business, and we quickly began to add more capabilities to provide across a broader spectrum of services to sell to our customers.

The second unintended consequence of consolidation was that our smaller number of more capable A&D customers woke up one morning to discover that they no longer had the resources they needed available to respond to the very substantial amount of DoD opportunities that remained.

While DoD acquisition spending had been cut in half, it bottomed out at some $65 billion, a huge market! The prime contractors no longer had the available resources to respond. They had either laid off many of their most capable people or assigned them to ongoing projects. To make matters worse, as the number of contractors went down, the intensity of competition for new contracts went up. The weak players were all gone. Only the most capable competitors remained. Every US government competition became a major battle. If a contractor didn't have the right people available for the fight, our opportunity was to become their proxies.

The phones started to ring. We began getting calls from our clients' CFOs, needing more services than we had ever sold before. They had done the math on our cost vs. benefit to them. The result was that our compounded annual growth rate at SM&A for the six years between 1992 and 1997 was a stunning 44 percent!

SM&A was growing like a weed and was taking more and more of my attention. That little voice in the back of my head began whispering to me. I began wondering if I had fallen into the age-old business trap of "starving my stars and feeding my dogs."

On cue, Ken walked into my office one day and announced, "Steve, I've been thinking about it. We need to sell CKC."

I looked at him in amazement, "What?"

"The business has real value now. With what's going on at SM&A, maybe the right play is to just sell it to a large institution that can carry it to the next level. You've got way too much to work on generating greater profits, and, frankly, with less aggravation."

I sat back and contemplated what Ken was saying for a moment. I replied, "Let's go to lunch and talk about it."

Several companies might buy CKC, including the parent of American Airlines (AMR), Lockheed, or Alaska Airlines, to mention just three. I was particularly intrigued by Alaska Airlines. We had recently negotiated a deal with them for the biweekly service of flights that they were starting up in the spring of 1995 to run between Anchorage, Magadan, Petropavlovsk, and Khabarovsk. Alaska Airlines had considerable inclement weather flying experience, had some cultural ties with Russia, and was about to become our first domestic passenger client.

Ken and I quickly arrived at a strategy for exploring the possibilities with all the potential players. Our two biggest concerns were making sure that our JV partners did not learn about what we had in mind until we were ready to tell them, and, most importantly, how Dennis would react to the idea.

I shouldn't have been concerned about Dennis. He thought this was exactly the right thing to do. His view all along was that this was a huge-scale endeavor. It was going to take several years to bring it to fruition. We were doing all we could do. We could only apply so much leverage. Dennis was also getting tired of the constant aggravation. It was completely understandable; he had a young family at home, and he was reaching his limit.

Ken agreed to take the lead in approaching potential buyers. He and Chuck went to work on building a presentation from the business plan and operating results to date. Ken was the consummate master of doing that kind of thing. He had been involved in many deals for Lockheed before becoming COO at SM&A. He focused on the top five prospective buyers, Alaska Airlines being at the top of the list.

We also agreed that the key to any prospective sale was keeping things together at CKC and continuing to grind away on incremental progress. We simply could not afford to let the business unravel with our JV partners while we explored other options.

16

MONEY, FUEL, AND
NEFARIOUS INTENTIONS

*"The moment our equipment leaves the Port of Seattle on a barge
for Petropavlovsk, it might as well be leaving for the Moon!"*

Airplane deicing was the single most important and most
expensive issue remaining unresolved. If we solved that,
then we didn't have to worry about the Russians putting out
bogus or inaccurate weather forecasts. Deicing 747s, DC-10s,
and L-1011s required a boom truck with a very tall hoist so that
an operator could reach the tail of the airplane and the wings, in
particular, to blast the ice off and coat the surfaces with a heated
solution of ethylene glycol. Without that piece of equipment,
the FAA would not certify Elizovo for wintertime, inclement-
weather operations.

We needed nearly three million dollars' worth of equipment
to solve this and other related support issues. I had decided by
1995 not to write any more big checks. Ken, Dennis, and I were
in complete agreement on that. We needed to keep things going,
but we were not going to pour more major investment capital
into CKC. We were going to sell it if we could, and hope to keep
some equity in the process.

The negative operating cash-flow issue was an inconvenience that we could live with for a while. We needed to find ways of hedging our bet on the equipment we needed. We needed to either lease the equipment or obtain loans to buy it. For the remainder of the 1994/1995 winter season, we serviced airplanes when the weather was acceptable and worked on having the Russians issue accurate weather forecasts. We just kept at it until spring 1995. Our real concern was for the following winter season, starting in November 1995. Chuck DeVore, my utility infielder, began focusing on how to get the money for the deicing equipment.

Some US export guarantee programs had been put in place by that point, such as the Export-Import Bank. They were agonizingly slow to deal with. There was also a federal program that guaranteed the exports of American manufacturers, but that program did not work for us because it required three years of operations to qualify. Also, it was specifically designed only for manufactured goods, not for services.

The US government and the financial system generally were very slow during the 1990s to recognize and react to the reality that service businesses were becoming an important factor in the US economy. The rules were designed to support manufacturing output, while services were essentially ignored. We discovered that we did not qualify for any of the federal guarantee programs. We didn't even qualify for the programs that had been expressly set up by Congress to promote entrepreneurship in Russia and her former regions that had broken away.

Without federal guarantees, none of the banks would underwrite us. As one leasing company expressed to me so eloquently, "As far as we are concerned, the moment our equipment leaves the Port of Seattle on a barge for Petropavlovsk, it might as well be leaving for the Moon! We have no expectation of ever seeing it again!"

The financial services industry justifiably worried about the potential for our business to be nationalized, or that the Russian authorities would simply appropriate our assets. The political risk was just too high. I wondered if our inability to arrange financing was nothing more than bureaucratic red tape or whether the financial system was trying to tell me something.

In November 1993, I testified as an expert witness before the US House Commerce, Consumer, and Monetary Affairs Subcommittee of the Committee on Government Operations. They wanted to understand better the issues that I was facing as a pioneering entrepreneur in the new Russia.

I explained that the inability to finance debt was fundamentally the most serious problem. CKC needed to take on debt in the form of lease obligations for equipment, rather than expecting me, as an individual, to put up the huge capital expenditures required to buy all the equipment we needed or to sign personal guarantees for it.

The banks were only too happy to lend the money. The leasing companies were only too happy to lease us the equipment. That is, as long as I personally guaranteed the obligations! To do so would have been a very risky and foolish move.

Ultimately, if it was in the interests of the US government to promote the rapid expansion of entrepreneurship in Russia, then we needed access to capital to make it happen. We needed the federal guarantees that had been promised to make that work, the same guarantees that they were giving in the manufacturing sector. The bottom line was that these guarantees were never going to happen. At least not within the window we had to work with. We didn't have the lobbying resources or the bandwidth needed to play in that game.

The fuel supply chain for Petropavlovsk also continued to be highly problematic. Kamchatka had two things that were strategically crucial to the Soviets: its location, and a deep-water bay. Its location was strategically critical for its military operations. The deep-water bay allowed porting of the Soviet Pacific submarine fleet year-round. The logistical challenges were only an irritant to the Soviets because the system was designed for strategic and tactical expediency, not economic efficiency.

With the nearest petroleum-refining capability some 1200 miles southwest of Petropavlovsk, the locals, and now CKC, were all utterly dependent upon fuel coming in by barge from the ocean port of Vladivostok. It had to come in by sea. There was no other alternative, and the fuel supply was becoming increasingly irregular and unpredictable.

The various players in the supply chain had soon realized the opportunity presented by our JV's increasing demand for fuel, and naturally, wanted to increase the cost of the fuel. The other problem was that we were not receiving all the fuel at the storage tanks at Elizovo. When a barge pulled into the harbor and began unloading fuel through a pipeline to the tanks at Elizovo, some 14 miles away, Elizovo would receive no more than 90 to 95 percent at the tanks. The people who managed that process could have been bleeding it off somewhere along the route and then reselling it, possibly to us. They could have been lying about how much they were actually pumping.

A third possibility concerned us much more: it could have been leaking out of the pipeline! If 10 percent of the fuel really was leaking into the ground, it would be an environmental disaster. What was our liability? Did that really matter in Russia? We were the easiest high-profile target to spin an elaborate yarn about. All the potential soap opera drama aside, we had a great moral responsibility to get to the bottom of this, and quickly!

Managing the fuel supply, the cost of fuel, and trying to get to the bottom of the missing fuel were never-ending headaches. The fuel was our Russian partners' responsibility to manage, and they weren't doing very well. Without cheap fuel and a reliable supply chain, we had nothing to sell. Without a credible accounting for the fuel, we could be facing a ticking time bomb.

We began receiving some very unsettling intelligence reports about a Russian official at Rodzer-Navigazia in Moscow we had worked with to open up the air routes. We knew he was former KGB. Later, this Russian official was transferred to Japan. The intelligence reports suggested that this guy was being bribed by the Japanese to try and shut us down, in the interest of keeping business up at Chitose. Around the same time this was going on, Viktor reported that his colleagues in Moscow suddenly became less cooperative than they had been. He did not know why and couldn't get to the bottom of it.

These intelligence reports made perfect sense to us. Chitose had a very good deal going with the cargo carriers, charging high fuel prices, high taxes on the fuel, landing fees, servicing fees, and so forth. They had been sticking it to their customers until we came along. Not only were we stealing business from them, but we were also creating leverage for the cargo carriers to renegotiate pricing when they did go there. We had become a thorn in their side, and it promised to become a much bigger thorn if something wasn't done.

There were too many people sitting in backrooms trying to figure out schemes for how they could take advantage of the situation for their benefit. The alignment of interests between ourselves, our clients, our JV partners, and the fuel-supply chain was hanging by a slender thread.

17

EXFILTRATION

"Steve, you don't want to get your sleeve
caught in the gears of history."

After the two US government agents left my office in June 1995, I sat for quite a while, thinking about what to do next. I had invested millions of dollars and three of my prime-time years in CKC. My management team and I had worked long and hard on this venture. It was our moonshot, and I had just been informed that the launch was scrubbed. Worse, the news had implications that would significantly impact not only my life, but also the lives of my people on the ground in Russia, and many other people involved in Russia and the US, starting with my family. I had a crisis of the first order on my hands, some tough decisions to make, and not a lot of time to figure out a plan.

We were facing an ever-increasing number of challenges in dealing with our JV partners. We were having difficulty getting prospective buyers to come to the table with offers. The negative-cash-flow bleeding was never ending. We still didn't have a solution for obtaining deicing equipment for the coming winter.

And now the national security authorities were hand-delivering the news that I was going to be taken hostage during my next visit to Moscow in August. Somebody was definitely trying to tell me something.

Reacting emotionally wouldn't help; it would only slow down my ability to deal with this challenging array of facts and endless suppositions. My thoughts turned to "the crevasse," as they had many times over my life in difficult situations, of how an unsurvivable mountain climbing accident had prepared me to deal with so many challenges in life. Finding a way to survive the unsurvivable had given me a sense of confidence about my instincts and a sense of purpose about my future. Becoming an aviator had perfected my ability to deal calmly in a crisis.

My concern was not fear for my life, but the people working for me on the ground in Russia. For sure I was not going to Moscow in August. That was a no-brainer. The real challenge was to figure out how to proceed so that none of my people on the ground in Russia would be taken hostage, or worse, in my place. So much was at stake: money, lives, futures—other people's and my own—and no end of unintended consequences. What were my options?

One of my greatest challenges as a CEO, and an aviator, has been learning how to deal with people who don't think through the unanticipated consequences of the actions they advocate. From employees, to clients, to executives, to boards, and to flight crews, people tend to focus on what they want to happen, or what they think is most likely to happen. Most don't put nearly enough thought and attention to potential unintended consequences. "What would we do if . . . ?"

For this situation, I began thinking about what the opposition would do if . . . ? The opposition always gets a vote! How would they respond to each of the options I think I have? This kind of "out-of-the-box" thinking requires considerable imagination. I like to start with the worst-case scenario. If we can't live with it, then we better have a plan to make sure it can't happen, not just hope that it won't!

There were some ugly, scary, and entirely unacceptable scenarios that could play out here. I had a lot of work to do. I thought it essential for the moment that the situation not be revealed to anyone interacting with the Russians. I couldn't take the chance that someone they interacted with on the Russian side was working for the opposition and would "read" them. What if, indeed, it was our Russian JV partners who were behind this? They'd be looking for just that kind of signal. Any abnormal change in behavior on our part might trigger a change in their plan. Perhaps they would grab Michael or Viktor, or both, and do so immediately instead of waiting until August. My people needed to exhibit business-as-usual behavior with the Russians.

Telling Dennis and Tom might have been helpful in the sense that they might have given me useful intelligence. But at what cost? No, it wasn't worth the risk. When they needed to know, I would give a cover story to Dennis, Chuck, Tom, Viktor and Michael. They'd understand, and they knew that I'd take care of them.

But I needed someone to bounce ideas off of right then. Ken was out of town that day visiting clients. How ironic, since he had also been out of town three and half years earlier when Tom had walked into my office at Lockheed, Sunnyvale, to pitch the idea that had brought us to this point.

I walked down the hall to Nick Kallay's office. Nick was SM&A's chief systems engineer. He is one of the most intelligent people I have ever known, a brilliant systems engineering director, and a client at McDonnell Douglas before coming to SM&A. His family had escaped to the West from Hungary in the 1950s. He had many harrowing stories about those experiences and strong opinions about how to deal with Russian thugs. I was very fortunate to find him in his office that day.

At lunch, I briefed Nick on my visit from the US government agents and the tactical situation on the ground in Russia. He listened intently while I went through the options floating around in my head. After I finished, he sat there a moment, and in his scholarly Hungarian accent, made a comment that has stayed with me ever since.

"Steve, you don't want to get your sleeve caught in the gears of history."

Fantastic! That said it all. Translation: "It's time to get the hell out of there!"

Irrespective of the why, who, and how, the risk/reward ratio on this venture had just become intolerable, and it was time to pull the plug. But how, exactly, were we going to pull the plug while minimizing the potential for unintended consequences?

Starting with the most apparent scenario with the highest risk, what if I sent a fax to my Russian partners informing them that I was terminating the joint venture, effective immediately, for financial reasons? Any, or all, of our people on the ground could be taken hostage in my place before we had time to get them out. Then the phone would ring, and I'd be told how they'd be coming home in pieces if I didn't come up with big money. Would the "powers that be" send the rescue forces needed to intervene if that happened? I didn't think so, and even if I did, would I be willing to bet my people's lives on what others might or might not do?

The government only cared about me being taken hostage because I was on the protective watch list and would, as the agents put it so eloquently, "result in an unacceptable international incident with no end of unintended consequences." They'd have to respond in my case. Not so with my people. My top priority had to be figuring how to get all my people out without anybody realizing what was happening.

I spent that evening rereading one of my favorite books— *On the Wings of Eagles* by Ken Follett, a story about a desperate rescue attempt of two Americans from an Iranian prison. The brief version of the story is this:

Ross Perot's EDS Corporation's biggest client in the 1970s was Iran. EDS was responsible for developing a modern Social Security and Health Care Administration for the Shah's government. Just before the Shah's overthrow in the 1979 Islamic Revolution, insurgent revolutionaries working on the program took hostage the two most senior EDS executives in Iran, using a "contract dispute" as cover, and locked them up in Tehran's Evin Prison.

As the revolution picked up steam, Perot hired Bull Simons, a famous retired US Army Special Forces colonel, to organize and lead a rescue mission into Tehran to get his people out. It's an incredible story and a miraculous achievement that Perot succeeded in rescuing his people without US government assistance. Perhaps I reread the story to remind myself not to try and repeat Perot's saga. It was imperative to avoid any kind of hostage scenario.

When Ken returned the next day, I took him and Nick to a place where our discussion could not be overheard; a place we jokingly called the "cone of silence." Actually, it was our building's emergency stairwell. It had thick concrete walls. The unusual design deadened the sound of our voices. By the way, we routinely had the entire SM&A facility, including the stairwell, scanned for listening devices.

Ken, Nick, and I went over the situation and the ideas that I had come up with overnight. After a lengthy discussion, we agreed on the outline of a sensible plan. We couldn't think of a better approach. But we kept trying over the next four months.

The six-point plan was this: (1) Double down on our efforts to find a buyer. (2) Keep working as if we were committed until reaching the decision point to pull the plug, but delay any commitments requiring significant cost. (3) I had until the end of October to decide not to pull the plug, the timing driven by the fourth point. (4) Unless I decided to continue for good reason, all our people would be extracted from Russia during the Thanksgiving holiday weekend of November 22nd to 26th, 1995. (5) A fax would be sent on the morning of November 27th informing the Russian partners of my decision to withdraw from the JV, effective immediately, for financial reasons. (6) Move the JV board meeting scheduled for August in Moscow to July in London, using Farnborough as cover.

Ken, Nick, and I also agreed that Dennis did not have a "need to know" for the moment. He would be briefed no later than the end of October so that he could participate in managing the extraction process, but probably much sooner, depending on how events unfolded.

In addition to the Americans we would have to extract, there were hundreds of Russians on the payroll. They weren't a concern. But Viktor and his wife, Sveta, were a significant concern. We'd have to get them out at the same time as the others. There were too many potential adverse consequences for them if we didn't.

I spent a great deal of time over the next month making lists of technical and logistical issues that would have to be sorted out and outlining a timeline, with critical events of how the plan would work. For example, how and when would Dennis and I communicate instructions with each of our people so that no one else knew?

Something had to be done immediately about the JV board meeting scheduled to take place in Moscow in August. I provided a very plausible pretense for why the board meeting had to be in London and at the end of July. It was believable because it was true. I made it all about the Farnborough Air Show. It is one of the largest aviation exhibitions and airshows in the world and, coincidentally, scheduled for late July.

The cover was all about my having impossible scheduling conflicts with my biggest aerospace clients. I offered to pay for the Russian board members to travel to London and to buy them VIP access tickets. And I suggested we have the scheduled February 1996 board meeting in Moscow. While the Russians were annoyed at the change of plans, they could not come up with a plausible reason not to go along with it. After some initial pushback, they agreed. I didn't know if the reason they were annoyed was because they lost their chance to kidnap me, because I had changed the plan, or because they just didn't want to go to London.

It was a challenge to continue acting like everything was fine. There were no written or verbal communications internally or externally that suggested anything was amiss. I told the US government agents in June that the August board meeting would for sure not take place in Moscow and that I would not return to Russia again for the foreseeable future. In fact, the next time I visited Russia wasn't until May of 2007; I suppose a long-enough self-imposed exile. Moscow was a very different place by then. It was no secret I was coming. I've gone back several times since, including in May 2014, with a delegation to meet with the Russian deputy foreign minister in the Kremlin.

It was a given that the FSB, CIA, and NSA were monitoring our communications. I was extraordinarily careful to avoid unintentionally revealing that anything was up. Since those in the CIA and NSA who cared knew better, the more I acted like nothing was going on, the more I assumed they knew that something was definitely up. I'll never know if they ever figured out what, until it happened.

Still, I hoped we might be able to sell CKC and salvage my investment, as well as the sweat equity of all who had participated. But I also didn't want to give up on the vision. We were the best hope for the people of Kamchatka, and if we were out, it would not just be the end of our dream, but theirs too. Hope isn't much of a strategy. But hope was all we had.

The CKC negative cash flow at this point was about $50,000 per month. Continuing to operate through November meant losing at least another $250,000. There was also the severance, the travel and living expenses involved for the people we'd need to get out, and reimbursement for any claims for abandoned personal property that they might leave behind. Small change compared to any hostage scenario!

I hoped that some of our financial initiatives would significantly improve the cash flow as the clock wound down. Closing contracts with new clients could only improve our prospects for a deal. The deicing equipment we needed for the coming winter was still not in hand, but we might be able to get a lease or a loan done and get the equipment barged over in time.

The board meeting in London revealed no indication of something going on with my JV partners, other than the usual nonsense. There was just no way to read them, working through interpreters. My interpreters, of course, had no clue that anything was up. I also had no sense of being followed. The board meeting turned into a two-day rehash of all the same discussions Dennis and Chuck had gone around with them during the last several months: "No, we aren't going to change the JV so the customers would pay the Russian side directly and then have the

Russian side give us our cut. All the client contracts would have to be amended, and the clients would never agree."

"No, we aren't going to dramatically increase our fuel pricing to match our competitors' fuel stop prices. It would instantly kill the business."

"No, we are not going to absorb the cost of the missing fuel. Oh, by the way, have you found out what's happening to the missing fuel? We need a credible answer."

"Yes, we are still trying to arrange for the deicing equipment for the coming winter."

"No, we are not going to pay the Russian side upfront for the cost to construct a new ICAO certified passenger terminal."

"Where is the proposal you promised for the terminal with the design, schedule, and cost details?"

The last point about the terminal was a doozy. Alaska Airlines was ready to sign a contract with us to begin passenger service between Anchorage and Elizovo the following spring. But the passenger terminal had to meet ICAO standards. Dennis and I talked about this opportunity extensively with the Russians. We were confident we'd be able to finance this, funded through the International Monetary Fund (IMF), or some other government-backed financing.

The Russians needed to prepare a draft proposal with architectural drawings, construction schedule, pricing, and an analysis of the progress payments required. SM&A people would clean up their proposal, and Chuck would submit it to the IMF on behalf of the JV. We had been telling them this for six months.

When the Russians finally gave us their proposal, it might as well have been handed to us on the back of a napkin. They asked for a ridiculous price, provided no architectural drawing or construction plans, provided no schedule, and demanded 100 percent of the cost funded upfront. Which part of "That will never happen in a million years!" didn't they understand? I was beginning to sound like Chuck.

By the time I returned to Newport Beach from London in mid-August, I had emotionally accepted that we were going to pull the plug. I invited Ken, Tom, Dennis, and Chuck into the "cone of silence" for a meeting. I delivered the "cover story" version of the bad news. I had reached the limit of my willingness to continue investing money. The board meeting in London had not gone well. Our JV partners were either incapable or unwilling to do their part. The U.S. government wasn't coming through either, with anything more than empty talk about loan guarantees, etc. It was simply too much financial risk for me to carry on.

Everyone was deeply saddened and disappointed by the news. Dennis was devastated. Each of us had our hearts and souls wrapped up in this venture. This venture had been huge in its potential success for all concerned. Ken was my COO at SM&A, but he was also an equity stakeholder in CKC. Tom was a Senior VP at SM&A and an equity stakeholder at CKC. Chuck was an SM&A employee on loan to CKC. He hoped that his CKC equity would give him the financial freedom to pursue his dream of a career in politics.

For Dennis, it was a different story. He was committed to CKC up to his eyeballs and didn't have an SM&A net to fall back on. He knew I'd take care of him. But it didn't make him feel any better. He had been here before, several times, with other ventures. We were quickly running out of runway. We couldn't make a sale happen unless Dennis was on board.

No one wanted to argue with me. Ken, Tom, and Chuck had understood that SM&A was the business that they and I had built our careers on. Without my full engagement in SM&A, it wasn't clear that it could scale.

I presented the group a list of what had to happen if CKC were to continue past October. We needed to achieve a target rate of flights, we had to close specific contracts, and we had to solve the deicing equipment problem. We needed a signed letter of intent from a viable buyer. If most of these things did not happen, we would pull the plug over the Thanksgiving weekend. If we were going to do so, we had to decide by the end of October. We needed most of November to get the logistics for our extraction plan in place.

One feature that I liked about briefing them was that it gave me added critical resources to help work through the details of the extraction strategy and how and when it should be communicated. Everyone involved understood that no Americans or Viktor could be on the ground in Russia if and when we pulled the plug. The reaction of the Russians could be one of "detaining" people over any number of pretenses. Again, I didn't mention the kidnapping threat. This was all they needed to know.

Thanksgiving gave us our best window. The Americans would be expected to want to go home for Thanksgiving. Refueling activity would be minimal then, with perhaps only three or four flights. We would not draw any suspicion if we were very, very careful. It was critical that none of this was conveyed to any of our people on the ground over there. It was strictly "need-to-know."

Things went on like this all through the remainder of August, September and October. Despite everyone's best efforts, it was clear that we were not going to make a deal with any of the prospects soon enough with a high enough probability to risk continuing. We wondered if some of the prospects might have had intelligence, perhaps from the opposition, that we might shut down. Perhaps they foolishly believed that if we did, they could pick up the pieces. It didn't matter.

Dennis and I worked diligently on the details of our extraction plan. The timing was critical. He talked with everyone individually and said, "I'm trying to put together a plan for people to get time off around Thanksgiving. What are your plans? When are you going to go home, and where are you going to go?"

We ended up with a plan for everyone, based on what they wanted to do, and when they were going to do it. In some cases, people wanted to go home to visit their families. Others, who had no plans, were tasked with cover assignments: "We need you to go [someplace] to do [something]." Perhaps it was to go to a meeting, see a vendor, see a customer, whatever. We needed a plausible pretense for each person to travel out of Russia over a seventy-two-hour period.

Each person only knew of his or her own plans, and perhaps one or two others. It all seemed perfectly normal. No one, except Dennis and I, ever saw the entire plan. No one could piece together what was really going on. There's a very interesting intelligence community term for this kind of exercise. It's called "essential elements of friendly information." You pretend that you're the opposition and figure out what you'd need to know to make sense of what was really happening. And then use misdirection to carefully communicate information that will cause the opposition to come to the wrong conclusions.

We prepared the entire plan on notepads so that there would be no trace on our computers for anyone to hack into and find. We never faxed any of it to anyone. We never talked about it in other than very general and vague terms in our offices. Specific details were only discussed in the "cone of silence" or in restaurants.

Viktor and Sveta were handled differently. Tom, who was, and still is, a very close personal friend of Viktor's, was detailed to rendezvous with Viktor and work out a plan that no one would know about, not even Dennis or me. We didn't need to know. We just needed it to happen.

November 23, 1995 arrived, and the Thanksgiving weekend began. Slowly and imperceptibly, people began to scatter. As cargo airplanes came through and were refueled, we used our jump-seat privileges to fly people out. Others took commercial flights through Moscow. By the time Monday morning came, everyone was out, including Viktor and his wife. No one had noticed.

One of my tasks during that busy November was to draft a long letter to my joint venture partners explaining why I had decided to withdraw from the JV and terminate all operations, effective immediately. All the assets on the ground at Elizovo were signed over to them in settlement of all claims that they might have against us. Any payments due the Russian side still in process as of Monday morning would be used to partially offset the value of assets I left on the ground at Elizovo. On Monday morning, November 27, 1995, my Russian partners arrived at their offices in Petropavlovsk to find my letter waiting for them, sent via fax.

The headline in the *Los Angeles Times* "Orange County" section read, "Steve Myers of Newport Beach cuts his losses in aircraft refueling operations at Russian airport. Rising demand can't save California Kamchatka Company. Suffering losses and unable to raise capital . . . ," etc.

I needed time to grieve. It felt like I had been in California before the Gold Rush and controlled the Port of San Francisco. I was so close to having achieved remarkable success—and yet I couldn't pull it off!

It was immensely frustrating and humbling. In retrospect, it is clear that some of the interests involved wanted us to fail. Several possible theories offer insight as to why this ambitious venture unraveled. First, there was constant feedback to Moscow about what we were doing in Kamchatka. We were beginning to put enormous pressure on the Russian Far East infrastructure. We were impacting their fuel-supply chain. We were impacting their banking operations. Not everyone was happy about it.

Second, we wanted to be the catalyst for Russian Far East economic self-enlightenment. If we had been successful, we would have made the Russian Far East economically independent of Moscow. How did "Moscow Central" and the Kremlin feel about that? We could easily have been making enemies we did not even know about.

Third, our Russian JV partners may have wanted to edge us out, perhaps believing they didn't need us anymore, now that things were up and running. They could have put out a story that someone was going to kidnap me, while they pretended to know nothing about it. It wouldn't be hard to make sure the CIA and NSA heard about it. A few staged phone calls would do it.

Fourth, the CIA understood my intentions but may have been stunned at how much progress we were making so quickly. They may have initially been excited about what we were doing because it gave them a window into the Russian Far East they may not have had before. Perhaps they changed their minds and decided that they did not want us to be there after all. The visit by US government agents may have been a fabrication intended to push me over the edge to get out.

Fifth, what if they hadn't been US government agents? Could they have been contractors for the opposition? Forging the needed credentials wouldn't have been hard to do. Who the opposition was exactly, could have been any number of players from the mafia, to potential competitors, to the people we were impacting the most: the Japanese, Koreans and other Russian facilities.

For example, a large, well-known commercial operator had been trying to set up a competing operation in Magadan. They couldn't get any of the cargo carriers to come there. We were killing them because we were better situated strategically and were there before them. This large commercial operator had many US government contracts and routinely hired former intelligence community personnel, just like we did. There's no reason why the Japanese or Koreans couldn't have done the same thing, and they had a lot more to lose.

We'll probably never know the truth of it. We do know that in the twenty-five years since we pulled out, no one has replaced us. This suggests to me that the agenda was clearly to kill it, not merely elbow us out. A commercial operator with the resources needed to edge us out would have been smart enough to start with an offer to buy us out instead of letting the JV collapse and the contracts with the cargo carriers default.

If we could have found a way to get the Russians to play ball for the long haul, we would have stimulated a massive multi-billion-dollar expansion on the Kamchatka peninsula. It would have been spectacularly good for the Russian people, for my people, and for me personally.

But not all the Russians involved shared our optimistic view of the future. Many were so fearful of being taken advantage of and things going badly for them. They didn't have the staying power. For them, like so many others in Russia, the agenda was to get enough money together to leave and get to the West.

A couple of years after we pulled out, I ran into two of our former Russian partners at the National Business Aircraft Association (NBAA) convention in Las Vegas. I was gracious, but their consternation was evident. They were respectful, though frankly, it was not a pleasant conversation. They reported that since we had pulled out, they had not been able to conduct a single cargo aircraft servicing operation. Understandably, they and so many others in Kamchatka felt that we had abandoned them.

Dennis made many trips to Petropavlovsk and Moscow. No one worked harder!

At a catchup dinner with Dennis a few years later, I told him about the US government agents visiting my office. I felt that he should know the truth of what was behind my decision to pull out. He just shook his head and said, "Wow! Steve, I look back on it now, and ask myself, why did we put ourselves in such high-risk situations so often? There were so many times when I was vulnerable. Maybe all that saved me was that I wasn't the prize they were after. You were the prize, Steve, your financial situation, and your intimate knowledge of so many government projects. Oh my! We were both very fortunate to get out of there in one piece."

It had been an enormously complicated endeavor with a grand vision. I was blessed with a tremendously capable management team. I am grateful to have known and worked with each of them. They brought enormous energy, enthusiasm, commitment, leadership, and courage. It was indeed a world-class venture, led by world-class people. I will be proud of each of them to the end of my days.

The truth is that not every entrepreneurial venture works out, no matter how well-conceived and led. A high-risk, high-reward situation is just that. Swinging for the fences is more likely to yield a strikeout than a home run. But entrepreneurial opportunities with the potential described in this book are extremely rare. If striking out is painful, the chance for an "at bat" in the majors is hard to come by.

My story began by paying homage to Lindbergh's aeronautical daring and observing that exceptional achievement comes from having the courage to knowingly embrace uncertainty. Adventurers, aviators, and entrepreneurs all share this essential quality. But where does our courage come from? For each of us, it's a deeply personal and unique discovery.

For Lindbergh, it may have been bailing out of a bi-plane, lost in a snowstorm and out of gas on a night mail run over Indiana. Or perhaps it was his trying not to pass out from exhaustion over the Atlantic. For me, it was on Mt. Rainier more than fifty-three years ago. At the bottom of a crevasse, I discovered that the cornerstone of the courage needed to embrace uncertainty, indeed to survive, comes from the eternal optimism within myself.

No matter the entrepreneurial outcome, I experienced the adventure of a lifetime. An adventure that most can only dream of. And I was reminded of something precious and joyful that will be within me all the days of my life.

EPILOGUE

Among his many achievements, Tom Heinsheimer was an avid balloonist. For many years he ran the Gordon Bennett Balloon Race, the oldest and most prestigious international gas balloon race in the world. In August 1990, Tom and Viktor Kerzhanovich organized several gas balloon events for a group of international balloon enthusiasts near Suzdal, Russia, located in the "Golden Ring" of old Russian cities near Moscow, famous for their white Kremlins and churches.

The participants included Tom's close friends Ed and Suzie Beall. Ed, a prominent architect, was particularly interested in the local architecture. As they socialized with Tom and the group, Suzdal city officials became interested in Ed's views of the feasibility of constructing a new hotel on the site of an existing dilapidated hotel. They saw a new hotel as essential to attracting much-needed tourism and revenue.

Officials from the Space Research Institute (IKI) in Moscow also became interested. They approached Tom and Ed about the feasibility of building a hotel on an IKI site to accommodate visiting scientists and engineers.

The lack of suitable hotels in the USSR was a serious impediment to economic progress and an opportunity waiting to be exploited. During a conversation about how to make something happen, Viktor told Tom and Ed about an American businessman, Paul Tatum. Tatum had recently been in the Moscow newspapers announcing the merger of his company with the Radisson Hotel Corporation and an agreement with Goskom Intourist and the Moscow city government.

Paul Tatum

It was rare to read about the success of an American businessman in a Moscow newspaper. Tom called Tatum to arrange a meeting. They took Tatum to dinner, where they found him to be friendly and cordial, and anything but encouraging.

"Guys, it's more complex than you could imagine. It's near impossible to create valid, legal partnerships with your Soviet counterparts. Don't even think about doing it."

They came away from that dinner with positive impressions of Tatum. They found him to be intelligent and enthusiastic, nothing in his behavior that would suggest the egomaniacal tag he'd eventually be branded with. They took his advice and wisely walked away.

Tatum's hotel did very well before the fall of the USSR. After the August 1991 Russian coup attempt, Tatum's prominence rose. The rumor was that he was personally responsible for the direct phone line between the Soviet White House and Gorbachev's camp.

But over the next three years, in a series of classic Russian maneuvers, Tatum's partners began maneuvering to take him out. Goskom Intourist was liquidated, and the Moscow city government became his new partner, along with a handful of vague Russian companies. The Russian visa renewal application for the JV's American general director was mysteriously denied, and the position taken over by Umar Dzhabrailov, a Chechen with substantial connections within the Moscow city government.

Several law enforcement agencies, including the FBI and Interpol, listed Dzhabrailov as a Chechen organized crime figure. A report in the Russian press called Dzhabrailov a "known contract killer, and one of a handful of Chechen mafia bosses operating in Moscow."

Tatum's situation quickly went from bad to worse. One of his bodyguards was beaten and stabbed, and given a message for Tatum: "Tell Paul it's high time he left for home." But rather than leave, Tatum doubled down. He increased his bodyguards and security. He called Dzhabrailov out in Pravda newspaper as a "genuine Mafioso" who "has threatened

Umar Dzhabrailov

he can kill me at any time."

Finally, after months of warring, Tatum was advised that if he'd pay Dzhabrailov and the Moscow city government one million dollars, Dzhabrailov would resign as a general director. But instead of making a deal, Tatum remained defiant, suing his Russian partners for thirty-five million dollars plus damages. One of the last things Tatum said to the media is, "They will have to shoot me to get rid of me." Not something anyone in a rational state of mind would say to a Chechen mafia figure.

On November 3, 1996, less than a year after CKC shut down on the other side of Russia, Tatum was shot eleven times with an AK-47. Shortly after the news of Tatum's death, Dzhabrailov and the Moscow city government took undisputed control of the Radisson Slavyanskaya Hotel and business center.

Tatum's murder sent shockwaves through the Russian business community and had American congressmen screaming for justice. But after a few months, all was virtually forgotten as the news media moved on to the next drama of the day. When I think of Paul Tatum, I'm reminded of Nick Kallay's advice, "Don't get your sleeve caught in the gears of history."

GLOSSARY

OF IMPORTANT NAMES

AKCORD The acronym for our Russian-American joint venture, Aviation Kamchatka California Organization for Reconstruction and Development.

Anadyr Viktor Shlyaev's (Viktor #2) home base and the most eastern Russian fighter base in the Russian Far East, located northeast of the Kamchatka peninsula.

Balabanov, Viacheslav (Slava) Deputy director of IKI (deceased).

Beall, Ed Nationally known architect and 1992 travel team member (http://www.ecbarchitects.com/).

Bering Strait Named after Vitus Bering, a body of water that forms a narrow gap between Alaska and Russia.

Bering, Vitus Danish navigator and founder of Petropavlovsk.

Birjukov, Vladimir Governor of Kamchatka during the 1990s.

Chitose City located in Ishikari, Hokkaidō Island, Japan, and home to the Chitose Airport.

CIS Commonwealth of Independent States, a regional inter-governmental organization of ten post-Soviet republics in Eurasia, formed following the dissolution of the Soviet Union.

CKC California Kamchatka Companies made up of CKC International, CKC Services Inc., and CKC Russia, Inc.

Colbaugh, Ken A terrific baseball player during his college days at San Jose State. A business operations executive at Lockheed in the 1980s. Chief Operating Officer of SM&A in the 1990s. Now living in Newport Beach, California.

Cox, Christopher Congressman from the CA-48 District in the 1990s and Chairman of the SEC under George H.W. Bush.

Crosby, Dennis Chief Operating Officer of CKC, now President of Inspire Logistics Group, Inc. and living in Chicago, Ill.

DeVore, Chuck Vice-president at SM&A and CKC, later a California state legislator, now living in Austin, Texas.

Efimov, Vladimir Chief editor of TV Kamchatka.

Elizovo Joint military/civilian airport at Petropavlovsk, where CKC operated.

Friedman, Dr. Louis Co-founder of The Planetary Society with Carl Sagan and Bruce C. Murray. He brought Tom Heinsheimer into the Soviet space program and was instrumental in getting the last-minute authorization for our flight from the Russians.

Gallev, Albert Director of IKI.

Geyser Valley Considered Russia's most beautiful national park, destroyed in 2007 by a mudslide.

Gurevich, Boris, Ph.D. Russian translator and financial advisor. Now living in Newport Beach, California.

Heinsheimer, Julie Healthcare manager of the 1992 travel team and Tom's very capable wife. Now living in Rolling Hills, California.

Heinsheimer, Thomas Chief scientist and vice president at SM&A, whose idea it was to go to Kamchatka, and 1992 travel team member. Now living in Rolling Hills, California.

Holkam Supermarket Grocery store in Petropavlovsk started by a Dutch entrepreneur named Holkam in 1992.

ICAO International Civil Aviation Organization, based in Montreal, sets standards used by all member countries for meeting minimum airport runway, overflight, and instrument landing criteria as well as requirements for passenger control and processing facilities.

IKI Russian Institute for Space Research in Moscow

Janisse, Rick President of Martin Aviation at Orange County (John Wayne) Airport in 1992.

Kallay, Nick Together with his family escaped from Hungary in the 1950s, settled in the US. Director of Systems Engineering at McDonnell Douglas in the 1980s. Chief Systems Engineer at SM&A in the 1990s. Retired to Montana to be a cattle rancher.

Kamchatka A region in the Russian Far East that includes the Kamchatka peninsula, Komandorsky Islands, and Karaginsky Island.

Kerzhanovich, Viktor Russian IKI Scientist and SM&A/CKC representative in Moscow, known as Viktor #1. Now living in Fallbrook, CA and a member of the technical staff at JPL in Pasadena, CA.

KGB Komitet Gosudarstvennoy Bezopasnosti (Committee for State Security), a combination national security agency and CIA of the Soviet Union, 1954–1991. The KGB's successors are the secret police agency FSB (Federal Security Service of the Russian Federation) and the espionage agency SVR (Foreign Intelligence Service).

Khabarovsk Located eighteen miles from the Chinese border, it is the second largest city in the Russian Far East after Vladivostok.

Klyuchevskaya The largest volcano in the Northern Hemisphere at 15,584 feet.

Korf Port village on the northern end of the Kamchatka peninsula, destroyed by an earthquake on April 21, 2006. More than eight hundred families were evacuated and the settlement abandoned.

Kozyrev, Andrey Russian foreign minister in 1992.

Kozyrevsk A village in central Kamchatka on the Kamchatka River that we used as our base of operations while exploring the area.

Kvacof, Vladimir Director of flight operations, Korf in 1992.

Linkin, Katia Our visa support angel.

Ludmilla Our cook during the July 1992 visit to Kamchatka.

Magadan Located 472 nautical miles to the northwest of Petropavlovsk across the Sea of Okhotsk. Stalin established the settlement in 1930 as a disbursal point for the gulags.

Mathis, Paula Wife of Steven during the time period covered.

NOAA National Oceanic and Atmospheric Administration.

Nome Located on the west coast of the Seward peninsula of Alaska, facing the Bering Sea.

Nyet Russian for "no."

Osipov, Yuri President, Russian Academy of Sciences.

Paratunka Resort & spa forty miles west of Elizovo Airport.

Petropavlovsk Main city and administrative, industrial, scientific, and cultural center of Kamchatka Krai in Russia.

Provideniya Situated on Komsomolskaya Bay across the Bering Strait from Alaska, the closest Russian airport to Alaska.

Rodzianko, Michael Operations manager for CKC at Elizovo Airport. The grandson of the last non-communist prime minister of Russia, Mikhail Rodzianko, who had led the abdication of Czar Nicholas II.

Rohrabacher, Dana Republican member of the US House of Representatives who represented the CA-46 congressional district during the time period of this book.

Sagdeev, Dr. Roald The director of the Soviet Space Research Institute (IKI), his "da" gave the final Russian green light for our flight. He is now a Distinguished Professor of Physics at the University of Maryland.

Samarski, Vladimir Helicopter wing commander, Kamchatka Airline.

Senchenko, Vladimir Vice governor of Kamchatka during the time period of this book.

Shenakova, Olga Air traffic controller at Elizovo Airport.

Shlyaev, Viktor Russian navigator who met our travel team in Provideniya, also known as Viktor #2.

SM&A Steven Myers & Associates Inc.

Stoner, Mike Freelance videographer and filmmaker, member of our July 1992 travel team.

Sveta Viktor #1's wife.

Tatum, Paul Led the first Russian-American joint venture, a hotel in Moscow, murdered in 1996 by the mafia.

Tolbachik A 12,080-foot volcano used by IKI for Mars rover testing.

Tverdokhleb, Aleksey Airport director, Elizovo Airport during the time period of this book.

Volodya Our driver in Petropavlovsk. A second Volodya, a volcanologist, served as our guide during our trip north to Kozyrevsk and Tolbachik.